Shaping Survival

Essays by Four American Indian Tribal Women

Lanniko L. Lee,
Florestine Kiyukanpi Renville,
Karen Lone Hill, and
Lydia Whirlwind Soldier

Edited by Jack W. Marken
and Charles L. Woodard

The Scarecrow Press, Inc.
Lanham, Maryland, and London
2001

SCARECROW PRESS, INC.

Published in the United States of America
by Scarecrow Press, Inc.
4720 Boston Way, Lanham, Maryland 20706
www.scarecrowpress.com

4 Pleydell Gardens, Folkestone
Kent CT20 2DN, England

Copyright © 2002 by Lanniko L. Lee, Florestine Kiyukanpi Renville, Karen Lone Hill, and Lydia Whirlwind Soldier

All rights reserved. No part of this publication may be reproduced, stored in a retrieval system, or transmitted in any form or by any means, electronic, mechanical, photocopying, recording, or otherwise, without the prior permission of the publisher.

British Library Cataloguing in Publication Information Available

Library of Congress Cataloging-in-Publication Data

Shaping survival : essays by four American Indian tribal women / Lanniko L. Lee . . . [et al.].
   p. cm.
   Includes index.
   ISBN 0-8108-4151-7 (alk. paper)
   1. Indian women—North America—Social conditions.   2. Indian philosophy—North America.   3. Indians of North America—Social life and customs.   I. Lee, Lanniko L., 1949–
E98.W8 S53   2002
305.48'897—dc21   2001042673

∞ ™ The paper used in this publication meets the minimum requirements of American National Standard for Information Sciences—Permanence of Paper for Printed Library Materials, ANSI/NISO Z39.48–1992.
Manufactured in the United States of America.

Contents

Introduction	v
1. Ways of River Wisdom *Lanniko L. Lee*	1
2. On Learning *Karen Lone Hill*	45
3. Dakota Identity Renewed *Florestine Kiyukanpi Renville*	91
4. Memories *Lydia Whirlwind Soldier*	159
Glossary	215
Index	217

Introduction

I

After the end of the wars with the Dakota, Lakota, and Nakota people in the latter part of the nineteenth century, the survivors were confined to areas reserved for them by treaty, small landscapes compared to the expanses on which they had previously flourished. With the buffalo virtually gone and other game scarce, the federal government decided that tribal people should be turned into farmers or ranchers. The belief was that they could be trained or forced into being like the whites who lived in neighboring areas. Then, the government turned its attention to the children.

It was decided that to guarantee that the children would be able to "assimilate" into white society, they must be educated in the American language and culture by non-Indian teachers. Their native languages and cultures would have to be obliterated. The mechanisms for accomplishing these goals would be the boarding schools. Enlisting the aid of organized religion, the federal government fostered seventy-eight of these schools within the first two decades of the twentieth century. Indian children as young as four or five were forced to attend these schools, which were usually far away from their families. These bewildered children were taken from anguished parents, grandparents, or guardians who had their annuities, rations, and other services withheld if they failed to comply with the demands of the authorities. (See Brenda J. Child, *Boarding School*

Seasons: American Indian Families, 1900–1940, University of Nebraska Press, 1995, p. 40. Child, an Ojibwe Indian from Minnesota and a professor at the University of Minnesota, was a boarding school student.)

Congress had passed a compulsory attendance law for American Indians as early as 1891, but there were evidently no laws requiring humane treatment of the children. In these schools, whether they were administered by the government or by the churches, students were treated like prisoners or boot camp inmates or worse. On February 4, 1938, Mrs. Isabella Strong of the Red Lake Reservation in Minnesota, trying to get her homesick daughter Claudia home from the Flandreau Indian School in South Dakota, wrote this to the superintendent there: "It seems it would be much easier to get her out of prison than out of your school" (Child, p. 47). Superintendents of boarding schools had absolute power over Indian children and even kept some of them over the summers to work in area homes or fields rather than permit them to go home for vacation.

II

Three of the four women whose stories constitute this book were boarding school students. Their accounts give graphic evidence of the mistreatment of native children in these schools during the middle and later years of the twentieth century. The fourth, Karen Lone Hill, was schooled on the reservation while living at home, but her teachers were also non-Indians.

Each of these women was born on one of South Dakota's nine reservations. Four of these reservations, Crow Creek, Flandreau, Sisseton-Wahpeton, and Yankton, are east of the Missouri river. The others, Cheyenne River, Lower Brule, Pine Ridge, Rosebud, and Standing Rock, are west of the river. These women were born into families speaking the Sioux language. In the east, on the Sisseton-Wahpeton Reservation in the northeastern corner of the state where Florestine Kiyukanpi Renville was born, the dialect spoken is Dakota, which Florestine heard during her childhood from her parents and relatives but was not encouraged to speak. In the west, where the remaining women were born, the dialect is Lakota. The remaining three women learned their language as children, mainly because the reservations in that area had less white presence, enabling those people to retain stronger holds on their language and cultures, though these were repressed as much as possible by the white government officials among them. It has been only within the last quarter of the twentieth century, mostly because of the establishment of American Indian institutions of higher education, that an intensive revival of tribal languages and cultures has occurred.

Lanniko Lee, who is a Minneconjou Lakota, was born near the Missouri River, which remains a strong influence in her life. She describes her childhood along the river in poetic language, evoking an early life of beautiful freedom and family happiness. This idyllic life continued until she was sent to boarding school, an act she calls "a government-designed madness." She especially focuses on the tragic effect on her people of the government damming of the Missouri River, beginning in 1948.

Karen Lone Hill's young life differed from the childhoods of the others, as she was born on the Pine Ridge Reservation in the southwestern part of the state and went to school there. When she was a child, her family lived among non-Indians in nearby Nebraska and experienced no prejudice, which she says she did not experience until she was an adult. As an adult, growing in awareness, she became involved in the culture and religion of her ancestors, taking part in their religious ceremonies. She remains on her reservation as the chair of Indian Studies at Oglala Lakota College there.

Florestine Kiyukanpi Renville spent part of her difficult childhood in western Minnesota, where her father worked as a farm laborer on land owned by a demanding bully, for whom she and her brothers and sisters also worked as child laborers. She attended elementary school in the area, the only Indian child in her class. Later, when problems broke up her family, she was forced to attend St. Mary's, an Episcopal boarding school in Springfield, near the southern border of South Dakota. Her experiences there might well have made her suspicious of whites and white institutions. A Dakota of the Sisseton-Wahpeton tribe, she now lives with her family near the small town of Peever in northeastern South Dakota. There she owns and edits a magazine entitled *Ikce Wicasta*, which means "The Common People," featuring materials focused on the tribal people of the region. The magazine, which includes essays, fiction, and poetry mostly by native authors, is committed to cultural reclamation and to increasing public awareness of the history and traditions of the Dakota people.

As a small child on the Rosebud Reservation in southwestern South Dakota, Lydia Whirlwind Soldier experienced happiness until she was suddenly taken at the age of four to St. Francis Indian School, nearly a hundred miles south of her home. She stayed at this boarding school, controlled by the Catholic Church, for most of her elementary education, but had to leave because her parents divorced when she was twelve, a family condition not tolerated by the church. Although she finished her education elsewhere and earned college degrees, her mostly traumatic experiences in the boarding school at St. Francis remain a central influence on her life. These and later experiences have convinced her of the importance of reclaiming and strengthening Lakota language and culture.

III

The life stories of these four native women germinated in a program that began in 1993 as a retreat for aspiring Dakota, Lakota, and Nakota writers. Working in collaboration with Elizabeth Cook-Lynn, the noted Dakota poet, critic, and novelist, Lowell Amiotte and Charles Woodard and others at South Dakota State University organized the first retreat, which featured Cook-Lynn and N. Scott Momaday as co-mentors. The retreat, which is now an annual four-day event held in the late summer or early fall at an SDSU facility on Oak Lake, twenty-three miles northwest of Brookings, has also featured nationally known James Welch, Roberta Hill, Laura Tohe, and Joseph Marshall III as co-mentors with Cook-Lynn.

As a result of the ongoing experience of this annual retreat, now co-organized by Cook-Lynn and Woodard, tribal participants have created a statewide group, which they have named the Oak Lake Writers' Society. Lee, Renville, and Whirlwind Soldier are founding members of that society, and Lone Hill is now also a member.

The achievements of the members of the writers' group, one of only a few of its kind in the country, have been notable. Besides helping foster the journal created by Florestine Renville, the group has published, with Augustana College's Center for Western Studies, *Memory Songs*, a volume of poetry by Lydia Whirlwind Soldier. And other writings by the group have been published in journals and magazines and in an anthology entitled *Woyake Kinikiyan: An Anthology of Dakota/Lakota Storytellers*, which means "Bringing Back the Stories." The retreat and the society's other activities have nourished the flowering of these authors, who have opened their hearts and minds to each other and to others, including students who have attended their readings and read their works.

The stories of the lives of the women are highly instructive to all of us. Even today in educating native students, we do not include parents in formulating practices and policies affecting their children as often and as fully as we should. Not consulting parents at all was one of the major failures of the boarding schools. Tribal children lived in close-knit extended families in early times. They still do if circumstances permit. Taking them from their families and placing them in schools far away from home created alienation and anger that were increased by punishment and isolation. We must learn from our mistakes. In all schools presuming to educate native students, we need to involve their parents and other family members more fully, and we must educate teachers to be more sensitive to the backgrounds and the feelings of these students.

Each of the women in this book indicates that she recovered her spiritual strength and sense of well-being by returning to the religious beliefs of her ancestors and the practice of their ceremonies. Returning to their ancestral cultures has enabled these women to triumph over efforts to break their spirits. Teachers of tribal students must be required to take courses that include materials on their students' tribal histories and cultures, and all children in our society should be taught the many important contributions native peoples have made to America in areas such as agriculture, art, government, literature, and pharmacology. These significant contributions are too often ignored.

It is a tribute to these four strong women that, despite often painful experiences in a society that has mistreated them and continues to be prejudiced against them, they have become remarkably well-adjusted human beings. We can all learn from their stories, which are enlightened documents of reconciliation and human possibilities.

* * *

We wish to thank the South Dakota Humanities Council for providing travel funds for initial work on this book.

Jack W. Marken
Charles L. Woodard

Chapter 1

Ways of River Wisdom

Lanniko L. Lee

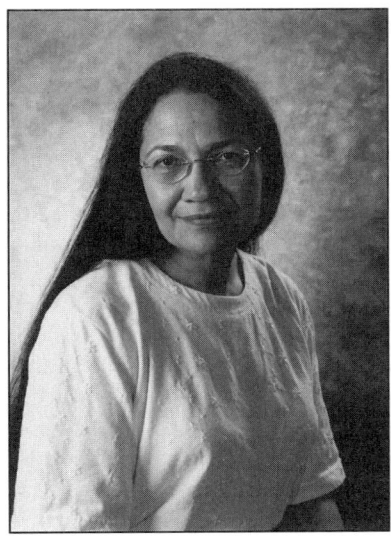

Lanniko L. Lee is an enrolled member of the Cheyenne River Sioux Tribe. She was born and raised near the Missouri River in the remote southwestern region of Armstrong, now Dewey, County.

After receiving a B.A. in sociology from Beaver College in Pennsylvania and an M.A. in English from the Breadloaf School of English of Middlebury College in Vermont, she taught English and American literature in high schools and tribal colleges on the Cheyenne River Sioux and Standing Rock Reservations. She has also taught at Northern State University and South Dakota State University. Her articles, book reviews, poetry, and tribal college student profiles have appeared in the *Tribal College Journal of American Indian Higher Education*, *American Indian Culture and Research Journal*, *Writers' Forum of the University of Colorado* at Colorado Springs, *Paintbrush Journal*, and the *Sioux Falls Argus Leader*.

Once I had a teacher who taught me many good things that had been the way of life for my grandparents. Even today I feel a strong sense of connectedness to a time and place that no longer exists. The river I knew provided a good way to live when the good life was growing up on the Missouri River when it flowed freely, unencumbered by the Oahe Dam. Seldom do I pass through a day without some connection to the river. My dreams and the gift of new thoughts reclaim those stories that shimmer and sparkle with life like the river that gave birth to them. My spirit, caught in the needlegrass like the cottonwood seed, is held fast to the place of my birth, forever fixed to that place, forever affirming to me that the river has shaped my existence. I am moved by its seasonal rhythm. I look forward to its changes. I look overhead each spring and fall and I am comforted by the ribbons of migratory fowl as they come and stay and go on again and again. Who I am today is clearly the work of the river and it continues to have a strong influence in my life. The river to which I refer is really a family of rivers including the Moreau and the Cheyenne, but it is the Missouri that shaped the dreams and visions of my ancestors long before it made a river thinker out of me.

My stories constitute a river wisdom of sorts. I have changed some of the names of the persons in this recollection out of respect and to preserve their anonymity. Some are children born of my grandmothers' imaginations and their special way of raising their children and grandchildren. Their stories and my experiences have helped me to appreciate the many blessings of life that come with having a keen awareness of the value of place. From childhood my heart has been of the river, where I learned belonging, fulfillment, personal safety. Having a memorable childhood means not only having shared a family place but also having had the opportunity to begin building a spiritual identity.

My grandmothers are gone from this world, but I continue to grow in awareness of who they were, because I live near the river, where there is constant interaction with them. I am a reflection of them. I find myself doing the arts I loved to watch them doing when I was a child. Moving in and out of their patterns of work, I understand more every day how I have them and how I now act on that reservoir of shared knowledge, shaped by the river, which was for centuries our home and the source of living power for all of us. It is imperative that this river power be shared, because a river childhood provides wholeness and a perspective worth remembering.

Also worth remembering is the human need to have a perspective on the world beyond, and a place on the land from which to have that perspective. My generation grew up learning that the reservation would forever be home.

Reservation life evolved into a way of life through necessity; it meant survival for the people, as it does for many Lakota people today. Still, the transient life has also continued. For example, young Indians traveling the path to self-determination went away from home for college education until the mid 1970s, when the establishment of tribal colleges slowed the exodus.

Lakota people have always known the need to travel was a necessity. In earlier times, they traveled to escape persecution and even death, to trade for the things they required which were not to be found along the rivers, to find better grazing for their horses, to replenish their stores of foodstuff from the bountiful river bottoms. These movements were essential to survival. At the height of their transience, their worldview was shaped by the gifts offered by tatanka, the prairie and woodland bison. These gifts were manifold- food prepared in various ways from the meat, shelter from hides used for teepees, bones used for religious ceremonies celebrating tribal and personal thanksgiving and spiritual guidance. Back then, the transient life kept minds resilient, open to creative possibilities, open to opportunity when it presented itself.

I, too, have had to move about. I moved away from home to get an education, and then I moved about for meaningful work as an educator. I was taught as a youngster to carry my load and so I have always worked to provide for my family and myself.

I attended college near rivers and some of my workplaces have been near other rivers, but after a time I returned to the land of the Big Roiling, the river which has made me who I am. Wherever I was, transcending experiences happened for me along rivers. My childhood river education began on the Missouri River in a place which once had been Armstrong County on the Cheyenne River Sioux Indian Reservation (CRST) in north central South Dakota. In the introduction to an unpublished 1940 souvenir program celebrating fifty years of reservation life, Tribal Chairman Luke Two Tails Gilbert describes the land:

> The Cheyenne River Sioux Reservation begins in the center of the Missouri River, ten miles north of the mouth of the Moreau or Owl River, this point being the southeastern corner of the Standing Rock Reservation; then down the center of the main channel of the Missouri River, including also entirely within the reservation all islands, if any were in the river, to a point opposite the mouth of the Cheyenne River; and up the same to its intersection with the one hundred and second meridian of longitude; then north along that meridian to its intersection with a

line due west from a point in the Missouri River ten miles north of the mouth of the Moreau or Owl River; and finally due east to the place of the beginning ("Celebrating Fifty Years of Progress at Cheyenne River Agency").

As a child I learned that the four corners of our reservation could be remembered by the rivers. Over the years, my father would tell his children that we could travel on the water around the Reservation to the camps and new districts to visit the members of the tribe. From Swift Bird Creek, named for Chief Swift Bird, into and up the Missouri were remnants of the Minneconjou, planters by the big roiling waters; further north on the Owl River, better known as the Moreau River today, lived in Oohenupa Tiyospaye, the Two Kettle or Two Boilings Band. Further north were the Itazipco Tiyospaye, the Sans Arc or Without Bows Band, and still further north and living along the Missouri were the Sihasapa, the Blackfeet Band, near the homelands of Sitting Bull, of the Hunkpapa or Campers at the Opening of the Circle, those tribal members enrolled on the Standing Rock Agency. Following the waterway westward across the uppermost region of the Cheyenne River Sioux Indian Reservation, spring thaws empty into Cherry Creek, Rattlesnake Creek, and Plum Creek, which converge and then empty into the Cheyenne River, where live most of the Minneconjou, Planters by the Water. Entering the water again, the Cheyenne River current flows east and empties into the Missouri. The little western reservation community of Cherry Creek is where my great-grandmother went to live.

My grandmothers, paternal and maternal, lived out their days along the Missouri River on the eastern side of the Cheyenne River and the Standing Rock Sioux reservations. My mother and her family were tribal members of the Standing Rock Sioux Indian Reservation, and her mother, my grandmother's people, are Hidatsa or Gros Ventre enrolled in the Three Affiliated Tribes of Fort Berthold Reservation in northwestern North Dakota. When I was a child my family traveled often to Old Kenel on the Standing Rock to visit Unci Susan Defender Jordan and all the way to Elbow Woods to visit Unci Martha Red Pheasant and many other family members, and we traveled as far west as Poplar and Browning, Montana, where lived my uncle Alvin and his family with other members of my mother's family. I remember these trips as being very long because each mile was marked by the great anticipation of reaching our destination.

Back in the 1950s, the river bottomland of Armstrong County was sparsely populated with fewer than a dozen Indian families; most were my relatives living like us south of the small towns of Ridgeview and LaPlante. Even the nonresident white ranchers who leased tribal land in that area were few. However, temporary help was brought onto the tribal lease land during spring and fall cattle roundups for Burton Mossman, owner of the Diamond A Cattle Company. During late spring and early summer, young Indian cowboys would ride horseback from the Cheyenne Agency boarding school to help the white cowboys from Eagle Butte and Dupree and other places. More ranch hands were also needed during branding season and again later in the fall, when the cattle were once again rounded up for sale, sorted, and then driven by horseback to the shipping corrals in LaPlante.

Except for these occasions, we seldom saw strangers moving about in our part of the reservation, especially by automobile. The relative absence of neighbors in the land south of Ridgeview happened because during certain times of the year, travel to and from our homes on the river bottom was nearly impossible, even for those of us who considered ourselves born of the river in south Armstrong County. Much of the land was gumbo, a clay soil that quickly turned sticky, the consistency of oatmeal boiled hard in axle grease. Days after a hard rain or a spring thaw, it looked deceptively dry, but many an impatient traveler found himself sticking fast in the mud. It seemed to take forever to dry.

Back then, the land was open, with few fences crisscrossing the native prairie short grass. On top of Fox Ridge west and south of Virgin Creek skirting the little community of LaPlante, only isolated scrub sage, prickly cactus, and gumbo patches of large waxy white flowers of the gumbo lily broke up the treeless terrain of rambling ravines and rolling green grass.

Even today, the treeless land above the river bottomland is still soft rolling prairie short grasses spotted with gumbo acres. Once, high above the prairie shelves leading to Fox Ridge, I looked back with my father over the subtle breaking slopes in the direction of the river. "Your grandpa used to say that this land is so open to know that you can see a lie walking through the grass toward you long before you can hear it," he said.

As often as the days were perfect with soft gentle breezes and golden shafts brightening the first of the prairie green, the spring thaws and summer rainstorms would wash out the old buckboard trails on which my family traveled up out of the river bottom. Those of us who lived on the river learned to read the skies. We would watch the old woman's long hair fan out across the bright blue, then break off into a growing layer of rabbit tails that would sink down and crowd close together until they would begin to boil into a dusty mat of gray hanging almost within reach.

Other days, when the sky was without a cloud, we could see the wall of blue thunderbirds traveling toward us from the west. The vanguard of angry white towers climbing higher and higher would tumble into itself as the bottom turned deep indigo blue. Through the swelling white towers, some Great Spirit of power would thrust itself up, then flatten out into the shape of the great mushrooms my Uncle Alvin cut from ash trees. Then the western sky would darken the land and the heavy raindrops would burst out of the low hanging canopy and pelt the trail dust, making it slick and sticky. Often these summer rainstorms lashed out and swallowed up those trails, center ridge grass and all, as frightened miniscule rivers ran wild. The flooding turned dry gray patches of gumbo the color of gunmetal into a greasy, shiny pewter-colored gray, evaporating any travel plans until the roads were dry once again.

But if supplies were needed and could be carried on horseback, my dad would ride up north some eighteen miles to the Frank "Short Log" and Bethel Tibbs General Store, the only store in the little community of Ridgeview. On a few such occasions, a visiting cousin or two and Dad and I rode to Ridgeview and then nine miles farther east to the commodity depot at LaPlante.

In good weather when the roads were dry, the ruts in the dirt trail were often so deep that the old Studebaker pickup truck or the buckboard and team would only creep along. Seldom did we ever travel purposefully anywhere in a hurry. How to get around those natural barriers of gumbo after a hard rain was not a question we entertained, since most of the gumbo patches were so large that they often reached down into the ravines we would have to ford.

In those days of my early childhood, we seldom left the bountiful shelter of the river bottom. The river provided us with all our needs. The cottonwood shelter was home to plenty of deer, raccoon, porcupine, squirrels, muskrats, and beavers. The river provided us with numerous birds, including mourning doves, ducks, geese, prairie quail and, when necessary, rails. And just above the cottonwoods along the slopes of the ravines and shallow creeks, the river provided us with cedar woods where antelope, grouse, prairie chicken, and partridge came in from the open prairie flats and fed on the evergreen berries.

The river provided food for every living thing, most of which we consumed. In the naturally occurring ponds and fresh running water of the creeks and streams which emptied into the Missouri, my family fished for bass, paddlefish, sturgeon, catfish, shad, pike, and many other fish, including even burbot, or eel pout. Along the shore we caught clams, mussels, turtles, crayfish, and frogs.

We also gathered and dried for use year round a generous variety of wild teas. We harvested the little white rice heads, rosehips, red feather reed, cattails, scrub oak acorns, juniper berries, chokecherries, buffalo berries, plums, sand cherries, juneberries, elderberries, wild grapes, and prairie stone apples, and the many mushrooms that grew on the ground, and even the "big-ears," the ash tree mushrooms that grew like melting stairsteps along the north sides of the ash tree. We dug and ate yucca, wild turnip, and a large variety of other roots, which grew along the hilly slopes leading to the river.

Medicine plants also grew in abundance along the river and they were gathered, dried, and kept for use when needed. Many families, including mine, kept a bundle of dried red willow bark and flower heads of numerous names and other plant stems, roots, and leaves which were used for medicinal purposes. All of these gifts were from a place far up the river where thundering waterfalls were steps leading to the big mountains and source of all things good for the people. The river brought it all to us, the birds, the animals, the fish, the trees, and all of their smaller relatives.

From the top of the last bluff and looking farther north, the ridge stretching across the horizon from east to west was the gravel road which became Highway 212, an important roadway dividing nearly in half latitudinally the Cheyenne River Indian Reservation. The roadway was important then and is equally important today as a passenger and transport carrier route to the relocated tribal headquarters in Eagle Butte and to communities west like Dupree and Faith and beyond to the Black Hills. Highway 212 stretches straight eastward until it crosses the present-day dammed up Missouri River. There the highway leaves the Reservation and passes over into Potter County, non-Indian land where intensive small grain farming is practiced and where few Indian families live.

Now come with me to the river bottom, where a five-year-old can run carefree between three houses, all different in form and structure. The first house is a dugout, an earth house built by my father, my father's brothers, Dave and Cal, and various cousins who came for occasional visits and always stayed for a few days. Dug out of a remarkably high hill, it provides ample room for the primary dwellers here—my parents and myself. There is also room and privacy for my mother's youngest sister Arlene, who visits my mother often enough, yet I greatly anticipate the times when she comes with my grandma and grandpa. Other occasional stayovers are my father's hunting and fishing relatives and some of his friends from across the river.

When other relatives come for two or three days and longer, my father goes to work and digs deeper into the hill, framing up the additional space with tree trunks the size of a man's leg and carving out another opening facing the southeast side. The front entrance faces the river. Big cottonwood timbers hold up the dirt-covered roof and the floor rises gradually up to the door to ground level. The main entrance is a third of the way up the hill. We can go with our coffee cups to the doorway and stand on a flattened-out area about the size of the interior living space to see over the tops of the cottonwoods to the river beyond. Along the entrance is a good mat of buffalo grass where I like to sit in the warm spring sunshine with my three dogs, Ripper, Shep, and Lady, and watch the birds float just above the treetops of the riverbanks.

There is a hitching post just down the slope a bit where Dad ties Big Red after he is through checking the cattle and where he hangs the saddle blankets to dry in the breeze. In the fly-speckled summers, Red's and Winnie's feet work the ground into dust bowls in which the chickens and the chickadees bathe. After a good rain, the bowls fill up enough for the dogs and me to play. Of all my dogs, Lady most enjoys wearing a mud coat. Sometimes, when the gumbo lily is in bloom, I pick several and push the stems into her mud-caked hair and shape a flowered-collar for her.

Not far down the river lives Unci Eunie in her three-room wood-framed house. I don't know how she came to live in this house. It is so unlike ours. There are steps leading up from the large common kitchen to another level where there is a sitting room in which Unci spends time doing quiet things like sewing and reading her Bible. At night she sleeps in this room, but I would never guess this from the neat and orderly way it is arranged during the waking hours. A bedroom is also on this level, where for a brief time my father's younger brother and his bride will stay until they can move into their own place.

Just down the hill from us is a log house with two big rooms. A Ben Franklin stove nearly blocks the doorway between the two rooms. Our menfolk stay here when there are more family visitors than places for them to sleep in the dugout or in Unci's framehouse kitchen.

These three houses along the river make up a world where people gather. My Unci draws them to her like a magnet. She knows about plant medicine and how to birth babies. She helps many women and gives them quilts for their babies and makes clothes for little children, too, especially for her grandchildren. She sews dresses, aprons, and shirts for her sons and their children. I have paisley, calico, gingham, and taffeta dresses all trimmed with tatting and ricrac also made by Unci. Anything Unci sees in the Sears catalogs or in the ready-made garments ads hanging from the dowel sticks in Barker's Dry Goods Store at the Old Agency, she studies closely and then she makes what she sees out of new remnant fabrics and recycled family clothing.

My father raises livestock along the river. We have cattle, horses, a few sheep, and even fewer goats. My Unci doesn't like the sheep, though she says they are especially valuable. She explains that, like the buffalo, every part of them can be used. Somehow she has learned how to work with the sheep's wool and though she seldom does that, she reminds me often of the sheep's usefulness. When she and I walk to the river to fish or to get water, we see the sheep grazing in the distance along the hillside. She calls them "hocospu," "scabs." "You never want too many of them," she says. "Too many of them and they make scabs of the land." She adds: "See how they even look like scabs there on the hillside."

From where we stand looking up at them in the morning sun, I can see the lambs sucking their mothers or chasing each other around the ragged outcroppings of sedimentary rock, sage, and shale wall. To me they do not look anything like scabs. I can hear them bleating and their mothers' deep low bawls in reply as they crop the grass. Their white, fluffy coats are beautiful. I never tell Unci what I think about the sheep, but she knows I love them. I fancy I can talk to the lambs since she and I have taken the frailer, weaker ones, especially the weaker twins, off their mothers and have given them to the milking goats to raise. They have become my special friends and they follow me around the yard trying to suck my fingers. Our dog Lady keeps a close eye on the sheep. When it starts to get dark, my father whistles to Lady to bring the sheep closer to the house.

I am the oldest child of my parents. A brother is two years younger, and the babies are twin brothers. After helping with the chores and after we have eaten our breakfast of kabubu bread with chokeberry syrup and scrambled eggs, it is my job to watch my younger brothers. Only this morning it is different. My mom, who is washing clothes, will watch the little ones this morning as they play near the clothesline.

My father brings the old mare around to the front of the house. "You and Sleepy Eye will take care of the sheep this morning," he says. "Uncle, Johnny, and I are going to work on the fence west of the house. Sleepy Eye and Lady will keep you company."

I am so happy to be given such an important job. I thank Dad for lifting me up onto Sleepy Eye and she walks slowly out toward the sheep, which are already out in the open, grazing on the lush grass in the big draw well beyond the trees. Sleepy Eye takes her sweet old time sauntering through the little flock until she is on the far north side of the flock nearly up the hill. She jerks her head forward, stretching her jaw high in the air, and loosens my grip on the reins. Then she thrusts her head forward again as far as she can and sinks her big face into the tall grass. For a little while I yank on the reins to let her know I'm the boss, but she's stronger and knows what she will do on the sheep-watching job.

After a time of unconvincing effort to get her to cooperate, I'm content to simply watch my father, my uncle, and my cousin at some distance on the other side of the yard. Mother is hanging the wash on the clothesline and lying next to my three brothers is Lady. I puzzle over Lady's loyally watching the babies, but then the warm sun make me drowsy and I stretch out over Sleepy Eye's withers, my head resting on my hands which are interlaced into her mane. Cloud shadows slide across the hills in the late morning breeze.

Suddenly I am awakened from my stupor by a loud swoosh, and a large, flat black shadow sweeps over Sleepy Eye and me and I can see the wings of a big bird swoop down into the flock and pick up a little lamb that's sleeping in the grass. The big bird jerks the startled lamb up into the air and her bleating cries are lost amid the flapping wings. I watch aboard Sleepy Eye as the big bird flaps the lamb up, up into the air and then glides over the house, straight toward the cottonwood stand along the river. Horrified, I slap the sleepy old mare on the side of the neck and dig my heels into her ribs, demanding at the top of my lungs that she move. "Get. Inahni, Hurry! Get up, girl!" I shout. Finally, Sleepy Eye leaves off her grazing and slowly raises her head, looks around, then begins to walk back down the hill, picking up speed with each descending step. Near the bottom of the hill and now on a dead trot heading in the direction of my father and his helpers, Sleepy Eye and I are bouncing along down the cow path when I nearly slide off her back.

"Dad-dy, Dad-dy. Did you see?" I stammer out the words to my father with each jarring jolt of Sleepy Eye's trot. "A big, black bird took one of the lambs!"

My father clicks his tongue and Sleepy Eye stops short. I crumble forward into her mane and once again nearly fall off her slippery back.

My father reaches up and puts his hand on my back. "Yes. I see we have given that eagle a meal, today. That little lamb and your baby brothers are about the same size," he says. Although his voice isn't angry, a frown comes over his face as he speaks.

"Now go over to the house and tell your mother," he says. "Then call Lady to go with you back up with the flock until it's time to eat. This time stay sharp, my girl. Don't let the eagle catch you sleeping in the sun again."

Deep in the night, the eventful day finally over, I toss and turn, dreaming of big black wings flapping in my face, then a family of eagles rising up into the moonlight with my brothers, tiny legs and arms dangling down while they sail over the rooftop and disappear among the cottonwoods.

"Hush, Hush, Ishtimila. Go to sleep, little one." Unci's soft voice is singing in the darkness from the rocking chair. "The eagle and the lamb have taught us to mind our work carefully," she says. "Now, go to sleep, little one, and rest. The sun will soon be up."

I drift off to sleep listening to Unci singing in her soft, melodic voice her favorite hymn "Abide With Me." In my dream I imagine Tunka Shila watching the day unfold; Sleepy Eye and I slowly moving about on the hillside, the lambs and the babies sleeping on the grassy green below; and the eagle sitting somewhere, too, watching until I doze in the warm sunshine.

Even though my tears have dampened my pillow in the night, by morning the event has taken on a new meaning. My little brothers are easier to mind; their demands are less troublesome and I seem to find more ways to make them laugh than before.

It's not far to walk down to the river to get water, to fish, or to gather sandcherries or currants. The walk with my Unci down the winding, sandy path from her wood-frame house is most always a happy time. Sometimes on these walks we carry buckets for water. Other times we carry our homemade fishing poles. Then I carry anticipation with me to the water's edge.

One favorite place, where the tall grasses bend over with the weight of their heavy seedheads on long stems, is where the current ripples open a wide place in the river. It makes that part of the river look like a country of water almost without border. It is a place where another world opens up, and from where I stand I see flatboats and ferries loaded with boxes moving down the river, or at other times I see paddleboats loaded with people slapping their way up the river. My aunts and I sit on the sandy ledge and wave at the passengers who, when they see us, wave back and call out. Overhead the magpies call out, too, and the lazy bullfrogs sunning themselves on the occasional branches of driftwood jump from their perches and dive deep into the lapping water.

On this grassy shelf I sit, a barefoot child with feet hanging over into a watery world of little waterjigs. I watch insects skimming along the surface, seed hulls and broken pieces of driftwood. I see the cottonwood leaves, their stiff tails up-turned and waxy, riding high up over the top of each river ripple, then slipping down into the curl of the tiny swell and up again on the edge of the current. Watching the waves lick the sand, turning the path to slick gumboshale, I see the holy work of energy and movement. Sometimes, I watch the water slip its long flat tongue into and out of the half-moon tracks of early morning whitetails. Water beetles scurry indiscriminately into and out of webbed and clawed bird prints in the shiny mud.

Occasionally, butterflies light along the rim of mud cups made by deer hooves and gently unroll their long black velvet tongues into the water to drink. Sitting here on the cool, grass-covered riverbank in the heat of the summer, I learn of summer things the way my grandmothers did. This mighty water flows freely past our houses, and then further down it flows past the Sicangu, the Yanktonai, and the Winnebago and eventually into the big Mississippi. This is also the one path that links us to our scattered bands in Canada. Those of us who have traveled this water highway have as point of origin our homes along its shores. Here the swollen tails of spring shrink to narrow, dried-up necks alongside late summer gumbo cracks. I know these jump-across places. It is in many places like these that stories live, stories to live by, stories through which we remember who we are.

It is in this place on this grassy shelf where I learn that everything has its story. On this path, a particular place called Butterfly Girl's Path, my grandmother told a story about pride. It is a story Unci Eunie, Minnecoujou Lakota who lived on the Cheyenne River Sioux Indian Reservation, told to me about a particular young woman.

Once long ago, there was a camp here south of Swift Bird, here on the river up there on the open meadow. It was a large camp circle. In the camp was a family with two girls. One of the daughters spent much time alone.

The people noticed that she was often at the river. Sometimes she would be gathering wood or getting water for the family. But most of the time she sat by the water's edge and peered at her reflection in the quiet little puddles near the shore.

One day in the late spring the time arrived to honor those who had faithfully kept the families fed during the winter. It was a time to honor the elderly who had come through the hard winter. It was a time to plant the summer gardens. All winter the women had busied themselves making gifts for this time of giving and for other special occasions. After all, tradition holds that to receive in times of need, it is good to use the strength of the body and a good heart to give away to others the gifts of thanksgiving. To have a good heart and good strength is reason to celebrate. It was at this time that the one daughter decided to honor herself.

All morning long the women of the camp and their girls carried the quilled moccasins, belts, and bags out of the tipis and placed them in a long line for others to admire. There were digging sticks, woven willow chairs, robes, blankets, and cooking utensils. And for the children, dolls and bows and arrows hung draped over or tied to the drying racks. Finally, the last of the fine gifts was gathered and the lone young woman carried to the stack an armload of shawls.

The people all assembled and the speaker for the family spoke of the great mercy of the Creator and prayers were sung to give thanks for the bounty which had kept him and all of his many family members in good health and sound minds. Other members of the family stood up to offer up their recognition of good fortune. When all was said and done, the father of each family called to those among the people to come and receive the gifts of his great fortune. The eldest, seated in the shade of the trees, received their gifts first. Then those much younger received their gifts. Though the line was long there was plenty for everyone to receive something and the family was pleased that they were able to be so generous.

Now it is not good to hold back gifts intended for others, but this is what the eldest daughter of the family had done. She had seen a beautiful shawl made by one of her aunts. The skilled aunt had captured dazzling colors unlike any she had ever seen before. The vivid colors were like the brightest summer sky, the starless night, and the white of winter snow. Upon seeing this shawl, she had hid it away when no one was looking, even though the shawl had been made to honor the younger sister.

After the giveaway and all of the gifts had been distributed, all of the family, with the exception of the oldest daughter, wore their simple clothes so the whole camp could see their humility.

Days passed, weeks passed, and the pride-filled daughter would take the shawl from its hiding place to admire its beautiful colors. Finally, when she reasoned that all thoughts were on other things, she wrapped herself in the bright blue shawl trimmed in white against a black background and walked to the river to admire herself in the quiet waters of coming dusk. She saw the blushing rose in the setting sun as it blanketed the distant shore to the west and wished aloud that she could have that color in the shawl, also. Overhead, the cottonwood women looked down and saw her shadow cast in the yellow sunlight.

Standing on a fallen tree trunk sprawled across the water's edge, the girl opened wide the shawl and admired the swaying fringes in the water. She pulled it tight around her and glanced back over her shoulder to see the beautiful design on her back. As the girl opened wide the shawl again, she heard a soft whisper in the leaves above her:

"For a season each year, in the time it takes for the red rose of sunrise to meet the red rose of sunset, all will admire you. However, so as not to encourage your dishonor to be repeated by other young women of the camp, you will wear the colors of the brightest day and the coldest, starless night in winter. These colors are a reminder that selfish pride cannot bring life to the people."

The girl turned around to see who had spoken. Only the dragonflies darting and dipping into the water caught her eye. She looked up and as she did, the sun sank behind the hill and the darkness rooted her to the spot where she stood on the river bank.

That evening her family looked for her when she did not return to eat the evening meal. They looked and they looked but they could not find her. After many hours of searching into the night, the family returned to camp in the morning to eat before beginning their search again.

All day they searched, until sometime after the long shadows stretched behind them to the east, when the younger sister remembered that she had seen her older sister walking to the river alone. Having heard this, the family rushed to the spot where the trail meets the river and called out. They called and they called but they heard no reply. Discouraged after much calling and whistling, the family stood quietly together, looking out over the watery horizon.

After a long while, the young girl's grandmother reached out her outstretched hands and grasped those of her daughter. With great sadness and downcast heads, they stood in a circle and held hands. Then softly, the grandmother began to sing the missing young woman's naming song.

As they held hands and sang softly in the golden light, a small cluster of butterflies, kimimila-skanyeca, fluttered into the family's circle. Overhead, the cottonwood leaves rustled gently around them.

Days passed and a great sadness came over the family. Each evening when they ate their evening meal, they were reminded of their missing member.

Each evening after the meal, the family members would walk one by one down the trail to the river's edge and call for the missing girl. Each time someone did, a bright blue butterfly would fly to the mud tracks along the trail and fan open and close its bright blue wings trimmed in white and black.

The older sister had become the blue damsel butterfly.

"I'm told that when young women too full of their own importance walk along the river, they see the blue damsel butterfly admiring itself as it drinks water from the deer tracks," said my grandmother.

"You look around carefully when you're down at the river," she said. "You'll see that little butterfly spreading its colors on the edge of the water. It likes to sit on the edge of the little puddles that the deer make. Do you know that the deer and the little butterfly admire themselves every time they drink? They used to be beautiful women who made too much of themselves. Don't forget that now."

One of my grandmother teachers grew up Minnecoujou Lakota on the Cheyenne River Sioux Indian Reservation and the other grew up Hidatsa (Gros Ventre) on the Fort Berthold. She later married a Hunkpapa from Old Kenel and moved to the Standing Rock Sioux Indian Reservation to have her children. These women were important teachers to me. Unci Eunie taught me about Butterfly Girl's Path. It is a place, a butterfly species and a story emblem of what this butterfly means to women of the Minnecoujou Lakota Oyate, the Planters by the Water People, and it is a glimpse of the way of life on the Missouri where this story was born. My Unci told me this story when I was very young, before my parents took me into the Old Cheyenne Agency to attend boarding school. I still do not know if the Ogalala of the Pine Ridge to the south or the Hidatsa, Arikara, or Mandan women to the north in Fort Berthold have the same story for this butterfly. I wonder if they tell this story or whether they have a similar story that ties them to a similar place along the water where they live and where blue damsel butterflies frequent the water's edge.

Along the river, or sometimes following the many creeks up the barren gumbo hills leading to the windy ridge and out across the hills that breathed and rolled along under their shaggy grass coats in late summer, I rode horseback with my father. On other occasions, I walked with the women of my family, picking June's summer cherries and wild berries in the draws and washouts, or searching deep in the tree cover of the river banks for sandcherries and currants.

Before the Army Corps of Engineers built the Oahe earth dam and pushed the Missouri out of its banks, I would stand on a sharp ridge we called Magpie Looking waving at the passengers aboard the riverboats as they paddled up and down the river road on their way to Pierre, to Mobridge in South Dakota and to Bismarck, North Dakota, and to other places along the way. Other times, the whole family would stop the busy work of loading firewood or water to watch them pass.

Our teams of horses harnessed to the stone boats or the buckboards always seemed grateful for the brief rest. Of necessity, depending upon the time of year, our teams of horses dragged home from the river bottom fallen trees for firewood or they hauled home big 55-gallon oaken barrels full of water for drinking, cooking, and washing clothes.

Often when my mother, my father, and his brothers moved off to the campfire to drink coffee and to rest, my mother's youngest sister and I would call out to the boat riders. Other times we would lie flat on the river bank fishing in the warm, summer afternoons. Sometimes we would whistle out strange sounds as we watched to see if the passengers spotted us hidden in the tree shadows. We would pretend that we, too, were passengers on the boats and that we were headed for Pierre or even to St. Louis, a city neither one of us had even been to, though we had heard the railroad workers refer to it in LaPlante. My mother had acquired an old Sears and Roebuck catalog somehow and we had spent hours studying the many items for sale between its covers.

In the winter, when the river was still itself and not a dam, we would lie on its frozen surface on a gunny sack full of straw, our fishing lines tied to sticks straddling across chopped-out holes in the thick winter ice. Then we would watch men and women start out across the ice bundled up like porcupines, making their way to wasicu farms where they worked or would trade.

When my father went across the ice, he nearly always took a horse. We knew he would be gone for several days. When he returned home, he always had several bags filled with spices for my mother, some fabric, other sewing things, candy, dried fruit like apricots and pineapple, and smoking tobacco, which he carried tied to his saddle. He also brought home groceries that were not a part of the government commodities. These were always a welcome treat.

On other occasions, when enough time had passed so that my mother's good humor was starting to spoil into long stretches of sullenness, my father would harness up the team and buckboard for our long journey to my mother's people on the Standing Rock Sioux Indian Reservation. Years later, he would start up the Studebaker pickup for the trip. We never visited my mother's family enough. In fact, to this day I refer to my mother's family as "her people" as my father did, even though I love them and yearned to be with them almost as much as my mother did. Back then too much time elapsed between our visits to Good Defender and Defends the Camp Circle country near Kenel, a little village on the Standing Rock Reservation.

Even today, I still yearn to know "my mother's people" better, and to spend more time with them. Because they are my family, I also have accepted that we must grow stronger in our need to be together. I feel a need to spend more time with them. I wonder if I, too, will be like the old women I enjoyed watching as a child. They would sit under the arbors reliving adventures of their youth because they had taken time to make memories together. I found such joy and admiration just listening to their treasure trove of stories, stories that evoked soft laughter and sighs that confirmed some shared understanding, comfort nods as they relived their youth in the telling.

All along that northward road to my mother's childhood home, I learned about our homeland and heard stories that fixed those places in my memory to make them mine. Our early trips northward in our old buckboard are rooted in memory, like the memories I still hold dearly of miles and miles of cottonwood stands all along the river bottom. We would wind our way up Prairie Chicken Creek in horse's time where we would cut across Bare Belly Flats (my father's name for this flat, barren ground of gumbo), then pick up the sometimes overgrown, two-wheel trail leading to Virgin Creek, after which we would cross over the top of the ridge to Swiftbird Butte before dropping down into the yawning valley of the Moreau River with its miles of gray gumbo.

On these trips, my father would tell of old places and events that made room in my mind for the land. For example, I would hear stories my father heard as a child and also stories he lived in as a boy growing into manhood. He was a good storyteller and his stories came alive for me, there along the greasy ridge top, in grass that swallowed up distant horse and rider in its late summer gold, on our way to Big Foot's country far away from my home.

On our first trip north to Unci Susan's home, we settled in overnight at two campsites and slept under the faraway campfires of the ancient ones overhead. Stories I heard along the trail during that trip and many times thereafter were richly painted with the lives of those who had lived in other times. Through tiospaye stories, I came to accept that I would know my grandmother, my grandmother's mother, my great-grandmother's mother, and that their stories would fill in the hollow ignorance of my young life like the stars fill up the deep hollow above me until the rising sun.

Mid-morning the next day found us descending the south rim of the Moreau River. Off to the east were scattered homes of Promise District people, nestled in among the cottonwoods and the wild turkeys that roamed this area of the reservation. Further westward along the shallow river were the White Horse District people. Crossing over the river, which was sometimes difficult after a summer rain, and ascending from the Moreau bottom, I saw Sleeping Woman Butte on the distant horizon. Her limbs stretched out gracefully to the point where her hands disappeared under the surrounding buckskin grass and lay pressed flat in the gumbo. Muted colors of dried chokecherry pulp and variegated strips of greens, yellows, and black, like Snapping Turtle's neck, painted the creases of her large, soft mounds. Thunderhead clouds overhead chased across her body, dragging their shadows over her. I remember asking my father to stop the wagon so I could see her wake in the bright morning sunshine. Her rounded, mother mounds reached upward while her head, partly submerged behind her right shoulder, faced to the north.

As I stared, the horses bobbed their heads and snorted off flies from their muzzles as they patiently waited. Occasionally, one of the horses would raise its hind foot high in the air and stomp the soft pad of overgrowth underfoot. Or shake loose a stubborn bluebottle fly with shoulder muscles that lay still and glossy until they moved like a rolling grass carp, then the horse's withers rippled, and finally its ears twitched. From where I sat next to my father, the horse's soft twitching ears made Sleeping Woman's feet look like restless toes inside dapple and bay horsehair slippers. It was my father's voice that broke the silence that early morning.

"She's like your mother. See how she has one hand reaching south into the river toward the Cheyenne Agency and the other reaching north into the Standing Rock. Even as she sleeps she looks homeward to her mother's bed." For a long time my eyes were locked on that grand woman of dirt, shrub, and mystery who lay on the horizon. I knew what my father meant for me to know about her and about our family.

My mother was sitting on the bedrolls behind my father's springboard seat with her left arm resting on the side of the buckboard. Her face had already begun to take on that smoothness across her forehead and the bridge of her nose that would appear whenever we reached this part of the trip. Her back rested against my father's saddle and her legs were folded back beside her. She was the living spirit of the woman I saw under the piled up form of Sleeping Woman Butte. Hidden under Aunt Celia's summer quilt that lay across her lap was yet another likeness to Sleeping Woman—her swollen belly still holding my unborn brother.

Our lives were woven into the buffalo grass that grew on the quick, yellowing high plains nearby and our dreams had become rooted in the red willow and the chokecherry stands or tangled in sandcherry shrubs that dug into the shallows; our spirits were shadowed among the cottonwoods along the Cheyenne, Moreau, and the Missouri. Our river life was an ancient way. Our river life was like the weaving and painting that goes on against the skyscape every spring and every fall when our mitigating relatives move overhead to their nestings in the far north, and then again to the far south. Like them, my family and I would move with, against, and on this great openness. And, like the antelope born into plenty grass and sweet water, like the one who ventures into new territory and runs until she drops her young under the cloak of the moonless night, I would know my home circle; I would know my territorial fringe, from the dirt to the thunderheads.

Then the tired sleepy woman large with child who rode behind my father urged us on down the trail toward Defender country, the place where my mother knew her childhood best. Now, with my days of musing, I imagine my mother as a small child, like I was then, vibrant and full of childhood's color. With the horses trotting down and around the gentle side of Mahto Butte, heading in the direction of Kenel, I imagine my nostrils flared like the team of horses up ahead. I would sniff the air, smelling Unci's tallow-tainted apron, warm chickens nesting and my waiting featherbedding, kerosene lamps and waxed paper windows, wet canvas cover and the sharp taste of the broken enamel water dipper that hung above the oak barrel just outside the front door. Then I would smell Lala's Bull Durham breath go past my ear as he would lift me up and out of the buckboard box. Fat orange chickens scattered like dried rolling tumbleweeds in the wind as I would run for the house and Unci.

No matter when we arrived, by evening the house was full of my mother's fámily, some from as far away as Fort Yates. I knew that her two sisters I knew from every visit would be there. Unci's brother and his family, and her niece and her family, along with assorted other younger nieces and nephews of my mother's, my cousins, would always make our trip north a celebration. Favorite foods would cover the kitchen table while welcome home gifts for Mother would find their way into Unci's pantry.

Meanwhile, we children, transformed by the sight of Crow Willow Creek behind my grandparent's house, became like prairie dogs as we slid down the shale embankment and chased one another into the deep hollowed-out pockets along the creek walls. We called them caves, though they were not true caves but boiled out holes caused by spring cloudbursts. All along the winding, twisted creek, until it split into Laughing Horse Creek and Wolf Woman Creek, we ran and hid from one another, or ambushed the ones who wouldn't wait for us to find them. We rolled down the bald, shale sidewalls of Crow Willow in those brief summer days until the sinking sun pulled us up onto the topside, into a galvanized bathtub of warm yucca water.

Later, leaving a half-eaten supper of fried bread and navy beans, we would sleep deep and sweet in the overstuffed feather tick mats in Lala's barn. Built of logs and about thirty feet by thirty feet, the barn stood about eight hundred feet from the house and served many functions—it was a tack shed, a pen used for foaling Lala's good mares, a milking station, a haymow, a place for the little orange chickens, and our sleeping quarters. As youngsters, my cousins and my young aunts and uncles and I looked forward to the visits to my grandparents, when we played all day and stayed up late into the night telling stories.

On those summer days Unci and Lala would always take us chokecherry picking. I remember the sky back then as being brighter and more brilliant blue than newly-laid robin eggs. My Aunt Arlene would be already up helping Unci prepare things for the day's trip along the river. We would have spent the previous night planning to follow the old sandy river road north toward Fort Yates.

My grandpa would have already eaten and could be found working near the corral, as he harnessed up the horses and put into the buckboard the cream can we always used to carry water for the day's trip. I would hear him humming as he tightened straps and filled the gunnysack with a mash made of oats, corn, and sweet stick (sorghum) for the horses. Frosty and Mr. Bucks, the old horses we could ride without a saddle or a bridle, were my grandpa's faithful helpers. They would patiently stand for him while he finished by loading the shovels, small lard cans, and the enamel water buckets.

In the house my grandma and youngest aunt were finished boxing up the big iron dutch oven, enamel soup bowls, utensils, seasonings, bread, peanut butter, corn wasna, papa (dried meat), dried onions, and corn for soup we would have later in the day. We would be out on the ridges and in the chokecherry stands well into the evening hours. I remember how the excitement mounted with each passing moment for us younger ones.

Having finished eating our oatmeal, my five cousins and I would grab our jackets and head for the buckboard. When we arrived at the back of the box, Grandpa shook his head and pointed to the house. Somewhat embarrassed by our forgetful eagerness, we threw our jackets into the back of the buckboard and ran back to the house to help carry the food and utensils.

We then leaped up onto the back end of the buckboard and seated ourselves so we could dangle our feet off the back of the wagon box. Unci and my aunt had brought blankets out when they came. They carefully arranged the blankets into a soft place to sit. All readied to leave, we sat as patiently as we could while my grandpa disappeared into the tack shed for his fishing gear which he placed under his seat. Then he climbed aboard the seat and clicked the horses into motion and we moved out of the yard and down the long slope to the river road.

The ground was soft and dry and the wagon wheels pressed down into the earth, raising a little layer of fine dirt onto the rim. I watched the dirt rise to the top of the wheel, then fall into the air, making a little cloud of dust. We took off our shoes and threw them further up into the buckboard and took turns jumping down into the soft dirt, then hung from our elbows as we dragged our feet in the dirt.

Along the way the magpies followed us, calling out as they flew from tree branch to branch. The bees were busy working out the nectar from the flowers which grew along the path. Every once in a while a curlew would bolt up into the air in front of the horses and hover near the wagon, all the while calling out its name. The water shone bright on the river in the morning. Everything was as it should be for a day of gathering wild fruit.

After a long while of dragging ourselves off the back of the wagon, we invented other games. We dropped a stone off the back of the box, drew a line in the dirt, put our big toes on the line and called out to Unci to give us the signal. Wigh a big smile on her face, she clapped her hands together and we ran like the wind to beat the others to the back of the wagon, and pull ourselves up into a sitting position to face the trail behind. After a while we tired of our various wagon tail antics and were content to just ride along, filling ourselves up with the beautiful June morning.

As we rode, Grandpa and Grandma commented on the way the washouts had grown from last year; they made note of how the gumbo patches were fringed with gumbo lilies in bloom. They asked each other the names of various flowers. One of my cousins spotted a dung roller that the wheels had just missed and he slid off the back of the wagon to pick it up. When he put it on the floor board, it was still holding a ball of dung between its feet.

"Unci. Why is this bug rolling up this stuff?" Dewey asked.

"It is said that this bug is making a new moon and when it is big enough a strong wind will come along and lift it up into place in the sky. When that happens then the two moons will talk to each other and we will know what is happening in places we can't see now," she replied.

"Unci, is that really true? Can the moon talk?" I asked.

"Right now the moon listens," she replied. "There's only one moon and so it only listens." She smiled at us as we watched the bug trying hard to hold onto its ball as the wagon floor bounced along. I had never thought about a bug having anything important to do, but after that day I would learn many stories that related the work of insects and animals as important to the way we think. On that day we had found two different kinds of dung beetles, one shiny black one and the other a brilliant metallic green one. Later I thought back to what Unci had said about the moon and I wondered if perhaps the green one was making another moon or another world for somewhere up in the great sky above.

Years later while I sat in a college sociology class, I learned the importance of one of the lesser Scarabaeidae, or dung beetles or tumblebugs, which we had watched intently on the floor of the wagon. I had no idea until then that this bug was an important icon to the Egyptian people of long ago. In fact, according to the lecturer, the ancient Egyptians considered the dung beetle to be sacred. The important work of the dung beetle was carrying the messages of the sun and relating life-giving messages as it symbolically rolled the earth. Later on I learned that several other civilizations recognized this bug for the same reason. So revered was the work of this insect that Greeks and Romans wore jewelry like the Egyptians to recognize the beetle's important work and its secret knowledge of life.

The wisdom of the beetle I learned from my grandmother as a

youngster; the wisdom of the beetle other civilizations celebrated I learned from my professor in a college classroom. There I sat half the distance across the United States in a college classroom, learning about the wisdom of dung beetles and realizing what a wise and wonderful grandmother I had who, without a Ph.D., had taught me as a child what my professor was relating to us as adults.

My grandmothers were busy women. They always had a working plan of how to carry out the duties of the day. The fact that Unci Susan held in her thoughts such simple gem things as insects and their importance made me ever grateful for having such a knowledgeable grandmother. I often pressed her to elaborate on some of her thoughts, but her replies were always pretty much the same. "The ways of life will reveal themselves to you," she said, or "all in due time, these secret things will become yours."

She recognized the importance of knowing the "secrets" of the insects, the birds, the fish, and other animals. I believe she believed as I did that there would be plenty of time to learn these important things. I believe that at the time she was telling me these things, neither she nor I had any thought that the river would ever change. I believe she felt that the ways of knowing we could learn from our other relatives—the animals and the plants—would always be there. I believe that, like me, she thought that any changes made in the river would be its own doing and not the result of some decision made by humankind.

But things would not be this way for long. In fact, those who did not have river knowledge would make decisions for the river and for all of us. Decisions potent with power beyond that of even our tribal leaders' ability to comprehend would come. The Pick-Sloane Project and Oahe Dam changes would occur and the river world as we had known it would cease to be. All of those many lessons that only a river world could teach would cease to be taught to my generation. Succeeding generations of young people would not know the harmony of life I remember experiencing on the river. Many of our people have said that back before the creation of the Oahe Dam, we had it all—the good, the bounty, and the health of whole families. For us, the change was a twofold startling event of devastating proportions. First, there was the loss of the river and an entire way of life and then there was the imposition of boarding school education and the breaking up of family togetherness.

I see a river shoreline of men and women, young and old, carrying water, picking berries, gathering firewood, fishing from the shore, fishing in their boats, setting up frames for smoking their catch, wading in the sloughs for cattail root, gathering teas of so many kinds, making toys for children from the fallen leaves and branches, telling stories of how we came to be a people, making furniture, women telling river stories to their grandchildren, children learning about the gifts of the river. I hear men singing; I hear women, old and young, singing as they work and live among the trees. I hear children's laughter, too. All family members are busy moving about doing what needs to be done to keep a family healthy as they laugh and work and have their time of learning what the river can teach them. These are the scenes that come to my mind; these are the sounds that I miss hearing when I think of how things have changed from my early childhood.

When the river waters stopped flowing freely with the construction of the Oahe Dam north of Pierre, South Dakota, families living along the Missouri River were displaced. The consequence of that construction was to set in motion a domino effect of negative changes for Lakota people. The tribal administration and council members who initially supported relocating families away from the river to a new place portrayed this change as the beginning of a future of progress and prosperity. However, forty years have passed and, for the most part, the promised improvements in the lives of those who were displaced have not occurred. I believe that the loss of the river and its reservoir of wisdom and resources far outweigh whatever gains there might have been.

I am reminded of this great loss every time I smell burning or singed hair, which evokes a memory of being taken away to boarding school. Somewhere buried in those early memories of loss and separation are the stirrings of a realization that began back in my early childhood. As far back as I can remember, I have never participated in a conversation lauding the so-called virtues of boarding school life; never have I celebrated my life on the open prairie ridge far from the river bottom. Instead, the first thing that comes to mind when discussions drift to childhood and boarding school experiences or to the way of life on some ridge-top town is how I am still deeply saddened.

When we were sent to boarding school, we became lost children. Through no fault of our parents, we were sent off in the company of other frightened children on a long journey into a government-designed madness. It would take much of a lifetime before some of us would find our way back from that journey. It was a journey that made mourners of our grandparents and our parents.

As a girl, I believed I would someday earn my Indian name by running away from those dreadful dormitories. I thought that if I ran away from the dormitories until I finally froze to death in the driving winter blizzards, trying to find my way home, I would be saved. Instead I found a secret territory of my own making which enabled me to endure the emotional suffering as well as physical separation from my family. I did that and then some. Because, ultimately, I believe, I became a tangle-root woman and clung to the survival stories of my grandparents. I grew in other ways to protect my spirit so that I could stand upright in the face of a harsh way to learn away from home. My choice was to turn inward to the strength my grandparents assured me was within all of us, but even so, it was hard.

My grandmothers had prepared me for the skinning nightmares that would fill my boarding school nights. At home, I had first watched them skin the deer that hung low in the cottonwood. As I grew older I helped them, learning that by death the deer had been transformed in two ways—first, their once living forms were released into the spirit world and second, as sacrifice, their bodies became food for us.

As I lay awake nights, thinking about my father and mother driving me to boarding school, I thought about the deer. Instead of walking out on the ridge with my father to study deer and other game tracks and listening to him tell of just how plentiful the deer or antelope would be in the late fall, I started to seal up inside like thick tree bark, even before we left for the Old Agency dormitories. My child relatives and I were stripped of home life and expected to accept dormitory life. I felt I had been skinned like the deer, torn out of a river place from a real life and expected to accept dormitory life. Dormitory life probably would not have hurt so much had I not known what I was missing.

Five, six, or seven years old, it didn't seem to matter to government authorities how old a child was for subjection to compulsory education. Youngsters were taken away from their families to boarding school or their families took them to the dormitories or suffered the consequence of going to jail. In either event, young children were gathered up and made to live away from home and learn about a life they never should have known.

I remember that it was already late afternoon when my father drove our old pickup to the west end of the playground square and finally stopped in front of the little girls' dormitory. "Oh, huh. We're here," he said, trying to make light of a situation that the heaviness of his voice could not hide.

He lifted me out of the pickup box and together with my mother we entered "the little girls' dorm." I stood in front of the matron's desk while she wrote things on a paper as my mother answered her questions in a flat monotone. When they turned to leave after a while, I followed them to the door. There, my father told me to be no trouble and my mother knelt on one knee to hold me tightly in her arms before the matron moved out from around her desk and placed her hands on my shoulders. Then the matron turned me away from the door and closed it. I could hear my mother's leather loafers fade away down the steps of the sidewalk into the sandy gravel where our old pickup was parked. I could hear my father slamming the hood, and the motor cutting into the brief silence.

Then the matron called to a girl to come out from a storage closet across the room. I stood in front of the matron's desk while she lifted my clothes out of the Hamm's beer box like they were dead animals that had started to rot and threw them on a pile in the middle of the room.

"She'll have to have issue," she told the girl, who looked about the age of my mother. The girl took a measuring tape from a drawer in the desk and, stretching it out from the back of my neck to just below the backs of my knees, she wrote a number on the paper about me.

"Do her hair before you take her to her room. And put her in with the ones who came in last night," the matron told the girl. The girl took me to a small closet, took out a clean white-ironed sheet, opened it up halfway, and pinned it around my neck with a safety pin.

I watched the girl carefully as she pushed me away from the closet and toward a table near the hallway, which was covered with another flat white sheet. Then the girl motioned for me to sit in the chair. When I didn't move, she demonstrated sitting down in the chair. Then she turned her head to one side, pressing one ear flat to the sheet.

"Sit down like this," she said, as the matron walked across the room and disappeared into the closet. I stood straight up and still beside the table. After a short time, the matron came out of the closet with a handful of fine-tooth combs in one hand and a jar of kerosene in the other. I pretended to watch the girl, but I could see the matron place the combs and the jar of kerosene on the table. When the girl started to sit up from her straddle-legged, slouched position, I jerked the sheet from around my neck and bolted out the front door.

"Stop her! Stop her!" The matron shouted to a couple of girls who had just walked into the room. I glanced back and saw that they stood confused in the doorway. Then the matron grabbed one by the shoulder and pushed her back out the door toward me.

I shot off the porch and down the short flight of steps across the gravel road to where my mother and father had parked earlier. I scanned the road for my father's pickup, but it was no longer there. I couldn't risk looking further around the tree-lined square. Instead, I sprang up on the little curb that opened into the playground square, out-distancing the two heavy girls chasing after me while the matron stood on the steps calling after them.

"Enacaneiooo!" I heard a bird call out above me, but I didn't look up. I ran past the playground equipment and down and across the road that led to the government workers' houses to the north of the road and west, back in the direction of the Old Agency Camp and the river. My legs swept out in front of me and stretched longer and longer, until I was tall enough to see far ahead of me across the bridge and deep into the cottonwood stand, where I could see the old trail. I ran with my stretched legs like a blue lightning runner, my ears pounding and pumping until a soft, warm rain began to fall and sap flowed from my eyes. My sap flowed in the rain until the road disappeared off to my right and the weeds grabbed at me. Glancing to my left, I saw a huge, red man hunched up on the ground with his head tipped fully back so that I couldn't see his face. Instead, I could only see his equally huge pipe, bigger than any pipe I had ever seen before, which he held close to his chest on one end. The blackened end belched smoke, pointing straight up into the air.

I ran until I found the trail where the weeds were higher than I was and followed it as my legs began to shrink back to their normal size again. My ear had begun to stop pounding and then I could hear my feet slapping on the path. I looked down and saw that I hadn't torn the sheet free after all and that my neck was raw where I had jerked on it. I gathered up the front of the sheet, doubled it up, and swung it over my shoulder, twisting it over the raw burn until I could reach the safety pin. Then I unclasped the sheet and rolled it up under my arm. As I did that, I noticed that I had not run through any rain at all but that I had wet myself.

"It won't be light very long," I thought, "and then I can rinse out my pants and socks and follow the deer trail down around the water's edge back to my grandmother's house down the river." I kept walking briskly, slowing up only long enough to listen to hear if there were any motors further up from the river bottom in the open clearing to the north or if I could hear tire wheels crunching along the dried grass skirting the washouts along the ridge. But I could hear only a killdeer calling and occasionally a dog barking across the river on the other side. I remember as I walked along the deer path that early evening, the soft, warm breeze flowing through the trees. Then cool, crisp night air that sinks into the deepness surrounded me and a feeling of comfort washed over me in the shadows of the tall cottonwood trees. I felt at home under the rustling leaves overhead.

As I walked, my thoughts drifted back to the scene I had fled. That first trip to the little girls' dorm would remain vivid in my memory as a mixture of childlike mystery, desire, and terror.

In my mind's eye, I re-entered the half-glass front door onto the flowered floor covering and saw sofas and armchairs for the first time. Unlike the long hardwood benches that lined the walls in the Bureau of Indian Affairs building where my father would sit and wait with other men to see the superintendent, the two long, wide, padded benches in the little girls' dormitory building looked soft. They made an angle and faced a large black box in the corner. Two other overstuffed chairs just like them flanked the hallway entrance that faced the front door. I thought about the big chairs. Those chairs were big enough for my three younger brothers and me to sit on and even sleep on when company came. We always seemed to need chairs when the priest came and when Molly and her family and sometimes Grandpa Joe and Grandma Jenny would come for evening services at our house. We could even eat on those big chairs, since our table was too small for chairs that size. They were big enough to play on and all three of us could even sleep on them.

Chapter 1

I thought about the flowered floor covering. I had never seen anything like it before. I thought about how my baby brother could crawl on it and not get slivers; it was so soft and pretty. It would not have been very practical when it rained or the snow thawed in our gumbo country, but it was pretty. Overhead, three large clusters of bright lights hung from the ceiling.

To the left of the front door was the matron's large desk. Behind her desk was another door that stood partly opened, and a gray cat was sitting there looking out into the big main room I later would call the living room. Between the desk and the hallway entrance was the table with the kerosene jar on it. I stood frozen in fear as I saw those two women moving against the black-shadowed trees in the background. They were combing kerosene into little girls' hair, then striking matches and watching the hair curl and burn off black and powdery to their smokey-white scalps. As I stood there almost smelling the singed hair, watching it turn brown then black, crackling as it curled, an owl swooshed down and set me running down the path again. I had still too many miles to go.

Exhausted, I walked in darkness until I reached Unci's house. She never asked me any qustions. She just heated a pan of water on the stove so that I could bathe, then put me into her bed, where I hunkered down deep into the familiar sweet smell of her blankets and cried. I could hear her softly moving about in the kitchen. The sounds of the pans and the smell of wood burning in the big cook stove finally eased me into a sound sleep. The next morning I awoke to the smell of bread baking and for a time I believed I had slept through a night of bad dreams.

A couple of days went by and I believed that I was safe with Unci. Then one day a black government car with lettering on the doors pulled up alongside the house and a man I knew stepped out. It was Bill Iron Moccasin. He was a man my father knew well. He visited with Unci while I stayed in the bedroom and listened hard to hear what they were saying.

After all was said and done, Unci encouraged him to leave me with her until my father could come to the Old Agency Camp. "Let him take her to school," she said, and Bill agreed.

So eventually, I became a first grader at Old Cheyenne Agency Boarding School. This was my introduction to an education filled with many contrasts, beginning with the learning of English. (I have changed some of the names of the persons in this recollection out of respect and to preserve their anonymity.)

"Class. Today we're going to study tense. Remember last time when I said that many of you are ready to learn about tense?" The teacher paced across the front of the classroom, her eyebrows drawn together. I recognized that look. That look meant trouble. I slumped down in my chair as far as I could get without sliding off onto the floor. I could see Willis Iron Cloud across the room. He raised his hands to make a triangle with his index and thumb fingers, and then he nodded his head, signaling that everything was going to be all right. His posture confirmed that he knew what was going on. Everyone in the class knew that Willie was the teacher's favorite. We arrived at that reasoning since he was the one she called on to pass out the papers, to wipe off the blackboard and to put the trash into the hallway for the janitor.

But sometimes Willie was in a bad mood and wouldn't cooperate, and became loud and obnoxious. On those days, the teacher didn't have the patience to be kind to any of the students. In fact, she seemed to bristle up and act strangely. We began to judge what kind of day we would have by the way Willie and the teacher related to each other as we began the lessons to be learned. In other words, when Willie was cooperative, he and our teacher Miss Hodges set a half-pleasant tone for the whole class.

Feeling a bit better but not enough to take a chance and look over Arlene's shoulder at the teacher's face again, I glanced across the room again at Willie. He was already fidgeting in his chair, a sure sign that he was ready to dive in confidently. Everyone else in the room was quiet, waiting for our teacher to turn and face us. That would mean that class had started and there would be no turning back. Once Miss Hodges launched into her lesson plan, we would be joined with her in a tug-of-war for understanding until one of us demonstrated that we knew what she wanted and then her determined drilling would let up. Our only other relief came when Ruth Hale would become anxious and start to wheeze, or when Willie was able to throw Miss Hodges off guard with his usual antics that sometimes got us all into trouble.

Miss Hodges stopped in full stride, pivoted on one high heel, then dropped the other high heel with a loud click on the hardwood floor. She folded her arms in front of us and began to walk slowly down the aisle closest to the door.

"Today I like my dog Sparky," she said, as she strolled down the aisle, her dress making a soft, scraping sound, like fresh cabbages being pushed through a hand shredder. As she strolled past Willie, he sat up straight and leaned forward with a smile on his face and waved very slightly at me behind Miss Hodges's back. I pretended not to see him, but inside my stomach began to relax a bit. I usually started each day with a knotted up feeling in the pit of my stomach before Miss Hodges started her routine. As the class lessons progressed, my stomach would either shift into a gentle, random twisting and audible gurgling sound or it would settle into a constriction that escalated to a low nagging pain as her voice became higher and louder.

"Yesterday I liked my dog Sparky." Miss Hodges continued up the next aisle with each step stressing the words "yesterday" and "liked." Her high heel accented the motion of her jaw as it jutted forward, her mouth clenching down on each word. Ann, sitting across from me in the aisle to my right, looked over at me with a frown on her face. I shrugged my shoulders and we both turned to Willie, whose smile faded only slightly.

"Tomorrow I will like my dog Sparky." Miss Hodges turned at the blackboard and stared at the windows made of glass bricks behind us at the back of the room. A silence hung in the room as everyone in the room readied for what Miss Hodges would tell us about tense. Finally, as Miss Hodges seemed stuck in her thoughts, Willie ventured out with a concerned look on his face.

"Miss Hodges, did he run away? Maybe Fred and me and some of the other boys could look around for Sparky when the bell rings. I bet he mighta followed you over here. He's probably eating scraps behind the kitchen." From the look on Miss Hodges's face, we could see that something was wrong as she walked toward Willie's desk.

"No! No! No!" she said, her head bobbing with each word. "Not my dog. I'm talking about tense. Tense, as in time."

"But Miss Hodges, you weren't telling us about tents, you just told us you really like Sparky," he said. I could see Willie was trying for one of his rescues and once again there would be no stopping him, which is probably why Miss Hodges liked him so much. He wasn't afraid to help Miss Hodges out when she got distracted. No, Willie wasn't like the rest of us, who sat back without a word as we watched Miss Hodges drift off into what she was saying, then turn on us with her pinched up forehead and her shrill, high voice.

"No. Willie. Not Sparky. Tense."

"Yes, Miss Hodges. It take a while to put up a tent. One time when my Uncle George was drunk and he was trying to help my big brother and me put up our tent at the Berthold Powwow, it took us almost all night. Then finally my mom said we should just wait till my dad came the next morning. We slept in the back end of the pickup that time and the mosquitoes nearly ate us alive," Willie offered generously.

"No, Willie, I'm not talking about that word, tents," she said. "I'm talking about the tenses we use when things happen."

"I know, Miss Hodges. That's when things happen. That was the time some dogs were barking and spooked some horses and they got loose and ran right into where we camped and knocked down a whole bunch of tents, even our tent. That's what happened."

"Listen, Willie. Let's start all over. I said, Today, I like Sparky. Do you hear how I said that?"

"Yes. You said you like Sparky today. But you said you used to like him yesterday too and if we find him for you, I bet you, you won't get mad at him. You'll like him because he'll wag his tail and lick on you and then you won't be mad at him."

"Wait a minute, Willie. Wait a minute. Oh my God, not another day." Miss Hodges's left hand was already shaking as she cupped her jaw in it and the deep wrinkles grew in her forehead. Somewhere off to the left of the room I heard Ruth's breathing start to labor, and my stomach began to cramp up.

"Get out your pencils, right now," she said, her voice loud and stern. "Willie, give everyone a sheet of paper from the paper stack. Now, write this on your paper just as I am putting it on the board." Miss Hodges abruptly turned to the chalk tray, picked up a long piece of white chalk and began writing in such hard, angry strokes that the chalk broke and fell in pieces out of her hand. She muttered to herself, picked up another long piece, and continued as before, until she had broken at least four long pieces of chalk and had written the sentence, "Today I like my dog Sparky."

We had reached an impasse, Miss Hodges and the class, with her insistence that she liked her dog Sparky and our waning expectations of sharing what we knew about tents and teepees. This confusion continued that day with only slight variations, and Willie reported after recess and after lunch that he and the boys were unsuccessful in locating Sparky for Miss Hodges. Finally, having given up trying to explain, Miss Hodges took her place at the far corner of the classroom, silently staring out the clear window panel in the wall of glass bricks. This would not be one of those times when she would go into one of her emotional outbursts that would almost certainly send Ruth into one of her crying and wheezing attacks, scare Anita into wetting herself at her desk, and cower the rest of us into frozen terror. On occasions like that she would smack the hands of frightened left-handers who momentarily forgot and tried to write with the "wrong" hand. I learned to watch out for those times so as not to get my hands smacked with the ruler. Instead, this day, she chose her more frequent response of the cold silent treatment, which also had the effect of freezing us silently in our seats, but making an easier end to the day for everyone, including Miss Hodges.

This day, however, would be quite different, not just because of the breakthrough to a new word meaning but also because of the future implications it would have for at least one of the students.

Later that afternoon, Miss Hodges's high school student worker Lillian came to clean up the classroom during the milk break. While we ate our graham crackers and drank our milk, Miss Hodges opened up to Lillian. Lillian, like many other high school students, was allowed to move about the elementary school assisting teachers with whatever they needed as a merit award. Back then, good students were given certain merit privileges and older merit students were assigned to help a teacher. Lillian asked Miss Hodges during the break if she required help with anything. Instead of answering Lillian's question, Miss Hodges stated that she was having a difficult day but that she was determined to teach the lesson she then described to Lillian.

I could see that Lillian was listening carefully and nodding her head sympathetically. I watched the two women as together they talked quietly for a time in the corner of the room. As Lillian spoke softly to Miss Hodges, she was visibly transforming and began to look less defeated. I imagined as I watched from the safe distance of the snack table that Miss Hodges had needed to unload to someone at least some of the grief she had stirred up for herself on that day.

However, Lillian did more than listen. She took the larger primer story tablets that Miss Hodges used when she read to us and flipped them over so she could draw on the backside of them. Using the big colored pencils, she then drew a picture of Miss Hodges's Sparky, asleep on a porch in the blue night with a yellow moon overhead. On a second page, she pictured Sparky under a sun with a bird in a tree, and on the third page, she drew Sparky sleeping again, but this time on Miss Hodges's bed, again with a moon in the blue night outside the window. Finally, on the last tablet, she drew Sparky, again under the sun, smelling a flower. Then Lillian wrote the "ed" letters on the blackboard behind the first picture, left the part of the blackboard behind the second drawing blank, and then wrote the word "will" behind the third and fourth drawings.

With Lillian's help, everyone in the class was able to understand that Miss Hodges's word was new and different from what Willie had thought, not only in spelling but also in meaning. It meant that different word endings of "like" would convince us that Sparky could count on Miss Hodges's affection all of the time. We had been fortunate to have Lillian come to our room when she did. By drawing pictures to unravel the confusing word "tense," Lillian had saved us from the wrath of our teacher.

This would prove to be the beginning of a relationship in which Lillian would come to our classroom to sort out our confusion by illustrating meaning for such words as lie and lay, sit and set, and raise and rise. In most cases, the fine points of our lessons were cleared up with the help of Lillian's chickens, bread, eggs, and other illustrations. On many occasions when Miss Hodges left Lillian in charge of the room, Lillian's illustrations became so elaborate that they would often exceed their original purpose and invite Lakota stories. These stories were about such things as chickens that laid eggs in unintended places such as felt hats, car seats, and old wheel hubcaps. On one occasion, someone in the classroom told of a cousin who had married a girl who not only put too little or too much yeast in her fry bread dough but didn't know how to cook at all, so the cousin had taken her back to Lower Brule.

We were quickly brought back from our story tangents whenever Miss Hodges returned to the room, however. Then we chewed English stones the hard way again until Miss Hodges would give up and let Lillian grind them up into pictures that made sense to us and finally into words that we could use.

The first year of dormitory life was like every following year, a monotonous routine that seldom varied. It consisted of getting up early, getting dressed in government issue clothing, combing our bobbed hair, making our beds the way nurses are taught to make beds, with tight square corners. Then came lining up single file in the hallway so the matrons or the "big girls" who helped the matrons could inspect to see that our beds were made before breakfast. Having met with approval, and donned our scarves and coats, we marched single file like little ducks to the dining room, which was a separate building at the far west end of the boarding school square or courtyard. Once in the dining room, we went through the food line cafeteria style and sat in assigned seats to eat our breakfast.

After breakfast we waited until all of those seated at the table were finished eating and then we once again lined up and filed back to the little girls' dormitory. Between breakfast and the first bell for class, we cleaned our rooms. This entailed scrubbing the bathroom, dusting the furniture, and putting away all garments and other materials in our assigned drawers. Each girl in the room did an assigned task and the tasks were rotated every few days.

After the rooms were cleaned in the few minutes before the line up call to go to the school building, the matrons and helpers again inspected the rooms to see that they were cleaned for the day. Then the bell rang for us to line up to march to the school building. The routine of our days was punctuated by different reasons for lining up and moving about the school. After school, time was left for play in the playground, which was the center square that each dormitory building faced. On the weekends, we played there and in the rolling hills behind the dormitory.

I tried to fit in and accept the situation of being away from home, but it was hard and some days were downright unbearable, I would get so lonesome. Thinking back on those times, what stands out as so unnatural was the fact that we children were separated at a very young age from our parents and grandparents to live in peer groups. We cried in each other's arms whenever we were lonely. But when we were sick or when we acted out our anger, we were isolated from each other as punishment. And to take suffering to the level of physical pain we were made to kneel in the hallways long hours into the night in an effort to "break us into good behavior," into orderly conformity. It was not enough that we children were forced to attend boarding school like our parents and some of our grandparents had, but our families, especially those who lived on the river, would have to endure yet another devastating event.

I remember kneeling in the hallway one night and overhearing the matrons talking in the living room. There was already talk among the other students and the adults around the school campus that the routine of life we were living would be changing.

During this period, when my father would come to the school to check me out on weekends, we would go to see Unci, where there was more talk about new changes. Everyone, even our grandparents, got together to discuss what the possible changes would be, and they reckoned with these coming changes in many different ways. On those visits to my grandmother, I recall, she took to praying in earnest. She told my father that the old women were praying and singing together that the river would continue to flow as it always had. The common understanding was that once the dam was built, the river would be held back, no longer able to flow with a true current.

I remember that the women's prayers, like their songs, were too old for my ears. At least this is what Unci told me when I said I didn't understand their words. The kind of life which would evolve out of that change in the river was hardly imaginable; but there was a general sense of loss in the air long before the water began to rise. Ultimately, the great Missouri River would become barren, deprived of its gifts for the people.

As the dam became a reality, barrenness came not only to the river, but also to the men and women, young and old. Sons and daughters of all ages living along the river swelled up with emptiness, like the river. Instead of being filled with confident contentment, many of the people filled up with anxious emptiness, a heavy sadness. I saw it in their eyes. Would we still be able to call ourselves Minnecoujou, planters by the water?

Each passing day that the river widened, we could see the water moving further up our meandering footpaths along the sandy shoreline. The little places we had built in our play were slowly being covered over by the water held back by the earth dam. Teary-eyed men and women spoke of hard times to come, as the first generation of young people would have to learn to live without the gifts of the river.

A few of the river mourners met this change by grafting their dreams to their children and their grandchildren. They saw something in the rising river and sang with a new understanding like new life-giving sap flowing through them, even though it was not like the good days they remembered in their own youths. Some of them were singing the ancient songs for mourning. They sang of the coming death to the river life that the people had known. One of the singing mourners was Bird Song Woman.

She was an example of how love for family helps to make one strong and brave enough to face even the sad and difficult life-altering event of losing the river.

Bird Song Woman knew the songs of every season. She could answer the burrowing owl, the chickadee, and the snow geese, but her favorite song and the one I especially loved to hear was that of the meadowlark. When I was a little girl she taught me to ride her Appaloosa gelding with just a hackamore and his warm hairy muscles rippling beneath me. On other occasions, I stood on an old wooden dynamite crate so I could knead the dough beside her when she taught me how to make bread. "Knead it till it speaks to you," she would always say to me, and the freckled mound of stone ground would speak and pop in her hands.

During one of those special times, we were making bread at the kitchen table when I asked, "Unci, did Lala ever live here?" She paused and looked deep inside me for what seemed like a long time. Then she sprinkled more flour on the dark walnut grease stain in the middle of the oak table where the sticky dough held fast. She was a twilight worker, quiet and slow. Her whole body gently swayed back and forth to the rhythm of her hands disappearing in and out of the dough.

"We used to live on the river bottom," she answered in her soft, lilting voice. "All of us and there were so many more of us then." The stubborn sticky dough slowly began pulling itself into one breathing heap. "That was before the dam."

I knew she was working herself up like the dough to tell me something special. She was a woman of many songs but few words and I was ready to hear what she said.

"Your grandpa could swim like a turtle," she said with a smile. "He'd take his little wild ones and his old bamboo pole standing out there in the lean-to, and the pack of them would spend the whole day down on the river. Just swimming and fishing and chasing each other through the cottonwoods, forgetting all about the sun." Her right hand disappeared into the speckled dough belly and a big bubble rose up with a sigh.

"Just about when I'd start to light the kerosene lamps," she and her smile continued, "I'd hear Grandpa's hoot out there in the dark. I'd answer him and wait. Listening. Sure enough, your daddy and the rest of them would all try it. Then one would giggle and after a while they'd be all broken up, laughing. They sounded more like a pack of coyote pups, but your grandpa didn't scold. He'd let them carry on their barking and yipping like that till they got to the hitching post." She paused and shook her head, her eyes dancing off her smile. I abandoned my post and my little mound of dough, climbed up on Jimmy's tall stool, and sat with my elbows riveted to the flour dust on the edge of the table.

"Then your Grandpa would make them take turns washing the sand off their feet. They'd all sit down around this table, all yipped out and quiet. They slept like bears in the winter after your grandpa took them to the river."

For a time just the dough spoke above the quiet shuffling about on the table as Big Ben ticked on from the windowsill in the background. Another bubble swelled up from the freckled dough belly, broke, and shrank back into the rubbery, moving mushroom. I watched her like a rock as she picked up the shiny glutinous lump, set it to one side, and sprinkled some flour on the big slab of soapstone on the water reservoir of her old wood-burning stove.

Then she lifted the heavy dough ball into her speckled blue dishpan, hauled the dishpan to the stove, and coaxed the dough out onto the soapstone. Reaching into the warming oven, she pulled out a clean, flour sack dishtowel and covered the resting dough. With one hand she opened the side door of the stove, stoked the bed of glowing sticks with the lid lifter in the other hand, and then slid in an arm of dry ash. She filled the white enamel cup that she kept on top of the warming oven for coffee, took a quick sip through the steam, and put the cup back.

"Days and nights were like that on the river until a man in a government car came around and told us we had to move. Some men in Washington had made a deal with some of those on the tribal council to build a dam. He told us that the government would move our houses up to the butte halfway across the reservation. Or we didn't have to move them and they would pay us, or we could move into the government house camp. We listened to what he said, but none of us wanted to move."

"Your grandpa's friend Milbert went to visit his brother over at Red Scaffold and he told everyone when he returned that there were no trees where they wanted us to move. There was no river like ours there, either. All of the old-timers were angry about the whole thing but few spoke out. Your grandpa said he'd live with the fishes before he would move to that 'wasicu' town up on the ridge.

"It was a crazy time. Some of us put in a garden like we always did and made pretend that the government man hadn't told us anything. Some people went to the tribal council and begged them to change their minds. A few of the older ones got all confused because they thought we were moving out to the Black Hills and they couldn't understand what all the fuss was all about. Well, they moved us up here before the winter set in and Grandpa came along, too. He spent most of his days deep in thought and a sadness came over him that we couldn't lift no matter what we did to help him," she said quietly.

"Then one sunny quiet day, after about three days of howling wind and blowing snow, Grandpa said he was going to see his cousin Joe. They would chop a new stack of wood in case the crackling cold was not over yet. After the sun went down it began to get real cold, like it does when you can see tiny little stars sparkling on the snow. Some men found Grandpa the next morning on Virgin Creek Trail south of LaPlante. He was almost home by the shortcut," she said softly, picking dough skin from her hands.

For a long time I had trouble trying to swallow. In the meantime Grandma had moved from her chair at the table, lifted the dough from the stove to the table and worked the soft brown mounds for the oven tins. I watched her as she gently fitted the loaves into the tins. I understood then why she took her coffee cup out to the clothesline on warm summer evenings; why listening to the birds as they settled down to sleep was so important to her. I realized then that she could easily have gone with Grandpa, but instead she chose to stay. In the end, she and all of the rest of us who left the river bottom would suffer broken hearts because of the great loss of healthy, productive families.

Every week on one of our reservations and in some Indian community, the media uncovers indirect and direct evidence of loss to families living without the ways of knowing afforded by the wisdom of the river. I believe the river provided the basis for healthy and whole families, and without it, all manner of assault has been made against those families to hamper their survival in all the ways that really matter. Government remedies are powerless to replace the gifts of wholeness provided by river wisdom that upheld ethnic identity and cultural learning, all very much a valid part of our human experience. Instead of stories celebrating and honoring human life, I hear and read of child abuse or neglect.

Eventually, the Indian Child Welfare Act was created to help with this problem. But youth gangs and teenage vandalism prevail on the reservations, and in large urban Indian communities. Juvenile boot camps and juvenile holding facilities are the current strategies for dealing with teenagers who are growing up without sound parental guidance. Domestic violence, abuse, and homicides make the tabloid headlines and momentarily capture the public's attention. Safe houses for single parents and their children and homes for battered women were created to help with this problem. There is elder abuse and abandonment, conditions unheard of before the reservations and forced government relocation of families into contrived community settlements divorced from culturally significant environments like the rivers.

Today, police, tribal, and Bureau of Indian Affairs law enforcement officers provide patrolled or security-protected homes for the elderly and the physically disabled to try to help them. Poverty still holds the reservations tightly in its grip, though seasonal federal community block grants attempt to provide economic well being in these communities. And finally, racial discrimination, that covert disease of the mind, continues to feed on a landscape thriving with ignorance. I now understand that the loss of the river has caused the kind of family degradation no amount of money or talk will restore without the restoration of the river.

Maybe this loss is finally being accepted as detrimental to more than just the Indian families who lived on the river, since recent news stories include acknowledgement that even certain native fish species brought to near extinction as a result of the dams are being restocked in the Missouri River.

Other recent news events are yet another irony being played out in the wake of catastrophic historical errors in judgment. I am reminded of the strong ties that once bonded the river families. Our ancestors have joined in the revelation of this wrong. We are learning of ancestral gravesites emerging from the ground because of the rise and fall of the water levels along the Oahe Dam.

"Everything has its story," my Unci used to tell me as a child. "If we pay attention and listen, we can learn many things about ourselves from everything that tells its story of how we are connected, how we are related." She once told me that she trusted people who not only knew this concept but also practiced it. For example, she once asked me, "Do you know what the word 'amen' means?" I recall that I answered her with another question.

"Does it mean the end?" I asked.

She replied: "A priest told me that it means all men agree. He explained that when we sing, we all agree to praise the Creator; when we pray, we all agree to give thanks and to ask forgiveness and we all agree to be humble. You must remember that not all men do agree, even though they say they do when they talk to the Creator and others with them hear them say what they tell the Creator."

I have often thought about her response. It didn't make much sense to me at the time, but something about her words was unforgettable, and now I am beginning to understand them. "All men agree" or "amen" is not the same as "Mitaku Oyasin," "We are all related" or "We are all relatives," which we say when we pray. I think that some of our elders, because of their imperfect understanding of English, may have thought that "Amen" and "Mitakuye Oyasin" were the same since they are both closures to prayer. Could this have been behind our eventual accepting to leave our beloved river bottom to move to the ridge top where our ability to be self-sufficient was made so difficult? I have often thought about the implications of this intepretation and many other variations of unsatisfactory interpretations over the years trying to come to terms with our loss of the river.

When I was in boarding school we were made to do everything together, as a group. There and in mission school, when we prayed, we prayed in unison the prayers we had been forced to memorize for religious instruction. And the prayers always ended with "amen." I remembered what my grandmother had told me and I remember mouthing the words in silence and sometimes even omitting them. Over the years, my grandmother's careful distinction between the two expressions has taken on a profound and disturbing understanding for me.

Back then as dormitory children, we were afraid to ask questions of those in charge of our young lives but I did have questions. Therefore, I, educated in the power of river wisdom, did not believe that perpetuating or elevating human values, attitudes, spiritual understanding, or economical well-being with the creation of hydroelectric power with the Oahe Dam was wise. Now, I believe the Oahe Dam to be very much a source of the inhumanity which has entered insidiously into families that were once held together by teaching and exercising with each other the rightful meaning of respect for all living things as it is expressed in "Mitakuye Oyasin." The river animals and the plants would not have agreed to leave their homeland and their absence in our lives is evident in our poor health and well-being.

We have been silent about what this great loss has been for us as people. We have been silent instead of crying out "Injustice!" We have all tried to make some kind of sense of our lives without the river. We no longer have the river's gifts and wisdom to help shape who we are. When we look around us, the evidence is clear that we cannot expect to survive let alone achieve healthy wholeness without an environment of cultural and spiritual significance, which is our river way of knowing. The poor quality of our present existence continues on as it is today, if we bury ourselves in the work of piecing together merely an existence.

Today, when I imagine with deliberation, I must strain to hear and I do, and what I hear is the unmistakable distant chatter and singing of the cottonwood trees along the river. I imagine I see gold leaves shimmering and dancing off their lofty boughs, dropping into the water and swiftly forming a bright yellow snake in the center of a rolling blue ribbon. I see in the distance the people as they once were, whole and healthy and truly a family of grandparents and parents with their children. There are daughter seeds anchored in the washouts and ravines leading to the water's edge. They were planted in the fertile soil of hope, patience, and native wisdom.

Chapter 2

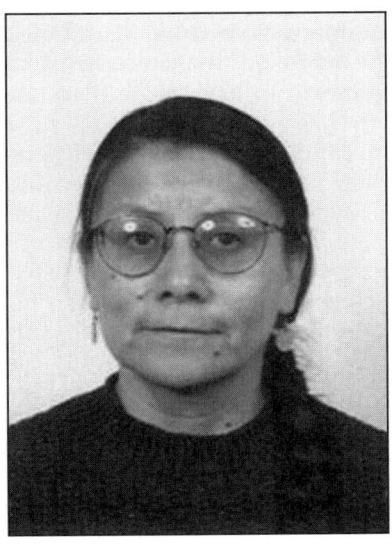

On Learning

Karen Lone Hill

Karen Lone Hill is an enrolled member of the Oglala Sioux Tribe. She was raised in Butte Community in the Porcupine District of the Pine Ridge Reservation in southwestern South Dakota.

Karen has a B.S. in secondary education from Black Hills State University and an M.Ed. in curriculum development from South Dakota State University. Since 1986 she has taught courses in Lakota language, literature, culture at Oglala Lakota College on the Pine Ridge Reservation. Her areas of research and publication are Lakota-English bilingualism, Lakota cultural history and sociology, Lakota legends and myths, and traditional Lakota arts.

To tell my story, I must begin with the lives of my parents, whose early lives influenced how they would raise their family and how they would feel about formal education. They believed that education was essential for their children because they had been deprived of it due to unusual circumstances, and because when they were growing up, traditional beliefs and customs were being set aside. My parents were forced to assimilate, a process which they seemed to embrace very positively.

I was born on May 5, 1956, in Gordon, Nebraska, approximately thirty-five miles south of Porcupine, which is a village in South Dakota on the Pine Ridge Indian Reservation. I was the fourth child of eight children. My parents, Llewellyn and Ethel (Weston) Lone Hill, had originally decided to have only one child whom they could "spoil," but their firstborn was a daughter who became ill and died at the age of two. Distraught and heartbroken, they accepted that misfortune as a sign that they were meant to have more than one child.

Their original decision to have one child was based on their own unfortunate experiences of losing their parents at young ages and never really experiencing family life. My father's mother and my paternal grandmother, Bessie (Rock) Lone Hill, passed away after contracting pneumonia when my father was one, so all he remembered was living with different relatives. He experienced living with his father, Sidney Lone Hill, and his stepmother, but eventually his father asked him to leave because of conflicts within their family. He then moved in with his older brother, Hobart, in Rapid City, where he eventually talked his brother into signing for him at the age of sixteen so he could join the Navy. Because of the instability of his home life, he never completed high school. He did have many learning experiences in his travels as a sailor and was well-cultured and literate in both English and the Lakota languages.

My mother's mother, Suzanne (White Bull) Weston, suffered from rheumatoid arthritis and died at the age of thirty-eight, when my mother was about sixteen. When my mother's paternal grandmother, Martha (Red Wing) Weston, became ill and could no longer care for my mother's youngest sister, Lucille, who was about three years old, my mother's father, Reuben Weston, asked her to quit school to care for her youngest sister because he believed their stepmother was unable and unwilling to care for her. My mother reluctantly quit high school along with her dreams of high school graduation and of joining the military, like some of her close friends.

Because of my parents' unfortunate childhoods, therefore, their goal was to ensure that their children received good formal mainstream educations along with a stable home environment. They also adopted a cousin of mine who became our oldest brother shortly after my oldest sister passed away. We never knew that he was not our biological brother until later in our lives. My two oldest brothers, Lamoine and Sid, attended a country school north of Gordon, Nebraska, for a short time, until we moved to Porcupine in the summer of 1960.

My father had worked as a ranch hand and laborer around Gordon, Nebraska, until that time. My memories of living in that area have always been positive. My father and mother formed close relationships with the non-Indian families where they lived and worked. They were so close that some of my bothers were named after some of my father's friends. My brother Lester Howard had the name of my father's uncle, Lester Lone Hill, while his middle name was for Howard Stauffer. My younger brother, Leonard Leo, was named after my mother's uncle, Leonard White Bull, while his middle name was for Leo Kearns. My father had chosen the name of Debra Lou for me if I was a girl, but in March of 1956, my older first cousin gave birth to a girl whom she named Debbie. Because they were at a loss for names when I was born, their friend Pauline Kearns suggested two names to my mother. She could choose between Karen Louise or Karen Doris. My mother chose the latter.

I still remember the dairy farm north of Gordon, Nebraska, where we lived. Every morning, my mother would have my two older brothers and me fetch a pitcher of fresh milk from a small building a short distance from our house. It was generally oatmeal for breakfast. I remember one particular morning when I noticed dark specks in the oatmeal. I asked my mother to remove them, but she was busy feeding and tending to my younger brothers. I began to cry, so she took my bowl, turned around and pretended to take the dark specks out of my bowl and throw them to the side. Then she returned it to me. Through my tears, I looked at my oatmeal and saw that they were still there. I began my wailing again, but nobody paid any attention to me. I was about three and a half years old. My mother and my brothers slowly finished their breakfasts and left the room. I don't remember if I ever ate my oatmeal that time.

Another memory I have of this place was when my father took all of us into this huge barn one spring. It seems he and Howard were taking care of some orphaned lambs and he sat me down with one of the lambs to bottle feed. At the time, I was oblivious to whatever else was going on. It was a comforting feeling, sitting there in the hay and feeding this helpless little creature.

It was shortly after this that my parents decided to move back to the reservation. My brother, who was fifteen months older than me, was to start kindergarten in the fall, so they decided to move closer to family. The summer we moved, I had just turned four. I remember my three older brothers started that fall at the Porcupine Day

School, which was a Bureau of Indian Affairs school. I threw a tantrum because I wanted to go to school with them. I didn't understand why I couldn't go and was very persistent. My mother and my brother Lester promised me that Lester would bring me papers to do. He kept his promise by bringing home his finished work and erasing what he had done and explaining to me how to do it. So I guess that was my "head start" in schooling. I looked forward to going to school and was well prepared.

The summer before I started school, there was an incident that strongly affected my life. My father had developed a work ethic and he believed that you needed to work for what you wanted and that you also had to live within your means. So he continued to work at his land leaser's ranch west of Batesland, South Dakota. We saw him only if we stayed up late or wanted to get up before five in the morning, but we always saw him on the weekends. When he got paid, the whole family would go into Gordon to purchase necessities, such as shoes for one or two of us and the groceries.

My mother always said that whenever people joined the U.S. military, they naturally developed a taste for alcohol because it was easily accessible to them. That was her explanation for alcoholism. She said that when they returned, they still had this acquired habit, or "addiction" as we call it today, so she tolerated my dad's occasional drinking with his friends and her relatives. Whenever my father was late in coming home, it was a cue to pack the bedding and go to one of the maternal grandparents' homes to "visit." I preferred to sleep in the comfort of our home, but it was also nice to break the routine and go to a relative's house to play with other cousins, even if it meant sleeping on a hard floor. We always had to be on good behavior without hospitality complaints of any kind.

Evenings at Grandpa Gilbert's and Grandma Nancy's were especially nice. One summer evening, we went "inkpata," up the creek, to Grandpa Gilbert's. He was my Grandpa Reuben's brother, so he would come and pick us up whenever my mother sent word. It was a sleepover and what my mother called "tiyukan"; in olden times, it meant the women and children leaving the house for the men to feast in. In the sixties, it meant an escape from the men who were assumed "partying."

We were never allowed to listen when the grownups visited, so we played outside until dark or until they made the bed and called us in. This one night, some of the Weston cousins and my younger brothers and I played near the spring at the bottom of the hill, and alongside the hill. We chased fireflies, or "lightening bugs," as we called them, as darkness fell. Once we caught them, we would smear them on our skin so we glowed for a short while. I never knew what the bug actually looked like, but it was an activity that kept us occupied.

Early in the morning the smell of frying bacon and baking powder biscuits awakened me. Grandma Nancy and Auntie Bena were already cooking. We were, in a sense, their guests. I would help my mother fold our bedding, go to the toilet outside, wash up, and seat myself on the long wooden bench on one side of the table. Chairs were uncommon in most of the homes in those days. That morning, I ate a small piece of fried slab bacon, a bowl of corn meal, and one baking powder biscuit. Then we loaded up our bedding and were taken home.

Other "tiyukan" times, we went "hutab," downstream, to Grandma Grass's house near Sharp's Corner. When we went there, we played with the Elk Boy cousins. Whenever we ended up at Grandpa Reuben's house, we had to be on extra good behavior because we were step-grandchildren. Whenever we got slightly out of hand, this Grandma would sneak out without us noticing. Then there would come this banging at the door and the entrance of someone named "Siyoko." She had donned her hideous mask, old raggedy clothes, and a broom she pointed threateningly at us kids. Everybody would be crying and screaming, clinging to Mom or hiding their faces to avoid seeing "Siyoko." She would leave only when everyone promised to be good and go to sleep.

I had never seen or heard my parents argue or fight, but this one particular summer day when I was four, I heard them arguing in the house. My dad came outside and told me to get into the car with my two younger brothers, who were two and three and a half, so I did. I didn't understand alcoholism, but I trusted my dad. He then took us into Pine Ridge to his older sister, Edna (Lone Hill) Two Dogs's house. He dropped us off and left, so we stayed with her for at least one night that I remember before my mother came and picked us up. Several years later, my dad became active with an AA group while my mom met with other wives in an AlAnon group. My brothers and I played with the children of the other members when they had their meetings.

The day my father dropped us off is my first recollection of my

Auntie Edna, who would play an important role later in my life. She was kind and gentle with us that first time because she knew we were homesick. I learned later from her that she had asked my dad if she could keep me. She was a traditional dancer and her intention was to teach me, but my mother refused to allow that. It was a missed opportunity to speak the Lakota language fluently and naturally and actively participate in a lifestyle that I had to learn later.

My aunt Edna's youngest child, my cousin five years older than me, spoke fluently. I have always felt that if I had been allowed to stay with her in that environment, I would now be much more comfortable with speaking the language. My parents both spoke the language in our home so all of us understood the language very well, but we were never required or even encouraged to speak it. Although Lakota was their first language, my parents understood English, so when they spoke to us in Lakota, we always responded to them in English. I never gave that much thought or questioned them until I became an adult. When I did question my dad years later as to why they didn't make us speak the language at home, he said the importance of speaking it never occurred to him then. He eventually harbored some regret, but his determination that we survive in mainstream society as adults outweighed that regret. It was dismissed as a trivial matter.

The following year, I entered kindergarten at Porcupine Day School with my older brothers. The kindergarten classroom was in a building set aside from the main school building. Years later, my mother told me that particular building had been called the canning kitchen. It was where another generation had learned how to preserve garden produce.

I was so proud to finally be going to school. I remember the first day of school. At the time, I couldn't understand why all the other children cried when their parents took them into the classroom and left. There was a slide set up in the classroom that I immediately began to play on. In reflecting back, I was always independent or wanted to be, so this was a perfect opportunity for me. My first reaction to all these crying children was to stare at them, wondering why they would cry. Years later, my cousin, Lorna Lone Hill, remarked that she always remembered that first day of school because I held her hand although she didn't know me. Our teacher, Miss Hendershot, assumed we knew each other because we shared the same last name.

I don't remember what I wore on that first day, but I remember in the days before school started, my mother cut off my braids and had my aunt Lucille give me a perm or "Toni," as it was called in those days. She wrapped and kept my braids in the cedar chest that she still has today. I laugh whenever I see my kindergarten picture because I looked like orphan Annie with all those curls.

She also ordered dresses for me from the Montgomery Ward catalog. The one dress I vividly remember is a red print corduroy jumper with a white blouse ruffled around the cuffs that had the slip attached to the blouse. Another new experience for me was using an indoor bathroom, so when it came time to go to the bathroom in this particular red jumper with the white blouse and tights, I fumbled unnecessarily with all those buttons. I completely undressed myself. It seemed I spent an eternity in the bathroom trying to get myself dressed when all I had to do was lift up my dress and pull down my tights.

The school Christmas program was one of the major events for the community. In the kindergarten, we rehearsed singing and performing "Up On The Housetop." I remember being up on the pullout stage with my class, set up in the gymnasium that also served as our lunchroom. The stage was in the spotlight, with the audience section in the dark, with some faces visible in the first few rows. We all sang at the top of our lungs and did our little routine. When we finished, we were applauded. For all I know, we probably just made a lot of noise, but our parents seemed proud of our performance.

Those winters seemed to be much more severe in the sixties. As a kindergartener, I remember an incident when snow had fallen and it was still snowing and blowing, and a huge drift had formed going down the hill where we lived. My mother readied us and sent us down to get on the bus. In those days, everyone had bus shelters built by the main road for waiting out of the cold and wind. As my brothers and I proceeded down through the snowdrift, I suddenly needed to go to the bathroom. As I told my brother this, I sat down in the waist-high drift and went without lifting my dress. My brother disgustedly took me by the hand and took me back to the house with my rear steaming. He pushed me back into the house and told my mother that I had peed my pants. Then they all went to school without me that day.

My kindergarten year was filled with many memories. I became Miss Hendershot's little helper. She always called on me for assistance. There was another girl named Karen in the class who contracted diptheria sometime during the year and was absent. A project she had us do prior to this girl's sickness was to spray paint little rubber bunnies, so it must have been just before Easter. She took all of this girl's belongings including her rubber bunny and burned them, so she had me help her with this task. In reflecting on this incident, I don't know if this teacher put me at risk. My cousin Lorna was also absent from school for much of the rest of the school year. I later learned she had polio.

I always completed my work before the other children. The "head start" in schooling that my brother had given me may have helped. I do remember that I was able to read and knew my numbers already when I started kindergarten. I did more reading and was rewarded by being given extra opportunities in the classroom. I don't recall any mistreatment or any type of harsh punishment of any of the children at this point.

There were no federally funded remedial programs at that time, but Porcupine Day School had a grade called "Beginner" that was between kindergarten and the first grade. Some of us proceeded on to the first grade, while some of the children, who I later learned were not ready for the first grade, were put in as "Beginners." So it was at this point that some stayed behind as others passed.

Culture-based education was nonexistent in the early sixties. It was virtually unheard of as our parents felt that it was the responsibility of the schools to teach their children mainstream values through a mainstream curriculum. It was not questioned because the assimilation process experienced by the earlier generations had taught them to be passive and accepting.

In the first grade, my teacher was Miss Ebner, who was a large, motherly type of woman. It was kind of like a repeat of my kindergarten year because I was able to read well, so once I had completed my lesson for the day, I was allowed to go to the back of the room which was set up as a reading center. I read all of the "Cowboy Sam" books. This was the grade where I began to really internalize the reading materials and developed the idea that I could go into somebody else's world, a reality different from the way it was in Porcupine or on the reservation. The readers used at that time included the characters of Dick, Jane, Sally, with Mother, Father, their dog, Spot, and their cat, Puff. They would go on occasional visits to their grandparents who lived on the farm.

This was enjoyable to read, but it was difficult to relate to because it was irrelevant to reservation life. Life in Porcupine was far from perfect. For one, I never knew my grandparents, and the families I knew had anywhere from seven to ten children. I was, however, able to relate to the farm life and milkman in these readers more than most children, because of my family's previous experiences living on a dairy farm. At least, I knew where milk came from.

In the first grade, we all sat in traditional rows. I don't remember what type of punishment or discipline was used with those students who misbehaved. I guess because I was eager from the very beginning, I was well-behaved. Also I knew that I didn't have a choice. My parents enforced regular school attendance and encouraged us from the beginning. I remember a girl who sat in front of me who sometimes wet her pants. There would be a puddle of water under her chair. I don't know if she was afraid to ask to go to the bathroom or if she had some sort of medical problem.

It was in this grade where manners and proper etiquette were learned. In the lunch room, we were taught how to properly use our silverware. It was a new experience for me because at home we never used a forks or knives. It was usually a spoon for every meal. At school, we had to eat everything that was put on our tray. I despised eating butter, raw onions, and the carrot/raisin salad, so I would eat everything else and then, if I couldn't sneak it to anybody, stuff the unwanted food into my mouth. Then I would show my clean tray to the teacher. Once she approved, I would put my tray away and then spit my unwanted food in the garbage can. I never got caught.

My second grade teacher was an African American woman from Texas, Mrs Gooch. She was probably about thirty at the time. This was about the time when I began to notice some abuse of certain children in the upper grades when they misbehaved. All grades had lunch together in the school gym where tables would be set up. We were able to witness a particular male teacher who would grab some of the upper grade boys by the collars and shake them up and throw them around when they misbehaved or talked back. Sometimes they would be placed in the trash can. This prompted me to behave and follow the rules.

It was also during the second grade when President John F. Kennedy was assassinated. Mrs. Gooch became hysterical and frightened all of us, mainly because we didn't know what was happening.

She was screaming and crying and went running out of the classroom. We stayed in our seats as we had been taught and wondered what the commotion was about. She returned later after she had composed herself and explained what had happened. It still didn't mean anything to us at that time. I remember watching the funeral on our black and white TV at home.

My mother was a learned seamstress from her student days at the Bureau of Indian Affairs boarding school's "practice cottage" caring for and sewing for young children. This was part of the requirement for the home economics class in the 1930s. She always owned her own sewing machine so she would also make my cousin Charmaine and me dresses. Charmaine and her mother, Lucille, lived with us from time to time because Lucille was a single parent and was also my mother's youngest sister. My mother treated us like twins. She was always concerned about our appearances and made sure we were properly dressed. She said it wasn't important to always have new clothes, but it was important that they be clean. It was about this time that there was supposedly a head lice problem at the school, so she had my older cousin, Kay, who she had heard was trained as a hairdresser, give me a haircut. I think she believed short hair would prevent head lice. It was about the time that the Beatles were becoming popular, so I was given a Beatle haircut. After I received my new haircut, I became infested with head lice anyway. It didn't last long, because my mother sat with me until she had them all cleaned out of my head.

I had the same teacher for the third grade. The second and third grades were combined in the same room with the same teacher. Many of my kindergarten classmates were now in the second grade, so we were reunited for a year. I had many cousins in the same room, so being familiar with each other, we managed to get into considerable trouble with the teacher. One cousin, Cheryl, supposedly was suffering with some kind of a kidney problem, so she had to chew Juicy Fruit gum. She was always generous and shared, which was against the rules. We would get our ears yanked if we were not discreet with our chewing.

My cousin Lorna was also back after her bout with polio. By this time, we were aware of our relationship, so when it came time for parent day and my parents showed up, she was very excited. We were told to continue working on our assignments when parents came, but she had to keep glancing at my parents to smile. She got a stern reprimand from the teacher that was at first just "Miss Lone Hill." Then it became "Miss Lone Hill," in a higher tone. I think she was told that day she had a "hard head." Whenever we didn't listen, we would receive a knock on the head and be told that we had "hard heads."

In the fourth grade, the husband of my second and third grade teacher, Mr. Gooch, became my teacher. I was pretty much well-behaved after witnessing what had happened to the older boys. I don't know why some of my male classmates would continue to misbehave and suffer the humiliating consequences of being shaken up in front of the entire class and tossed around. All of the girls, including me, tried to be proper and well-behaved. But there were a few of the boys who were very studious and well-behaved. Everybody knew that they received excellent grades and were academically inclined. In thinking back, maybe the boys who were always getting into trouble with the teachers were not academically strong, but were more athletically inclined and excelled in that area.

In the fifth grade, my teacher was a short motherly white teacher by the name of Mrs. Patnoe, from the Black Hills area. She was short, shorter than many of the students, even with her heels. She was older than other teachers. Her short hair was totally white and beginning to thin. Her classroom environment was different from the others. Her desk was at the back of the room facing the backs of all the students. Whatever her reason, it seemed to work, because everybody behaved and concentrated on the assigned tasks.

During this time it became apparent that I would need to wear eyeglasses. At the beginning of the school year, I sat at the very back of the room. The writing on the board began getting fuzzy as the year progressed, so I would have to make numerous trips to the front of the room to see the chalkboard. I was moved to the front row nearest to the chalkboard, but I would still need to get up to read the writing. Finally, it must have irritated Mrs. Patnoe enough that she referred me for an eye exam. My first pair of eyeglasses were what they called "cat eyes," which were in style at that time. They were heavy black-rimmed frames that were sharply pointed in the upper top outer corners.

I always attributed my need to wear eyeglasses to a bicycle accident I had with my cousins Charmaine and Faith the summer before my fifth-grade year. My older brother, Sid, was lucky enough to become the owner of a new red bicycle. My cousin Charmaine borrowed the bicycle and rode it down to Faith's house. When we were out of sight from everybody, we all got on the bicycle, Charmaine in the seat, I sitting on the seat above the back wheel, and Faith sitting sidesaddle on the front bar between Charmaine and the handlebar. Then we went down a hill that was dirt and pretty rutted. Charmaine lost control and wrecked us. They both flew over the handlebar. Unfortunately, I was stuck behind the seat and one of the handlebar ends hit me in the right eye. The others were okay, but I received a shiner and it swelled immediately. Charmaine became hysterical, screaming that my eye had fallen out. Then we went home, where my mother put packs on my eye and Charmaine's mother gave her a terrible spanking.

It was also at this time that I felt that because my older cousins had become cheerleaders, I needed to do the same. It made sense: my brothers and cousins were involved in basketball, so I needed to feel a part of that experience too. Things began to happen and change within my life. My cousin Charmaine, who was in the same grade with me, became interested in boys. She had a crush on this eighth grader, so she assumed that I was also interested in boys. I remember she set up a meeting for me with this other eighth grade boy that she felt I should like. I walked into the fifth grade classroom one morning before anyone had arrived and here was this eighth grade boy that my cousin had told to meet me. It was an embarrassing and awkward situation. I didn't know what to say or do. I think I turned red and ran out of the classroom. I was humiliated.

Another time, my cousin Charmaine and I were entered in this spelling contest being hosted by the Porcupine Day School. I was in the fifth grade oral portion and she was in the fifth grade written portion. As we were walking along outside the building awaiting our time, she suddenly saw her eighth grade crush. Not knowing what to do, she punched me in the kidney unexpectedly. It felt like a charlie horse at the time. I later developed a kidney infection. I was prescribed huge yellow capsules that I was able to swallow in the beginning, until I felt better. Then I would pretend to swallow my pills, and hide them behind the bedroom door. However, my mother found the pills and reported it to my dad. He was furious and said that if I didn't take the rest of my medication as prescribed, he would have to force the pills down my throat. I didn't understand his concern for my health at that time. I vaguely remember that when I was six, I developed pneumonia, but my mother said my dad refused to hospitalize me as the doctor had suggested. My older sister had died in the hospital four years before I was born, so I think he feared losing another daughter. My dad's concern to care for me during my illness was understandable.

I went everywhere with my parents whenever school wasn't in session. They were active Presbyterians, so I usually ended up going with them to the annual Presbyterian Mission Meetings held for four days in August. The ones I remember attending were held in Cannonball, North Dakota; Ft. Peck, Montana; Santee, Nebraska; Sisseton, Cherry Creek, and Wakpala, South Dakota, so I must have attended for at least six years. The Sisseton Mission Meeting included a visit to my mom's Flandreau relatives, particularly her Grandma Jeanette Weston. We took an extra day or two that year. On the way, my dad took time to drive us through the South Dakota State University campus. He told me that was where I was going to attend college. I must have been ten or eleven at the time, so he planted the idea in my mind that a college education was in my future.

My sixth grade teacher was Miss Williams from Ainsworth, Nebraska. She was also an older lady, taller than Mrs. Patnoe and not as gentle. She was a strict disciplinarian. In earlier grades, I had only seen male teachers rough up the boys. In this classroom, boy or girl, if you didn't behave and continued to talk back, she would grab you and shake you up. Her face would turn red and the flab under her arms would shake. It never happened to me, but I saw it.

I still continued to be actively involved in extracurricular activities at this time. Because my older Lone Hill cousins and older brothers excelled academically and athletically, the teachers also expected me to perform in the same manner. My academic learning and training was to be competitive, which was different from our Lakota cultural values, but I wasn't aware of those at that time.

At home, my mother was teaching me skills that were to come in handy later in life. I remember her cutting blocks of fabric when I was still very little and, although I was not yet coordinated enough, telling me to sew them together as she showed me. I sewed them together with the needle and thread she gave me. The stitches were maybe about a quarter to half an inch long, but I was proud of myself for completing some blocks. If anything, it taught me patience because I would have to sit and do my sewing while my cousins played outside.

The reason I wasn't interested in boys was because I was surrounded by six brothers by this time and I would rather just avoid boys altogether. I always wished they could have been sisters instead, so I wouldn't have to be the only one helping my mother with the dishes and the cleaning. I was so happy and relieved when my younger sister was born in 1965.

In anticipation of womanhood, my mother began telling me early on that once I began my menstrual cycle, I would no longer be a child. Her maternal grandmother, Ella (Pine Bird) White Bull, taught her proper female etiquette, so she was merely passing the information on to me. She said I had to respect my brothers during my menstrual cycle by staying away from them because "they would smell me." I don't know if this was a "scare tactic." It worked, although it made me wonder. I was told I could not step over any of my brothers' belongings and should not be near my brothers—that was the rule. Traditionally, this began the process of separation of the sexes and the beginning of adulthood.

Sex education was not taught in the schools or even discussed at this time, so I had to believe what my mother told me. I had noticed some of the older girls with stains on their dresses at school and it made me wonder, but I didn't know who to ask or even how to ask. My mother told me that as soon as I began my menstrual cycle, I was to tell her. She also said that in the past, there was a woman who had refused to tell anyone that she had begun her menstrual cycle and so she had gone crazy. I don't remember how I told her when my menstruation began, but I know it was uncomfortable. It was also a time when Lakota ceremonies were not being publicly practiced, so it was something that seemed shameful rather than a proud event as it had been in the past.

Another story I remember my mother telling me was about a little girl who cried over nothing. Finally, after many attempts to soothe her, her mother put her outside the door where her continuous crying could be heard. When the crying ceased, the mother went to get her, but the daughter was nowhere to be found. They searched for days, but never found her. Years later, somebody spotted a wild horse with a beautiful long mane in the herd. It turned out to be the little girl who had cried over nothing. The horses had taken her away from her family and adopted her and she couldn't return to her family. This story was told to me because I was very sensitive and sometimes became weepy. That was her way of teaching me that I needed to learn to control my behaviors.

An experience I had about this time that didn't make sense was when I was about eleven or twelve after I had begun my menstrual cycle. My mother's grandfather, Samuel Weston, had been a Presbyterian minister, so my mother's family members were all Presbyterians. He was a Dakota of the Mdewakantonwan band that called themselves Santee. As part of the assimilation process after the Minnesota Uprising of 1862, many converted to Christianity. Some became ordained ministers who moved to the western South Dakota reservations as my great-grandfather had done. My mother also said her grandfather was a skilled carpenter who built houses in his spare time.

My father's grandfather, Amos Lone Hill, had donated that portion of his land where the current Presbyterian Church is now located, so naturally they also became Presbyterians. My parents wed and became members of that Presbyterian Church, as did all of us after we were born. I was taught to attend church on Sundays, so I would walk to church alone or with my mother. One Sunday, as I sat in church, I became very uncomfortable. All of a sudden, I had this feeling that I should not be in a place where there was prayer while on my menstrual cycle. I could not explain my feeling at that time. Up to this point, I knew nothing of our traditional Lakota practices and beliefs. This came later in my life, but when a woman is on her menstrual cycle, I learned, she should not attend any of the sacred Lakota ceremonies. That was the reason for the isolation of women in traditional times.

Christianity was strongly practiced among the majority of the community members and by my immediate and extended family during the first twenty years of my life. Religious instruction was a part of my life while at Porcupine Day School. I believe we were all given religious instruction one day out of the week for about half an hour at the end of the day. All the ministers or priests from each denomination would converge upon the school and we would all gather into our little groups. There were Catholics, Episcopalians, Presbyterians, and maybe Baptists. It's funny, but I don't remember exactly what we did during that time. The Presbyterian group were mostly Lone Hills, Westons, Rocks, Red Eagles, and some more kids who lived east of Porcupine.

There were many programs for kids within the community at this time. I remember that on specific nights, the school gym was open for physical activities. The bus would pick us up and return us home by 9:00 P.M. Snacks of graham cracker frosting sandwiches and juice would be provided. I don't recall for sure who the chaperones were in the evenings. It might have been the teachers. There was also a simulated Boy Scout program combined with a tribal youth program that my older brothers belonged to about this time. I remember them camping at the Oglala Dam one summer. My brothers shared stories of sleeping in small tipis, learning to tie knots, swimming, and canoeing. My dad drove the rest of the family out to Oglala one afternoon to visit them.

There was a short-lived Girl Scout program that I belonged to. The Girl Scout leader was Cordelia Attack Him. I remember being excited about the proposed activities, but then I don't remember how many of them ever materialized. I remember hiking around in the hills above Porcupine behind Our Lady of Lourdes, selling Girl Scout cookies, and attending some sort of parent gathering at the school.

Another program that attracted many of us was the 4-H Club. It became an after-school activity for sixth and seventh graders. We were exposed to many different activities and projects during this time. The one I remember the most was clothing-making. All the materials were purchased by the extension services. We were allowed to select our own patterns, fabric, and whatever else was necessary to complete our projects. Mine was a lime green floral print culotte dress that was the fashion of the time. Our completed projects were entered into competition with other local and regional clubs. My culotte dress placed in the competition and went to the state fair, where it received a blue ribbon. I was allowed to keep and wear my dress afterwards. This was my introduction to sewing.

All of the programs available to the youth had an assimilationist perspective. The Lakota values, culture, and history were never mentioned. We were never taught to appreciate our Lakota heritage. As far as the programs were concerned, we were mainstream society kids. It would have been worthwhile to learn Lakota artwork, music, and dance at this stage of our lives, but it was overlooked.

Another part of being a 4-H Club member was summer camp at Camp Bob Marshall in the Black Hills. At first, it was difficult to adjust to a different environment. We were accustomed to the dry heat on the plains; so no matter how hot it got, it was tolerable. Camp Bob Marshall had cabins that sat among the pines near a small lake. There were at least eight bunk beds for the campers and one single bed for the chaperone in each cabin. We had to furnish our own bedding, but many of us didn't own sleeping bags, so we took sheets and blankets that didn't quite do as good a job as sleeping bags would have. The nights were cool and damp, and we had to rise early to chilly mornings. All campers met outside in the center on the dew-covered grass where we had to recite the 4-H pledge before breakfast. Each table of about twenty campers competed after each meal to have the neatest, most ingenious table of stacked dirty dishes and utensils to win. I don't remember if we ever won anything, but it was fun and noisy.

The campers were other Lakota children from other Pine Ridge districts and children from other counties in the state who were primarily white. We were mixed with other Lakota children and with white children in our cabins. The night before we left camp was reserved for the talent show and competition. Each cabin had to brainstorm ideas early in the week and practice. The mixing of children did prove to overcome any prejudices that may have existed. Everyone learned to work together as teams to compete against other cabins of children. It was sad at the end of the week when it came time to say good-bye to children we had befriended.

Another camp I attended was in Sioux Falls. I don't recall how I was recruited or who came to my parents for their permission. It was a camp with deaf children. It was definitely a new learning experience for me. In order to communicate with them, we had to learn sign language in a short period of time. I remember sleeping under the stars somewhere outside of Sioux Falls side by side with this other girl from Porcupine and discussing how we had ever got to be in that situation. But it was a positive experience, and probably helped prepare me for acceptance and understanding of learning differences.

I tried out for cheerleading every year after the fifth grade and made the team each time. I also joined the track team, but I only did this so I could stay after school a little longer to be around my friends. About this time, I was becoming restless. There wasn't anything exciting at home. My life there consisted of helping with the cooking, washing dishes, sweeping and mopping the floor, and baby-sitting my little sister.

My first summer youth job was at the Porcupine Day School when I was about thirteen years old. It consisted of assisting with the cleaning of the classrooms and the kitchen. Maybe my earnings weren't much, but my dad took me to the bank and had me deposit my money into a checking account. He said at the end of the summer that I could buy my school clothes. This was my introduction to capitalism. I worked almost every summer after that.

My seventh grade year was the last year that I spent at the old school. My teacher was Miss Hunke from Indiana. She was quite thin and tall. For history, I remember reading from a South Dakota history text and learning about American history. Although it was a South Dakota history text, no mention was made of the tribal presence at the time it was settled and South Dakota became a state. One project was to write about one of the U.S. presidents. Mine was about Franklin Pierce. I think it was only because he was the first one I could find. Our classroom was an old building set away from the regular school building because there weren't enough classrooms in the main building. My mother said that building was where white dances had been held in the past. They had many good times in that building.

Up to this point, all the teachers and the principal were non-Indian. The principal up through maybe fifth or sixth grade was Mr. Jamruska and then Mr. Ballard. Then Louis Whirlwind Horse became the first Indian principal at the old Porcupine Day School. Anthony Whirlwind Horse followed his brother to become the second Indian principal of Porcupine Day School. Anthony Whirlwind Horse was still the principal when the move to the new school building took place in 1969. The curriculum changed to include Lakota arts and more cultural integration with the hiring of these Indian administrators. Arthur Amiotte was hired as the art teacher and more cultural activities were included in the curriculum. This was the beginning of cultural inclusion in the curriculum. It was a major initial step toward holistically developing Lakota children and including the community in that process.

I was in the first class to graduate from the new Porcupine Day School in 1970. Our eighth grade teacher was Mr. Katt. I remember the fashion was mini-skirts and big chunky heels. My friend Denise Pourier and I would walk down the hallway to our classroom at the other end of the building. Our big heels echoed up and down the hallway as we made our walk.

I remember being philosophical for one of the first times during one of our recess breaks in the eighth grade. I asked Denise if she ever thought about what was beyond the sun, moon, and the stars.

I told her that life was infinite. I don't remember her exact response, but her facial expression said "are you crazy?"

After graduating from the eighth grade at Porcupine Day School, I went on to Oglala Community School, as it was called back then. It was still operated by the Bureau of Indian Affairs, although its dormitories were still open to all students who required housing. If you were from one of the outlying districts where buses didn't make a daily run, you were able to stay in the dorm. The bus did make a daily run to Porcupine, so I started out as a day student.

As a freshman, I tried out for cheerleading again and made the team. I remember not knowing anyone from my old school when I decided to try out. I did remember this other cheerleader from the Manderson Day School, Janice Janis, who was also a student there at OCS. I approached her and asked her if she wanted to go for the cheerleading tryouts. She hesitated, but I convinced her that we could make it and practically dragged her down to the gym. We didn't have anything planned, so we yelled and did our jumps. Janice and I both made the junior varsity cheerleading squad and later the varsity for both football and basketball. She eventually became my best friend throughout high school. We had to move into the dorm where we became roommates. Our friendship lasted the entire four years at OCS.

It was an easy transition from grade school to high school because one older brother, Lester, was a sophomore and the other, Sid, was a junior. My older cousin Happy was a senior and also a varsity cheerleader when I entered as a freshman. Happy and her older sister, Norma, had supplied me with hand-me-down clothes while I was in grade school. Their grandma and my grandma, "Unci" Eva, occasionally checked me out of the dorm along with Happy and gave me a ride back to Porcupine on some weekends. Both of my brothers were also into sports, so I wasn't alone. This is when I first met my niece, Jeaneen. She was a junior and she proceeded to introduce me to all her girl friends as her little sister. I felt proud because I didn't have any older sisters and went along with it. She was what we considered a "town kid" because she lived in Pine Ridge. I was included in her circle of friends who were all town kids. So actually I had two older sisters looking after me.

As entering freshmen, we were all placed into the basic courses at the beginning of the fall semester. I was eventually removed from the basic math class and placed into an algebra class with sophomores and juniors. I didn't question their decision because they told me I was ready for algebra. In retrospect, I am thankful that I was challenged. I was also placed in a debate class with juniors and seniors. The English class I was placed in as a freshman consisted of researching and writing. I did choose to take the home economics class in foods rather than sewing. My rationale for that one was that I already knew how to sew and make clothing from my 4-H Club days in grade school.

In the fall of our freshman year, we were all taken to the library for some sort of testing. I later learned it was IQ testing. This marked the beginning of constant hassling by my journalism teacher, who felt she needed to develop me to my fullest potential. I believe she felt it was her duty to pile on work and her expectations of me were high. Once when I was slacking because of peer pressures, she remarked disgustedly that I was capable of doing more and better because my IQ was quite high. She said it was the second highest out of about the seventy freshman tested. I resented being singled out. Out of stubbornness, I rebelled and deliberately did what was minimally required of all students. This was when I decided that I didn't want to be academically competitive with my friends. It was peer pressure and I wanted to be like everyone else—I didn't want to be labeled as "above" everyone else.

I had many learning experiences as a high school student. I was always eager and open to new experiences. I joined the Spanish club and the foreign studies club, was involved in class fund-raising activities, and was inducted into the National Honor Society while I was a sophomore.

In the summer of 1972, I lived in Hamburg, Germany, for eight weeks as an exchange student. We raised some of our spending money, but Youth for Understanding funded our trip. There were twenty-five students who made the trip that summer. There were five from OCS, five from Holy Rosary Mission (now known as Red Cloud School), five from Todd County, five from St. Francis, and five from Cheyenne Eagle Butte. About half went to France and the rest of us went to Germany. This was my first conscious awareness of myself as an "Indian." The Germans were thrilled to have us in their midst. Their curiosity and expectations of our culture were enormous and overwhelming for me. I was disappointed that my upbringing was more of the mainstream white society.

After this experience, I always remarked to my parents and relatives that I had to go all the way to Germany to sleep in a tipi. The Germans had Indian clubs and expected us to inform them of our ways. There was one instance of doing a dance performance for this crowd of people. Prior to our trip, we were informed to take a shawl, and whatever else we would need to dance. My Aunt Edna made me some hair strings. We were not well-informed as to what we would be doing, so it came as a surprise. The majority of us had never danced at a powwow before this time, but we felt obligated to perform, so we did. I remember one of the girls commented that she had never danced before and was a little embarrassed. I told her that maybe the Germans wouldn't know the difference. They were thrilled with our performance and we were relieved that we only had to do it once. I was amazed at their knowledge of our culture.

The only powwows I had attended in my life had been the annual Fourth of July Powwow in Porcupine and maybe one or two days of the annual August Pine Ridge Powwow. The Pine Ridge Powwow doubled as a Sundance during the day and a powwow during the evening and night in the 1960s. I didn't know the difference at that time.

At the beginning of our journey, we traveled by bus to Detroit, Michigan, where we met with representatives of the Youth for Understanding Program. Then we flew out of Detroit to Paris where half of our crew got off. The rest of us flew on to Hamburg. The families chose us before we arrived, so they were waiting to take us to their homes. I lived right in Hamburg, along with Lenny Brewer and Karla Cuny. My other friend, Janice Janis, lived outside of Hamburg on a cherry orchard farm. We were able to get together occasionally during the summer, so it lessened the homesickness.

Janice's family invited us out to the farm one day, so Lenny, Karla, and I traveled on the train alone out of the city. Her family provided a case of beer for us, so we drank while we visited. We all ended up going out to the orchard to eat cherries and began horsing around. I fell into an irrigation ditch. At the end of the day, we had to return to the city. While we waited for the train, we went looking for the bathroom. The train left with Karla and the tickets by the time we returned. The people at the station didn't understand English as we tried to explain our predicament. They finally called someone who understood some English; they laughed and put us on the next train into Hamburg.

Most of us were sixteen and at the legal drinking age in Germany, and most of the family meals were served with beer. It was a culture shock for sixteen-year-olds in a foreign city. We did eventually learn to use the subways and get around the city with the assistance of our host brothers or sisters. They usually accompanied us everywhere we went. Sometimes we would call each other and go on our own. Once we got together and went down to the main station to play on the escalators. It was the fascination that attracted us to that place. The lower level was always deserted, so that was where we went to run up and down while we visited. When we tired of that, then we went to look through the shops on the main floor.

In the summer of 1973, while my two friends Janice and Karla attended South Dakota Girl's State, I was sent to Washington, D.C., for the Washington Workshops. This was a national government workshop for high school students across the nation. I was among eight American Indian students who attended this weeklong event. It was also the first time that I had traveled alone. The other students represented the Turtle Mountain Chippewa, the Hopi, the Navajo, the Cherokee, and the Zuni. The seminar was quite intense, but I managed to find in the phone book and contact my second cousin, who lived in Falls Church, Virginia. She invited me to spend the night with her daughter, Clarice, who was my age, so I got permission and took a cab to her residence. It was unexpected for me, and a surprise for Clarice, whom I became close to when her parents were actively involved with the Presbyterian churches in South Dakota.

During my senior year at Pine Ridge, I began thinking about life after high school. I know my dad had told us that once we turned eighteen and graduated, we were on our own. We could no longer live at home. That was on my mind constantly. I knew I wanted to attend college, so I mentioned this to one of my teachers, Mr. Sanders, who taught math. He asked what I was interested in. At that time it was the medical profession. He said I needed to strengthen my math and sciences, so he encouraged me to take additional classes, even if it meant taking them independently, and he volunteered to tutor me.

I had nearly enough credits to graduate when I entered my senior year, so I was approved to do some work study. I started out in the store that was on campus, but switched to working as a tutor in the math department. That year I took Algebra II and Chemistry, although they were not required. This was at a time when Indian females were not expected or encouraged to attend college. We had a male counselor who encouraged my older brother, Lester, to attend college and assisted him in filling out his application for Dartmouth. He was accepted, but instead chose to attend a technical college in Laramie, Wyoming.

It was a disappointment to me that I wasn't given the same advantages and assistance as my brother, but this strengthened my determination to attend college. In the spring of 1974, I expressed my intentions of college to my dad, so he told me to get the applications and he would help me fill out the paperwork. My dad was always supportive of me and never critical. I received two spankings as I was growing up; one was when I was about eleven or twelve and I decided to try drinking beer with some of my Two Eagle cousins and little brothers and the other when I was supposed to be looking after my little sister when she swallowed an ice cube. The latter I knew I didn't deserve and I was devastated. I ran far back into the hills behind our house and stayed for hours until my mom came after me and coaxed me into going home. I loved the solitude.

That night as my dad was filling out my college application at the kitchen table, he commented on how well I had turned out. He told me how easy it was to raise me—that I always knew the right thing to do without being told. I wasn't much trouble. He also told me he had confidence in me that I would succeed in anything I decided to do. He cautioned me that life would be a challenge not only because I was a female, but because I was Indian. Although I wasn't a full-blood, I would never be totally accepted in the dominant culture because they would always see me as Indian; and I had already experienced some prejudice living on the reservation because I was not a full-blood. My dad said I would be somewhere in between. He reminded me that no matter how high and far I went, "Don't you ever forget where you grew up." In other words, he said, remain humble. It was an excellent father-daughter talk that has remained with and influenced me throughout the years.

My girlfriends and I had talked about attending these different out-of-state universities and what we were going to do after high school and college. Marriage and kids were not in the picture. But the reality was that I needed to consider the distance from family and the expense it would take in getting there and back, so I decided on Black Hills State College (now university) in Spearfish. It was far enough from family yet within driving distance.

It was also during my senior year when my life took a different turn. I was probably among the first waves of high school teenage pregnancies. In the past, unwed mothers were shipped off and never spoken of. High school teenage pregnancies are a common occurrence today. My parents were very disappointed. I never heard the end of my "careless mistake" and what shame I had brought on my brothers from my mother. My mother was old-fashioned and believed this only happened to "bad" women who were raised with no values. She questioned what had happened to my values. I had no answer. I now believe it was a part of my rebellion. I needed to express my individuality and test my limits by challenging existing values and practices.

I was seven and a half months pregnant when I graduated from high school. I chose to continue and graduate rather than drop out and finish later. It was at this point in my life when I realized that I had been going through the motions; I had attended school and learned because it was the required thing to do. I had done what people wanted or expected me to do. Grade school and high school were passive experiences for me. Now, I knew that as soon as I turned eighteen, I would be free to make my own decisions as my dad had warned us. He said he had done his job of childrearing. The only catch was I wouldn't be able to live at home. He said I was welcome to visit anytime, but it was time to start a life of my own.

In the spring semester of my senior year, I continued with school and with my work-study and purchased baby clothes with the small amount of money I made. It never occurred to me to apply for welfare. I guess I had no knowledge that I would be eligible. I doubt that my dad would have allowed that anyway. I had a stormy and abusive relationship with my daughter's father, so marriage was out of the picture. I lived at home and became a day student, attending school in fear that he would physically harm me while I was on campus in Pine Ridge.

He did hurt me on several occasions, substantiating my fears. That was when Mr. Sanders became aware of the situation I was in and asked me to work as a tutor in the math classroom for my own safety and protection. I was deeply grateful for his concern. My daughter's father had dropped out, and therefore was not allowed on campus, but he continued to harass me. Once at the end of the day as I was boarding the bus for home, he came out of nowhere and forcefully dragged me into his mother's car and drove off. Nobody attempted to help me. I was verbally and physically assaulted at his mother's home until she returned home from work. She apologized for his behavior and drove me back to my parents' home in Porcupine.

Through all this turmoil, college remained my goal. I decided to take one day at a time. That summer, I worked for the summer youth program again and purchased additional baby clothes with my earnings. My dad remained calm despite my mom's disappointment that there would be no marriage. My plan was to proceed with college; I was set to live in the dorm for the fall semester, and my parents were going to care for my baby.

My daughter was born on July 10, 1974. Everyone expected a boy; I had six brothers and one sister and my daughter's father had four brothers and no sisters. The night of July 9 was a full moon when I went into labor. As I sat outside under the trees in front of my parent's house throughout most of that night, I felt alone. I didn't want to disturb anyone, so I endured the pain quietly with the soft rustling of the leaves that night. Toward dawn, I awakened my mom, and my dad drove us into Pine Ridge. I was in labor for most of that day until Kim was born about 5:23 that afternoon. My mom always commented that I contributed to the arthritis that she later developed. I would squeeze her hand with each contraction. My daughter's father came in later before I left the hospital to sign the paternity papers.

Adjusting to motherhood was difficult, so I was thankful that I lived with my parents. My mom assisted me enormously in that first month. I was in a situation where I could allow my parents to raise my child or I could accept the consequences of the earlier immature decision I had made. It was clear that my daughter was my responsibility, but I was naive about how to get my life in order. My dad encouraged me to continue with college as planned and said he and my mom would care for my daughter. For how long was left open-ended.

At the end of August, 1974, my parents drove me to Spearfish so I could start my career as a college student. My roommate was a white girl from Piedmont, South Dakota. My childhood experiences of living and traveling allowed me to accept my roommate as another human being. We treated one another respectfully. On registration day, an advisor asked me what major I was going to pursue. I told him the medical profession, so I was registered for two general requirement courses, with biology for majors and a chemistry course. These two included labs. The first month of college was busy, as I tried to keep up with the homework and all the lab work in the evenings. Part of the biology lab included going into Spearfish Canyon to collect different algae. I didn't own a vehicle, so I had to hang around those students who did.

The loneliness I experienced in being separated from my daughter and also from my family was immense during that time. Then, as I became more familiar with life on campus, I met other Indian students, some who lived in the same dorm. I was never into slang, but they called each other "skins." Some I had befriended were from the Rosebud, the Cheyenne River, and the Pine Ridge Reservations, some were from out of state, and some commuted from Rapid City. Soon I was questioned as to why I didn't hang around with them very much and why I was always so seriously studying while they partied and were having a great time.

I was easily influenced, so I joined them as much as possible. Then my studies began to suffer. I fell behind and my mind just wasn't into it about halfway into the semester. Nonetheless, the Indian Studies counselor had begun assisting me in finding an apartment so my daughter could live with me in the spring semester. Well, my mom got wind of my college social activities and began issuing her threats as often as possible. The major one was that if I didn't marry my daughter's father, she was going to give my daughter to her father. I believed her, so in November, I left college without dropping my classes. I went home to reluctantly marry my daughter's father.

In the spring of 1975, I returned to Black Hills State College to begin my second semester. I had received some Ds and Fs for the fall semester, so I returned on academic probation. I was more prepared than the previous semester because my daughter was with me. I had settled down, quit the partying, and had become a responsible mother and full-time college student. I believed that marriage would change my then husband, but the domestic violence only increased. I was confused because I had never witnessed domestic violence to this degree. I had seen my parents argue one time when I was about four, but I had never seen my dad physically abuse my mom. I didn't know what to do or who to turn to. This continued for a year and a half.

Despite this, I continued to attend my classes and received passing grades. My major changed from medicine to English. As a mother and full-time student, I felt that I could not devote the time required to the study of medicine. It was also at the college level that I was introduced to Indian Studies, which became an awakening; classes were offered in American Indian history, culture, literature, and the Lakota language.

I then realized I didn't have a real identity up to this point. I was aware that I was Indian, but my formal elementary and secondary education had taught me mainstream values. In high school, among other Lakota students, I didn't feel the need to compete to be better. I was comfortable being equal to my Lakota peers. That was my Lakota conditioning. But in college, I was surrounded by non-Indian students and knew that I must put extra effort into my studies to remain in good academic standing. I began competition with myself at this point in my life. With guidance from my dad, I learned that once you made a commitment to do something, you persisted until it was completed. With that in mind, I committed to achieving a college degree. However long that was to be, I knew I was there for the duration.

I signed up for the Lakota language class taught by a non-Indian. He would mispronounce words, so I would tell him after class. I ended up helping him with correct pronunciation and usage in class. It was about this time that I also realized that something was missing in my life. I had grown up on the reservation surrounded with the Lakota culture, yet we had been taught primarily to become mainstream society citizens. There was this sense of pride that came over me as I sat in that Lakota language class. I felt like the expert and that it was acceptable to be Indian.

My freshman English II class was devoted to the study of minority literature, primarily that of African Americans, because of their recent struggles in the sixties. *One Flew Over the Cuckoo's Nest* was one of the required readings in one class; I remember the Indian guy in it as being the silent one, yet he made an impact. In the seventies the American Indian movement had become quite active, so Indian values were becoming evident on some college campuses and were reflected in the curriculum. In my American Indian literature class I read *Black Elk Speaks*, *Lame Deer: Seeker of Visions*, and other books that subsequently introduced me to the spirituality of Indians. I also took a course called American Indian women that reinforced my belief that Indian women throughout the centuries had been equal to their male counterparts. It was okay to be independent and maintain femininity simultaneously. This accumulated formal knowledge set the stage for who and what I wanted to become.

My desire to gain control of my life intensified. My love for knowledge and understanding increased while my personal life remained imperfect. Motherhood was a given; I had accepted full responsibility for the welfare of my infant daughter, but my marriage had deteriorated. From the beginning I was subjected to verbal and physical abuse. Once, after being falsely accused of infidelity and beaten, I attended class anyway the following day. I couldn't chew and if bruises were visible to the public that day, it didn't matter. On my walk to class, I began thinking of my future. Then the realization hit me; if I continued in this marriage, I may not have a future to worry about. Then what would happen to my daughter? It was then and there that I decided to get out of that marriage. It took about another year before I became legally divorced.

It was still as if I had to get the approval of my parents who believed in the institution of marriage and had been married for nearly thirty years by that time. It was my dad whom I approached and confided in. He wasn't aware of the severity of the abuse problem and convinced me to keep trying. He wasn't convinced until the summer I stayed at their home with my daughter, and my husband arrived drunk and my dad had a confrontation with him. Then I had his blessing to divorce my husband. At this point, I wasn't aware of the importance of respect for women within the Lakota culture. My husband had shown his disrespect and disregard for my physical and emotional welfare because of his alcoholism. We separated that summer when my daughter was two. My mom did stay with me for the remainder of summer school to baby-sit. I was left without a vehicle and had to walk across town to attend classes and do my work-study in the college library.

From that point on, I became a single college parent. I returned to Black Hills State in the fall as a junior majoring in English in the secondary education program. By this time, many of my freshman partying friends had dropped out and were gone. Other Indian friends came for a semester or two and dropped out, but I persevered. My cousin Debbie and another high school girlfriend Paulette would come to stay and baby-sit occasionally. I once told my friend Paulette that by the time I had reached my twenty-first birthday, I felt like I had lived a lifetime; I had a child, had been married and divorced, was near completion of my college education, and was happily living independently.

Little did I know that this was only the beginning of the most incredible learning journey in my lifetime. In the year following my divorce, I concentrated on my studies, withdrew from college social life, and spent time with my daughter. I was talked into going out one night a month with the girls. I was reluctant to date and when I did once, I was cautious not to become seriously involved. My disastrous marriage had taught me not to trust anyone. My goal was to complete my degree, find a job, and have a fulfilling life with my daughter.

My daughter was a beautiful baby. She was born with thick black hair, a tiny pug nose, and big dark eyes with long eyelashes. She usually got everyone's attention and my life pretty much centered on her. Then I noticed she had quit talking—she no longer made any attempts to talk after the age of two. I took her to the pediatrician and expressed my concern. He examined her and said that physically there didn't seem to be anything wrong. He said she just needed time. She understood when people talked, but it was like she had withdrawn. She laughed and cried, but I could not get her to talk. I knew she had witnessed the domestic violence and physical abuse that I had been subjected to. Her father had kidnapped her from our apartment one night when she was two and a half years old. I felt some guilt that I had somehow contributed to her condition by allowing her father to have that control over our lives.

I spent hours in the college library reading everything I could on child speech development and child development in general, although that wasn't my area of study. I even signed up for a class called Psychology of Personality that wasn't required. It was a search to understand myself. When my daughter was three; I told her how much I loved her and that I would never leave her. I told her that she no longer needed to be afraid of her father and that he would never hurt her or me anymore. She listened intently and cried. I held her tightly and we both cried. That was the close of that chapter in my life. After that, we both adjusted to being a single parent family. She still never attempted to talk, but she was a happy child.

I was determined to be a different type of mother. My parents had been so busy raising eight children that we had not had much individual attention. Our basic needs were met, along with discipline and guidance, but affection was absent. In response to that experience, I learned to be affectionate and gave my daughter a great deal of positive reinforcement. She grew up with discipline and a lot of encouragement. My parents had come from the end of an era that had attempted to destroy the Lakota family unit. In order to expedite the assimilation process, children had been taken from their families and sent to boarding schools far from cultural influence. Some of my grandparents and great-grandparents had been forcefully taken and sent to boarding schools, so it was understandable that their parenting skills were lacking and it reflected in the way I was raised.

As I neared the completion of my degree, I began to have thoughts of finding a teaching job. I mentioned to a friend of mine that I wanted to relocate to Reno, Nevada, to live. It was a dream and when I was asked why, I answered, "I don't know." Later, ironically, I expressed a desire and was approved to do my student teaching at Pine Ridge. It was ironic because it was there that I had rebelled against the journalism teacher for her high expectations of me. It was like I wanted to go back to show her that I was capable of achieving success on the outside. Her prodding actually had benefited me.

During summer interims, I would return to Porcupine and spend time at my parents' home with my daughter. Sometimes I would stay a week and then allow my daughter to stay for up to another week with her grandparents. She was their only grandchild and they enjoyed having her spend time with them. I also wanted her to be exposed to the Lakota language.

It was in May of 1978 while we were staying at my parents' home that I experienced a disturbing dream. They had just recently moved into their new HUD house built on their land, so my mom told me to sleep in their bedroom that night. Their bedroom was located on the northeast corner of the house with one eastern window that I left open that night.

I fell asleep and was awakened by a light accompanied by some commotion coming from outside the window. Someone began talking to me. It was like I was conscious, yet I could not comprehend what was happening. I panicked, and my first impulse was to jump out of bed, close the window, and pull the blind. But before I was back in bed, the blind went up and the window opened. Then the voice sternly began talking again and showed me a written text over and over. I kept turning my head in avoidance and telling him that I didn't believe in what was happening to me. I pleaded to be left alone. I lied, telling him I went to church every Sunday. Then suddenly, he was gone. I was wide awake, sweating and shaking. I had my daughter pushed against the wall in my attempt to get away from whatever or whoever had been there. I looked at the window and around the room, but there was silence. My daughter hadn't been disturbed by whatever it had been. I went back to sleep.

The next morning, I mentioned the incident to my parents and brothers. My brothers kidded me by saying maybe I had DTs. I argued with them asking how I could have DTs when I didn't even drink. I had not been much of a drinker since my daughter had come into my life. I couldn't explain this experience, so it was temporarily dismissed.

My final year at Black Hills State was the fall of 1978 and the spring of 1979. I had attempted one class, The Mass Media, several times. It was required for English majors. But I had dropped it each time because it was a seminar type of class and I adamantly refused to work in a group. Group work had not been a part of my formal conditioning. My formal K-12 education had focused on individuality, not interaction within groups. I hoped somebody else would eventually teach that class and teach it differently, but the original instructor was the only one who ever taught it.

I subsequently met with my advisor and explained my situation, so he suggested I speak with one of the English professors to see if I could take it as an independent study. I met with Dr. Ronnie Theisz and he agreed to supervise my independent study. Dr. Theisz spoke with an accent and had recently worked at Sinte Gleska College, now a university, on the Rosebud Reservation. He had done research with Lakota tribal members on the Rosebud and Pine Ridge Reservations, and he also sang with the Porcupine Singers, so I was comfortable with him as my supervisor. I concentrated on one aspect of the media: film. My research focused on the portrayal of American Indians in film from the silent era to the 1970s. I learned that many stereotypes of American Indians emerged through film. The research also allowed me to understand that in order for learning to take place, there has to be a certain amount of relevancy to my life.

Another worry in my senior year was passing the Junior English Proficiency Exam that was required of all education majors. Some of my girlfriends who were elementary education majors told of the difficulty of the exam and the retakes that were often necessary. My dilemma was that I was an English major, so if I failed on the first try, that would be total embarrassment. Having taken English grammar and composition courses, I felt the pressure. I was relieved that I passed it on the first attempt.

I moved out of Spearfish in the spring of 1979 after completion of all my coursework. Because of the housing shortage on the reservation, I moved in with my parents that summer and commuted to Pine Ridge to complete my student teaching in the fall. I was nervous about the prospect of teaching adolescents, as I wasn't much older than some of the seniors. I was twenty-three. My fear was that they would not respect me. Some of my high school teachers were still there, but there were also new faces. My assignment was teaching freshmen and sophomores, so that widened the age gap. The curriculum didn't allow for any creativity to include Lakota cultural information. I had pranksters who kept me on my toes, but by the end of the semester, I knew I had gained their respect. I had the opportunity to use some of the classroom management skills that I was taught. I learned to adjust my teaching to meet their needs and soon realized that flexibility was the key.

Before the fall semester ended, one of the regular English teachers suffered a head injury. A student had hurled a stone through an open classroom window. As a result, that teacher requested that he be given the remainder of the school year off. So the principal called me in and asked me if I wanted a temporary teaching job. I agreed, and that was my first teaching job after completion of my degree. It consisted of teaching the upper level English classes. That was a challenge with the seniors, because they were nearing graduation and were antsy. I put myself in their shoes as I taught because I wasn't too far removed from that situation myself. I was attuned to their antics and the communities from which they came. Chances were, I was related to some of the students or was friends with their brothers or sisters. I was one of them.

It was in a high school literature class that my 1978 experience came back to haunt me. I still had my books from college that I sometimes referred to. The collection of stories entitled *The Man to Send Rain Clouds* had one by Anna Lee Walters entitled "Come, My Sons." That story seemed to jump out at me and reminded me of the text that I was sternly shown in my 1978 experience. Other things I experienced during that time also reminded me of that night. It was something that a stranger said or did unintentionally. I was confused and shared my concern with a colleague who taught Indian studies. He had already been involved with the traditional ceremonies and was more aware of such things. He shrugged and said I needed to see a medicine man to have what I had experienced interpreted. He said people had dreams and they were reminded only four times. If they paid no heed, they could be killed in a number of ways. He suggested I see Dawson Has No Horse.

I had absolutely no cultural knowledge up to this point. After work, I returned home and told my dad what I had found out. I was still a little confused and afraid. He was also at a loss because traditional knowledge about dreams was not a part of his upbringing. He was in deep thought for a while and then he told me to go see his sister, my Aunt Edna. He suddenly remembered that my cousin had a dream and had been assisted by an older medicine man and had become involved with ceremonies and the sweatlodge recently. He assured me that she would know what to do and how to advise me.

The fall of 1979 marked the beginning of my involvement with the profound cultural knowledge and practices of my ancestors. It was like entering into another level of consciousness. On the first visit to my Aunt Edna, she advised me on what I needed to do. She taught me how to make tobacco ties and told me that there was going to be a ceremony or "lowanpi" that very night. I attended and asked for an interpretation of my dream. The first thing they asked was whether I would like to accept what was being offered me or if I wanted it wiped away. I thought briefly and said that I would accept. I thought it was going to be something simple, but it turned out that my great-great grandmother had chosen me to receive her gift. She had been a courageous woman who assisted the Lakota people by using her medicine and power to heal. She lived to be an old woman. My cousin then explained that if I accepted her gift, I would need to learn about it. He said I needed to participate in the Sundance. He added that people couldn't learn by watching and observing, they had to experience it. That was learning. He didn't want to hear me say that I would attend the Sundance and learn about it before I actually did it.

The experience I had in 1978 was a calling to the traditional ways. Only then did the text make sense. I had read "Come, My Sons" while I was in college, so that was the only manner that I could be reached—through my books.

The summer of 1980 was when I first Sundanced. Then I began attending ceremonies and going to the Sweatlodge regularly. Subsequently, there were many more dreams that served to guide me in my everyday life. I was transformed in many ways through these experiences. I suddenly was able to put my life into a new perspective. All my childhood experiences and memories that didn't make sense, the formal schooling experience, parenthood, and unanswered cultural experiences became clearer. Everything fell into place. I needed those experiences to understand myself. I learned that I was here on this earth for a purpose. All people were here for a purpose.

It was easy for me to accept this philosophy; while I was in college, I had taken biblical literature and had learned that the Bible is an excellent piece of literature. It is a history of the Hebrew or Jewish people and it contains all genres. I learned through class discussions that the Bible was adopted by Christianity and used to control mass populations. They then persecuted the Jews. This was when I questioned that philosophy. It was hypocritical. I learned there was a section on reincarnation that was deleted because the church heirachy didn't feel the people would accept it or were not ready for it. I learned through our traditional teachings that reincarnation was possible and that philosophy was accepted within the Lakota culture. With that in mind, I proudly continued to actively participate because I knew that my ancestors possessed a spirituality that encompassed all aspects of life. It was a valid philosophy and is still being practiced.

My dad had always been an open-minded individual who supported us in whatever we chose to do, so he gave his approval. It was a learning process that would define who I was as an individual. My mom, on the other hand, clung to her Christian beliefs. She was appalled that I would turn my back on the church and take my five-year-old daughter to "those things." She said something terrible would happen—those things were "the work of the devil." She said it was something that was done long ago, but now those times were gone.

Then there came a time when my dad became ill, as a result of his diabetes. My Aunt Edna suggested that I have a doctoring ceremony for him. My dad agreed, so I prepared everything as I was instructed. When the time came to go to the ceremony, my mom reluctantly agreed to go along. There, the songs and the prayers changed her mind. She later acknowledged that there was no difference between our traditional way of praying and the praying of the Christian church—we all pray to the same being. She became a strong supporter when some of my brothers also joined later and changed their way of life. They became drug- and alcohol-free.

In the ensuing years, I relied completely upon my inner faith and beliefs. My daughter became seriously ill at the age of ten. Our doctor in Gordon, Nebraska, ran a series of tests, but could not determine what it was. She prescribed penicillin and said that if that didn't help, I was to take Kim back for more tests. She had been ill for about two weeks and had already lost a considerable amount of weight in that time. Then I happened to stop in to visit my Aunt Edna with my daughter, who had become listless and pale. My first cousin, who had been visiting there, took one look at my daughter and told me that her daughter had the same symptoms and had been diagnosed with leukemia. Her daughter was a year older than mine, but through the ceremony and medicine, her daughter had been cured. At her suggestion, I inquired at the ceremony and it was confirmed that she was in the beginning stages, but through the interpreter, the spirits also said if I had a doctoring, the spirits would help her. Within four days, my daughter was able to eat and it was as if she had never been sick. I never took her back to the clinic for that illness again.

Another incident that strengthened my belief in traditional ways was when I became ill. In the early eighties, I blacked out for a second one afternoon while I was visiting with a group of ladies before a sweat. It frightened all of us, but I brushed it off. After that I would get dizzy spells occasionally. Then in the late eighties, they became more frequent and were accompanied by a slight pressure at the back of my head. I noticed I was beginning to lose my balance and was bumping into things. I decided it was time to visit my doctor when I leaned over in the shower and fell. She immediately referred me to a neurologist.

I refused to share my condition with my family, because I didn't want them to worry. I attended a traditional ceremony on New Year's Eve to ask about my condition. Although deep down I knew, it still shocked me to hear that I had a tumor. I had to make the decision on whether to rely on medical technology or on my faith in our traditional ways. I chose the latter, and the tumor was removed through ceremony. I was still seen by the neurologist and had an

MRI, but nothing showed up. I recovered and all my symptoms disappeared. I had a wonderful patient-doctor relationship with the Gordon Clinic female doctor who was aware of my beliefs and practices. She was encouraging and commented that we were fortunate to have our traditional ways.

On my follow-up visit with the neurologist, I questioned him again about my tumor. He was bewildered. He couldn't confirm that it was there because nothing had shown up on the MRI, but he said that there were definite symptoms of a tumor. I explained the doctoring ceremony to him when the tumor had been removed, and my recovery following it. He commented positively that our traditional practices were respectable and that we needed to do whatever was necessary to maintain our health.

Earlier, my short-lived job as a high school English teacher ended, because there were no other vacancies on the reservation. So my three-year Chapter 1 hiatus began. I applied for a Chapter 1 K-3 reading/language arts teacher position at Little Wound School. I was hired for the 1980–81 school year as a remedial teacher. That job included testing and tutoring the students in specific areas. Once again, although this was not my area of expertise, I wholeheartedly accepted the challenge. It was more exposure to another level of learners.

Then in 1981, there was a Chapter 1 coordinator-teacher vacancy for grades K-8 at the Porcupine Day School. I decided my one-year experience at Little Wound School was sufficient to warrant my application. Surprisingly, I was hired. This was my introduction into supervision and additional exposure to different levels of learners. I was twenty-five and much younger than my Chapter 1 aides; four of whom were my aunts. The only cultural aspects of the Chapter 1 programs at both Little Wound School and Porcupine Day School were the students and the teacher aides. I worked for two years in the Porcupine Day School position, and then graduate school sounded appealing.

I had taken the GRE and had begun receiving letters and brochures from different universities. One graduate program that impressed me was the public policy program at Carnegie Mellon University in Pittsburgh. I applied and was accepted, so I resigned from my Chapter 1 coordinator-teacher position. Then I attended the eight-week summer preparatory program in Pittsburgh, leaving my nine-year-old daughter with my parents. I had planned on familiarizing myself with Pittsburgh before I moved with my daughter for the fall semester, but it didn't turn out that way.

It was such an intense program as we were warned beforehand, that at times I was actually brain weary. We all had to take pre-calculus, technical writing, and computer classes. I learned later that we would be taught to write our own computer programs. We were given anywhere from forty to fifty calculus homework problems to do every day and all of our technical writing assignments had to be done on the computer. Up to this time, I had never touched a computer keyboard, much less turned on a computer. It was an overwhelming experience. I survived academically, but I had second thoughts about moving my daughter to Pittsburgh.

Despite reassurances from my African American roommate about how Pittsburgh's environment had been cleaned up and about the recent reduction in crime, I wasn't convinced. She was from Washington, D.C., and was accustomed to city life. On one trip to the 7–11 convenience store, we arrived shortly after a robbery had taken place and police were still milling around. It was a culture shock. On the reservation, robberies were rare, so this incident didn't fit my schemata. So, I regretfully passed on this educational opportunity because of its location. Deep down, I wished there was such a program somewhere on the great plains within convenient driving distance to the reservation. I didn't feel like I had failed in this attempt, because my family had become increasingly important, as had my quest to understand myself through spirituality.

Shortly before my Pittsburgh adventure, concerns about my daughter's education had arisen. Because she had been diagnosed as "speech delayed" in the kindergarten, I was told that she could not be in the regular classroom. They placed her in a self-contained special education classroom, much to my dismay. In the spring of 1980, she was scheduled for a screening and medical exam at the University of South Dakota Medical School in Vermillion. They were not able to explain the reason for her not speaking. They examined her mouth and throat and said that physically she was capable of speech. Her hearing was excellent. She possessed reasoning skills. Fetal Alcohol Syndrome was new, so of course, they had to ask me if I had consumed alcohol during my pregnancy. I was offended. The final report read that she possessed "angelic features" and "showed no signs of FAS or FAE." Later she was referred for an MRI and a CAT scan in Rapid City; the CAT scan showed that she had suffered very small seizures. They were so small that we hadn't noticed. They then prescribed an experimental drug that I later discontinued because I feared that it would damage her liver.

That was when I began questioning and disagreeing with the student labeling employed by the formal education system. This was in stark contrast to traditional Lakota philosophy and beliefs. I had taken my daughter to a doctoring ceremony and was told she was different and gifted. Because she didn't possess the ability to speak, her other senses had become stronger. One in particular was her ability to read minds and probably understand body language. They also said not to worry, that she would speak one day. She had developed her own sign language, using gestures that she had created to communicate with me. Eventually, I accepted my daughter's condition. It strengthened me as a person and gave me the ability to accept all people who are different. It was a lesson in humility and compassion. I am thankful for that experience. Although my daughter is handicapped in that manner, my prayers are always with those who are in worse situations.

I became a very protective mother because of her condition, but I also knew my daughter had to learn to fight her own battles. She was an intelligent little girl and learned quickly how to manipulate me. I worked in the same school that she attended, so I had to quickly learn how to work amicably with my colleagues. She picked up on the personality and style differences I had with her special education teacher, so she began telling me stories of how she was being abused. I confronted her teacher; we exchanged harsh words, but worked it out. It turned out that my daughter was the one who refused to work. I had a talk with my daughter and threatened that I would personally punish her if she continued. That was the end of that.

In the summer of 1983, Porcupine Day School created and advertised a position for an Indian studies coordinator, so I applied and was hired. I worked for another year at that school in an attempt to develop the Indian studies program for K-8. This was another challenge because it operated on a shoestring budget with no other staff and my office was in a trailer house set apart from the school. There was no direction or input from the administration or regular teachers as to exactly what they wanted, so I purchased a variety of American Indian textbooks. I was not into developing curriculum at that point and we could not purchase an Indian studies curriculum because none existed.

In the spring of 1984, I had a dream that led to my first "hanblec-eya," or vision quest. It was about the same time that national TV televised a movie called "The Mystic Warrior." I didn't have a choice because I had a dream that I was to go, but my cousin, Beldine, volunteered to "hanbleceya" at the same time as me. I approached all my spiritual experiences open-mindedly. I was asked if I was afraid shortly before I went. My response was, "How can you fear something you know nothing about?" My dad and mom were there to support me. Dad later commented that I did well and he could see that I approached it with confidence, while he said my cousin had an expression of anxiety on her face. We both survived the night, but she said she would never do it again. My brothers teased me and wondered if we did as the two boys did on "Mystic Warrior"; talking to each other during the night and asking if the other had a vision. I went again many more times after that. Some were because I was instructed through dreams and others because I volunteered to go as a "wopila," or thanksgiving for the health of my family members. This taught me to understand the balance of receiving something and then giving back of yourself.

In the summer of 1984, I noticed a vacancy announcement from Oglala Lakota College for an Indian studies instructor. I applied, was invited for an interview, and was hired in August as a full-time faculty member. This was my initial introduction to adult education. This was by far the greatest challenge of my teaching career. I quickly learned that I had as much to learn from the students as what I presented to them. Some of the students brought experiences and perspectives different from mine. I was immediately intimidated by some of the students older than myself. The majority of the students were my age and older at that time.

Tribal colleges were established in the 1970s to meet the needs of the reservation communities. Prior to that time, students would attend off-reservation colleges and universities, but a majority dropped out and returned. The tribal college founders believed that if the students stayed within their cultural environment and if their culture was integrated into the curriculum, the students would succeed. Oglala Lakota College had adopted the integration of the "Lakota Perspective" into all courses taught. Fifteen hours of Lakota studies are also required as part of the core requirement for all degree areas. The "Lakota Perspective" and the fifteen hours of required Lakota studies courses were designed to give the students a cultural foundation for the workplace upon graduation. Another dream of Oglala Lakota College was to produce Lakota speaking graduates. Although that has not yet happened, many graduate with an awareness of and a greater appreciation for the Lakota culture.

The first five years at the higher education level were a great learning experience for me. I was able to experiment with and use my prior educational training. I taught an overload in my first semester at Oglala Lakota College, but that was before I was informed of what a regular teaching load was. The only difference between elementary and secondary teaching with adult higher education teaching was the academic freedom. The academic freedom permitted at that level allowed me to develop curriculum to fit the needs of the students. I had finally found my niche. Our Lakota studies department consisted of two full-time faculty and one department chair for the first four years. Then the department chair was hired as the vice president for instruction, leaving the chair position vacant. The former chair asked me to apply for the position, but I initially didn't give him a definite answer. I wasn't sure at that point on whether or not I wanted the additional responsibility. But in 1989, after five years of full-time teaching, I became the department chair. Then I became 50 percent administration and 50 percent teaching.

In 1998, I realized that in one year I would mark the twentieth anniversary since I had graduated from college and I had not gone back to graduate school yet. I had promised myself in the beginning that I would work to gain some experience. Then I would return to graduate school, but after almost twenty years. I had seen the South Dakota State University West River Graduate Center summer schedule in the paper, so I decided to give them a call. That was the beginning of my career as a graduate student. I drove to Rapid City two evenings a week for two summers, two fall semesters, and one spring semester. I also continued to work full-time. My goal was to complete my M.Ed. in curriculum and instruction before the year 2000.

I unknowingly had been using the integrated theme-based (ITB) approach early in my teaching career because I had found it to be very effective with my students. I didn't have a name for it until I enrolled with the SDSU West River Graduate Center in the summer of 1998. It was in the adult curriculum and instruction class that I realized I had been using the ITB approach, in which the teacher serves as facilitator and guides the learners using context-based instruction, thus making learning relevant. The focus is on collaborative learning and on the adaptation of instruction to different styles of learning. Teacher flexibility and an excellent teacher-learner relationship are necessary for this approach.

My formal education conditioning from kindergarten to high school and even into college had been focused on individual learning. My informal learning through my participation in ceremonial practices and every day family living had given me a new perspective on learning. In the latter, things were accomplished as a group. There was a set goal, and everyone had a role to assist in the accomplishment of that goal. The leader served as the facilitator. I took this model and adapted it to the classroom with amazing success because the Lakota students had been involved in their own learning experience.

By then, I was convinced that both my formal and informal educational experiences had shaped my life. Both were necessary to develop me as a unique individual. It took the formal process to develop my left-brain functions so I could understand and survive within mainstream society. The left-brain functions are: linear, logic, science, analysis, mathematics, reading, writing, details, facts, and goals. It took the informal process to develop my right-brain functions so I could understand and survive within my own culture. The right-brain functions are: nonlinear, creativity, spirituality, holistic, perceptive, imaginative, dance, art, music, and feeling. After a lifetime of learning, I was finally able to say that I was balanced and secure with my identity.

My learning journey had begun the moment of that first memory at the age of six months, although I didn't understand until I began asking questions of it as a young woman in my early twenties. A "holy man" once told me that learning is infinite—that one continues to learn until the very end. The only catch is you have to be open to grasp and internalize it and then give back in a positive manner so it benefits others.

I have learned that the difference between formal and informal learning is that formal learning tends to be more concrete and overt, while informal learning tends to be more abstract and covert. A goal of the formal process is the attainment of status through materialism; one is forced to receive an education to attain diplomas and degrees in order to be somebody. The goal of the informal process is simply to understand and accept oneself in order to better serve others.

I have learned over the years that Lakota medicine and holy men are the most knowledgeable people; they are a combination of the medical specialists, herbalists, psychologists, historians, and teachers. Many are chosen to serve their people at an early age, so their need for higher formal learning was limited. Yet they are the ones who assist others to understand themselves. They serve as the intermediaries between the common people and the spirit world by retrieving historical and cultural information, collecting and preparing herbs that are prescribed for different illnesses, and informing and answering questions. They are the honored ones within traditional society because of their knowledge and stature within the community. My perception is that they are equal to or beyond those with earned Ph.D.s.

Living within a society that acknowledges both types of learning, I've had to learn to play different roles. Although I have received a formal mainstream education, I become simply a mother, daughter, sister, niece, cousin, or grandchild when I participate in our sacred ceremonies. I am no more important than anybody else—then I become equal. I am on a different level when I represent our people on the outside; I can be the educator and administrator, but always with the people's interests at heart and always mindful of my cultural teachings.

In retrospect, I am amazed that my formal and informal learnings were able to merge. There were times in the beginning when I had my doubts about my right-brain experiences. Once I allowed my left-brain to begin questioning why, and when, and doubted what I was told in the ceremony about my future. Then I was given a right-brain experience that quelled that. Open-mindedness and unlearning linear thought, logic, and science were the keys to getting in touch with myself. I still had respect for formal learning, but it was also important to detach from it to become a whole person.

In my earlier years, my dad served as my mentor. Although he never graduated from high school, he read everything he got his hands on. His reading combined with his lifetime experiences with people from all walks of life served to make up a part of my informal learning. In his later years, he would sit in his wheelchair at the kitchen table, with reading glasses on and a book in his hands. I cherished his words of advice and the wisdom he offered on how to exist in this world. My brothers received the same advice.

He was the one who saw early on that I was stubborn and, according to him, "narrow-minded." He also said that I needed to learn to control my temper and be less judgmental. It wasn't wrong to be worldly, he said, but a person's worth was within her heart and mind. I resented being told of my shortcomings, but I worked calmly to change some of them.

I had also come to terms with the fact that I had lived in a dysfunctional environment around me because of alcoholism. It was another struggle to keep from being pulled into the behaviors associated with alcoholism, such as family conflicts, workplace conflicts, gossip, and jealousy. Once, when I refused to become involved, I was accused of "acting too good." In the world of alcoholism, the Lakota cultural value of generosity is quickly misconstrued. Somebody wants to borrow some money, and you know it will be used to purchase alcohol, so you refuse. Then, you are not a "good Lakota" because you are not practicing generosity. I have said that I will not help somebody to his grave. I have learned to deal with the negative criticism and gossip that come when you experience success by letting the wind carry it away.

I have learned from my experiences that the only person I need to compete with is myself. After reading *Desiderata* (1927) by Max Ehrmann, I took it to heart, and those words have remained with me since my undergraduate days. The part that most influenced me was, "Avoid loud and aggressive persons, they are vexatious to the spirit. If you compare yourself with others, you may become vain and bitter; for always there will be greater and lesser persons than yourself. Enjoy your achievements as well as your plans." The entirety of the piece closely resembled the Lakota philosophy that I was taught as I participated in ceremonies. It was "wowahwala," the gentleness and meekness that can only come from within.

My entire life had been shaped through formal and informal educational experiences; and my self-esteem was nurtured by my parents, family, and teachers. I had never experienced prejudice or racism until I became an adult, and then I was able to accept it as the other person's problem. It happened at one of the stores in Gordon, Nebraska, when I filled my gas tank and went into the store to pay. The clerk was unfriendly, and tossed my change on the counter. I didn't say a word. I excused her because I thought she was having a bad day. The next time I went there, I received the same treatment. I then mentioned it to my cousin Debbie, who lived in Gordon. She said, "Yes, they can't stand to see Indians with money and driving nice vehicles." She said some of the non-Indians harbored some jealousy toward educated Indians. That was new to me. If they only knew how I had struggled to survive in two worlds. I never went back to that store again.

It reminded me of an opposite experience back in 1989 on a trip to Georgia. On our trip home, we stopped at a gas station somewhere in Tennessee. The clerk was a young man who asked us where we were from. We told him "South Dakota," so he enthusiastically said, "Oh, you're some of those 'good Indians,' what are you doing down here?" He then proceeded to tell us he was Cherokee and something else, although he clearly didn't look Indian at all. We remarked to each other that we would never hear such a compliment in South Dakota or Nebraska.

I had taught non-Indian students at Oglala Lakota College who were teachers at the local tribal schools. It was mandatory for them to take Lakota studies courses because it was a requirement of their contracts. One student was from east of the Missouri River in South Dakota. She was born and raised there, but didn't know a thing about South Dakota tribes and their histories. She was apologetic that she was never taught anything about South Dakota Indians. She had become so impressed with the Lakota studies courses that she took more than the required number. She said, if it were up to her that she would recommend that South Dakota tribal history and culture be taught in all of the South Dakota elementary and secondary schools.

I have taught a college Lakota language methods course that consisted of Lakota bilingual speakers. Their frustration level was high because they realized that the pedagogy necessary to teach Lakota culture using the language didn't fit the existing educational models on the reservation. It is necessary to make a paradigm shift that will be conducive to Lakota student learning.

Attainment of knowledge through formal and informal education is the key to understanding the world. My vision for the future of Lakota children is that they must be taught by Lakota teachers who use the Lakota language as the medium of instruction. It is apparent that a formal education is necessary to survive in mainstream society. It is also apparent that informal traditional teaching is necessary, but does not fit the current mainstream model. According to Lakota speaking educators, the Lakota language could become endangered as fluency rates drop with the aging of its society. The younger Lakota generations no longer speak the language. And without the language, we would also be in danger of losing our culture.

So, it is time for tribal governments to transform the current school systems to better serve the students and their communities. As Vine Deloria Jr. stated in his essay "Knowing and Understanding: Traditional Education in the Modern World," "Education today trains professionals, but it does not produce people." With that in mind, it is up to the families and communities or tiospaye to develop these individuals in a culturally appropriate manner.

Chapter 3

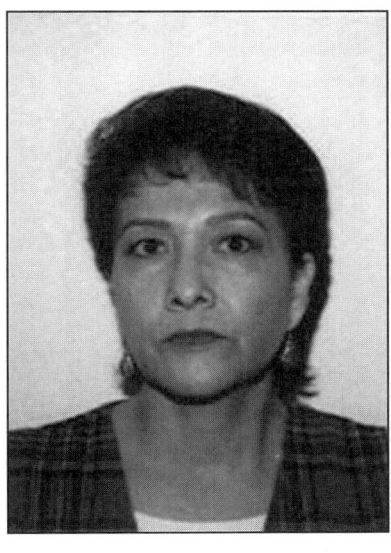

Dakota Identity Renewed

Florestine Kiyukanpi Renville

Florestine Kiyukanpi Renville is an enrolled member of the Sisseton-Wahpeton Dakota Tribe. She lives and works on her home reservation in northeastern South Dakota.

After completing extension courses through Weber State and South Dakota State University, she attended Sisseton-Wahpeton Community College, earning her degree in 1989. Her time there was pivotal, the beginning of a healing journey through learning about Dakota culture and spirituality. She earned a B.A. degree in journalism from South Dakota State University in 1995. Then, after interning at *Lakota Times*, she established her own publication, *Ikce Wicasta, The Common People's Journal*, which she edits and publishes. This journal focuses on the history and culture of Dakota and Nakota people. Her writings have also appeared in *Woyaka Kinikiya* and in several other publications.

I am a Sisseton-Wahpeton Dakota woman, born on the Lake Traverse Reservation in the northeast corner of South Dakota. I can't say "born and raised" on the reservation because my family moved away for a while when I was a small child. My father, Robert Renville, who was ⅝ Dakota, was born in 1895 and was 51 years old when I was born, and my mother, Blossom Keoke Renville, who was full-blood Dakota, was 26. My father died in 1980 at the age of 85, and my mother died in 1967 at the age of 47. They were both born and raised on the reservation.

My father's father, Peter Renville, was married twice and had twelve children, but they didn't all live to adulthood; my aunt Laura Renville Bird was, until recently, the only living member of that family. (Laura Bird died in 1999 at the age of 96.) My father's mother was Sarah Sheldon Renville, who was Grandpa Peter's second wife. My father was married more than once too. His first wife died while giving birth to twins who were stillborn. His second wife, Irene Brown Renville, who was my half-brother Kenny's mother, divorced him while Kenny was still a baby; she died several years ago. My mother was his third wife, and together they had eight children. She was one of nine children born to Jacob Keoke and Etta Grant Keoke. Only one living daughter remains from that family, my aunt Arlene Keoke Eldridge. Recently a cousin informed me that the name "Keoke" is a white perversion of the traditional Dakota name *Kiyukanpi* which means "makes room for them." The name Grant was given to my maternal grandmother's family by a teacher who couldn't pronounce or write their traditional name. Their name was *Si Hanska*, Long Foot.

I don't know the educational history, if any, of my paternal and maternal grandparents. Both my parents went to boarding schools for a short while and experienced harsh treatment there. My father ran away from one of the schools he was sent to and made it back to the reservation and home. My mother and one of her brothers became so sick at boarding school that they were eventually sent home—to die probably, but they didn't. It seems that the only way their father Jacob Keoke could get his sick children home was to write a letter to the agency superintendent and plead his case. When I questioned my father about his school experiences, he told me about only two.

He said that when he was about fifteen years old, he and one of his male cousins were sent to either Carlise Indian School, or to the boarding school in Genoa, Nebraska, I can't remember which. Like many other Indian children before them and after them, they ran away, and made it home. But it was when he was at the boarding school at Old Agency (Tipi Sa), here at home, that he witnessed what was done to a little boy who spoke Dakota instead of English. The little boy, about six or seven, he said, was stripped and plunged into a tub of icy water. As he described the scene, I could hear the anger in his voice as the words came out in chunks. His bushy eyebrows were pulled together in a scowl, and his hands and arms rigidly cut through the air as he demonstrated how the little naked boy was plunged into the water. I am guessing, but I think my father witnessed it because it was done as a lesson for all of the other Indian children. When my father told stories like that, the strong emotions the memories evoked were evident and obviously painful—my father was tenderhearted toward small children. Sometimes there was a note of finality in his voice, like the subject was closed and he wouldn't speak about it again. And sometimes he didn't.

Because I heard stories like that and experienced racism, it was difficult for me to understand why he felt so strongly about us children learning and speaking English rather than Dakota. It was only when I learned about Dakota history, culture, and spirituality that I finally understood my father's strong feelings about the language issue. It also helped to learn about the plight of other tribes and their experiences with federal government policies toward Indians in general. It was my father's difficult personal experiences, and what he learned as an adult, that made him want his children to learn the English language, and to speak it well. Dakota was his first language and he thought he had a difficult time expressing himself the way he wanted to in English, but I thought he expressed himself well. The only difficulty I observed was in his struggling to find the right word sometimes to say succinctly what he wanted said. But I struggle with that, too, and I learned English first. It wasn't until I was in my thirties that I felt brave enough to disagree with my father on the language issue. I argued that I could have learned English anytime in my life and that I would rather have learned to speak Dakota first, but that's not the way he saw it.

All of us children grew up hearing the language spoken, but we don't all understand it to the same degree. Mandis, Roberta, and Adrienne understand it better than I do. For part of her childhood, Adrienne was raised by our *Kunsi* Emma Redearth Grant, my mother's grandmother, who spoke and understood only Dakota, so that's what Adrienne learned. For a long time she couldn't speak it, but with the help of a Dakota language refresher class at Sisseton Wahpeton Community College a few years ago, she says, she is able to speak it better and better as she gets older.

I was eight years old when our *Kunsi* Grant died in 1954. Both she and my grandmother Etta Keoke were widows and they lived together. Because we lived on the reservation until I was five, I had opportunities to hear conversations between my *Kunsi*, my grandmother, my mother, my father, and several uncles and aunts. My aunts and uncles lived with Grandma Keoke off and on, so there were always extended family members around who talked in Dakota rather than English. Now when I hear my language spoken, it is very familiar-sounding. I have no trouble making the vowel and consonant sounds, or in saying words and phrases, but I can't speak it conversationally. There are times when I am thinking about Grandma Keoke and her place, and very clearly, I hear her and my mother talking to one another. Sometimes I hear a whole sentence spoken, with their particular voice inflections, but I cannot repeat it. When our family came home from Minnesota to visit at Grandma Jemima Jones', the experience was similar. My father and mother would sit at her table with other adult family members, talking Dakota and laughing. The only time my parents spoke Dakota in our home was when they didn't want us to understand what they were talking about.

My husband Owen had comparable experiences. He lived long enough with his grandmother Amanda *Tiomanipi* Owen, who was just "*Kunsi*" to many community members, white and Indian, to learn and speak the language. But when he spoke, it was like a woman spoke, so he was teased mercilessly by his uncle. Consequently, Owen stopped speaking Dakota, but like me, the language and its sounds and words are still very familiar to him. When thinking about *Kunsi*, he, too, can hear her speaking in Dakota, but is unable to repeat fully what he hears. As we talk about our problem with speaking our language, we are able to remember more words and phrases.

Remembering some of these experiences with the Dakota language also reminds me of the things other Indian people said about those who spoke the language fluently, but couldn't speak English very well. They were called "big Indians," which meant they were looked down on for speaking "broken English." I now understand that those kinds of opinions about other Indians were influenced by ongoing white tactics intended to divorce us from everything that was cultural and tribal. We were acceptable only if we imitated white people and behaved like them, and some of us believed and accepted the propaganda.

Once when I was in boarding school, a new girl came in the middle of the school year. She was very dark, had a traditional last name, and spoke Dakota well, but not English. So most of the girls avoided her because they said she acted like a "big Indian." At first I didn't want to associate with her either because some of the students said she was lousy with head lice too, but then I reconsidered because I remembered how it was to be ignored and to be without friends when I was in public school. As for the lice problem, we all had to go through de-lousing even though we all may not have had lice.

In my opinion, boarding schools not only denied Indian children their right to speak their own language, but also stripped them of learning how to be relatives and good Dakotas. Some were taken away so young and kept away for so many years that they were even forgotten by some of their younger siblings at home. When they finally went home, they were strangers. Being away in boarding school denied them the privilege of learning how to be good Dakota parents, of learning how to raise and treat children according to our cultural precepts. So when my mother and father married and had children, their parenting skills were limited, and perhaps lacking in some areas. Both were somewhat authoritarian, like those put in charge of Indian children at boarding schools. They didn't tolerate questions about their decisions or their motives, no matter what they did.

Traditionally, the Dakotapi (this is the old way of pluralizing the word versus the currently pluralized "Dakotas") weren't an authoritarian people, and we certainly didn't treat our children harshly, or hit them like white people did with their children. So even though my parents were authoritarian in some ways, my father never spanked me; instead, according to my sisters, he spoiled me. I remember my mother spanking me once when I was eight or nine years old, and I remember it only because I told some children at school that my mother had spanked me so that they would think she was mean. After I had done that, I felt completely disloyal and ashamed. If she spanked me before that, I don't recall it. When we stayed with Grandma Keoke, or our aunts and uncles, we were never physically punished. At Grandma Jones', there was no authoritarian behavior displayed either. My older brother Mandis said our father never spanked him and that our mother hit him just one time. His recollections of Dakota discipline are like those of many other

Indians who have said that if wrongdoing was observed, the child was spoken to in a normal voice and warned about the consequences of his or her behavior. Then the choice was left up to the child.

My father frequently told the story of how his cousin Elijah disciplined his son Edmund. If Grandma Jones thought her grandson Edmund needed correction, she would remind Elijah about it. But the most that he would do was to say in a soft quiet voice, "Edmund, don't do that." Even after all the years we had been exposed to white authoritarianism, some of our people were still unable to behave in the manner the whites would have liked us to. You know, like the Bible says, "spare the rod, spoil the child"? Although Grandma Jones would remind her own son to discipline Edmund, I know she could not have physically punished any child; she was too kindhearted and gentle.

The early years of my life on the reservation must have been fairly secure and stable because my memories of that time make me feel like I belonged, like we had a place to call home, although we didn't own the house we lived in. Those feelings are the complete opposite of what I've experienced in the white-dominated environments that I've been in throughout the rest of my life. The two major settings that impacted my life were the white schools and the white churches we attended.

Every time we went to any functions on the reservation, it included almost the whole family, unlike some white functions where children are excluded, or where there aren't any elderly people. In fact, I can't recall having gone to anything where Indians of all ages weren't represented. So we children were exposed to a seemingly balanced society in our Indian world. Allowing family members to be exposed to all facets of reservation life was still happening even after I returned to the reservation and attended high school in the 1960s. For example, one time I went with my mother to pick up my dad at a tribal council meeting and saw children inside with their parents, or playing outside. I think I was surprised by that because I was accustomed to the way white people did things, where children were not allowed at political meetings. And I wrongfully and ignorantly thought that was the way it should be. For too many years the white man's teachings were the ones that influenced my thoughts, behavior, and learning. White people continue to have a problem with seeing children of all ages in attendance at tribal community functions because in many white world settings it is still "adults only."

During my first five years on the Lake Traverse Reservation, my father was gone frequently, usually working out of state, and we spent a lot of time with our paternal grandmother Jemina Jones, who lived a walking distance of a half mile east of us. Those times are the warmest and fondest memories that I have of my childhood and of our family life. My older brother Mandis's and oldest sister Roberta's memories are of riding the work horses, playing in the barn, and staying out at night with cousins and friends doing "fun," but innocent, things. It was a time when we were truly happy, before we moved away from the reservation. All the elements for making memories were there—love, safety, family, belonging, independence, and pride. Once I learned about human development, my recollections of those first five years of my life strengthened in me the understanding that our Dakota culture and traditions were good for us, although that's not what I believed for many years.

Sometimes when I reflect, a lump forms in my throat, and I wish we could go back to that time and start our lives over with all of the things necessary to make us an emotionally and spiritually whole family. The pain I feel is knowing that the kindness and goodness in my father and mother, Robert and Blossom Renville, and in my brothers and sisters, were later perverted by alcoholism. I can't remember any of my family members turning anybody away when help was needed. My sisters' homes are still almost always full of extended family members, with their own children or grandchildren, and sometimes with foster children who need a place to stay.

My pain, and anger, too, is caused by knowing that alcohol has always been used by white people against Indians "to steal, to kill, and to destroy," to borrow a verse from their own sacred text, the Bible. But is that widely known by ordinary school children, or even students in colleges and universities? Not really, because according to the largely accepted viewpoint of white people, it was their ancestors, the pioneers, the mountain men, the fur traders, the risk takers, who settled the *wild* west and made this country great. And we are viewed negatively worldwide as reservation Indians, lazy and drunken. This opinion is still too prevalent, and the root cause is lack of education and accurate information about American Indians. Accurate ongoing education about American Indians needs to begin in the primary grades and continue right on through college; after all, that is the American ideology for learning the basic subjects of reading, writing, and math.

What I mean is that I hear and read stories about education, and many of the comments made about it by educators are that learning can and should occur throughout one's lifespan. It doesn't end when any level of formal education is finished. Frequently I hear on television that learning is lifelong, and white Americans advocate that, but it is untrue, apparently, when it involves learning about indigenous people. On this issue ignorance is accepted. I hear white college students complaining about having to take a class on American Indian literature or history, and having to attend a conference event that features something on Indian culture. They are content in their ignorance about us, but that isn't as true when education involves learning about African Americans, or other cultures.

As for my family's spirituality, we were exposed early to the Episcopalian belief system through our attendance at St. Mary's Church, one of the oldest mission churches on the reservation. It was about one mile north on the Bureau of Indian Affairs road east of our house, but because we walked most of the time, we probably had cut-across paths. The most familiar scenes that I remember are the Lenten services and wakes held in people's homes or at the church guild hall. Now whenever I smell freshly made coffee at one of the church's functions, and taste a minced ham (bologna) sandwich, I am transported back to the gas-lit guild hall and the time when I was a little girl. The soft hissing sound of the gas lanterns and the sound of a male voice rising and falling in the Dakota dialect would make me drowsy. Then the sound of Dakota voices singing hymns would awaken me. Remembering how certain individuals sounded or led the others in singing helps me remember names and faces of people who have been dead for many years.

My Grandma Keoke was well-known for her high soprano voice that could be heard above all others. Her son, my Uncle Mark (Marquette), was just as well known for his singing voice. Now when my sister Adrienne and I attend functions where there is Dakota hymn singing, others frequently reminisce about our grandma's and uncle's voices. I think that happens because Adrienne has a good voice like our relatives, although she sings alto.

One other thing that older Dakotas tell us of is seeing Grandma walk to church, which was three and a half miles one way. In fact, she regularly walked wherever she went, just like her two sons,

Uncle Bob and Uncle Mark, and her two brothers, Grandpa John Grant and Grandpa Paul Grant. None of these family members ever owned cars. And when Uncle Mark was in the Army, he hitchhiked wherever he needed to go, or where he needed to be. There are still some Dakotas who walk today, but it is not like it used to be.

I read about similar experiences in *Choteau Creek: A Sioux Reminiscence*, by Yankton Dakota Joseph Iron Eyes Dudley. Many events were very familiar-sounding, especially the church-related activities and the meals that sometimes followed. Although I can't recall specific details of our family doing some of those things, there must be bits of memories stored in my subconscious somewhere of our family participating in related activities. Sometimes while reading the book, I experienced warm feelings of love and belonging as I imagined myself back in my childhood on the reservation. I gave each of my sisters a copy of the book, and Adrienne said she could "just see" everything that Dudley described.

Most Dakotas carried their own hymnals and prayer books to church functions, and that still happens today. Books aren't stacked in the backs of pews like in white people's churches. I suppose white people would speculate that in the Indian community hymnals couldn't be left in the churches, because they would soon be stolen by someone. But my philosophy about why Dakotas don't leave their hymnals and prayer books in the church is because to them their spirituality is a very personal and individual and continuous experience, like traditional spirituality was before white people came and forced change upon us. And like many others before her, my mother always had her own hymnal. So when I became an adult, I made sure I had my own too. But my hymnals were Presbyterian. When I married, I switched churches and district membership. I went from being an Episcopalian at St. Mary's Church in Old Agency District, to being a member of Big Coulee District and the Ascension (*Iyakaptapi*) Presbyterian Church. However, later on I inherited my mother's hymnal and my Grandpa John Grant's too. I think I was given those hymnals because I have always sought a deeper spirituality. I now have a Dakota Episcopal hymnal and prayer book too. It's useful to have both because today many services, whether they are Episcopal, Presbyterian, or Catholic, include songs from both hymnals that are familiar to all three churches.

I can only guess about the influence the church and its teachings back home on the reservation had on my mother. She disliked powwows and Indian dancing, and wouldn't allow us to go to any. But my father loved both Indian singing and dancing, and would go despite my mother's feelings about them. My dad liked *wasicu* (white) dances, too, and was such a good dancer that he was sought after by many women, but that was before my mother entered his life. Dakota women and white women alike told me some of these things about my dad only after my mom died. I think the abhorrence of traditional practices and dancing particularly, white or Indian, may have been passed down to my mother by her mother. One older tribal member recently told me that her parents used to dance, too, but once they began going to a Christian church, they remained completely silent about their dancing, and they destroyed everything that was traditionally Dakota. Speculating, I think something terribly traumatic happened to our people during and after the 1862 war in Minnesota that made some of them try to remove all vestiges of their cultural heritage. So, having parents, and even grandparents, who had opposite viewpoints about traditional activities contributed to the confusion that many Indian families experienced about our culture and spirituality.

Some families became Christians while others just stayed apart, but they did not practice traditional spirituality either. The federal government and the mission churches that were established on reservations were directly responsible for this separation among tribal members. When our tribe was finally transplanted here with the creation of the Lake Traverse Reservation, my great-grandfather Gabriel Renville refused to give up practicing Dakota traditions. The Indian Agent, Reverend Adams, who was sent here by the government, and with the Presbyterian Church's blessings, condemned Gabriel for keeping his *heathen* ways. Gabriel had three wives, danced, participated in the sweatlodge, and prayed with the Pipe. In a letter, Agent Adams accused Gabriel and his followers of being lazy and unproductive. Yet, they were just as productive as those who became Christian farmers, and in some cases even more productive. But Indians experiencing success without embracing Christianity was not what the government or the churches wanted. Conflicts among tribal members about the two ways of life helped the government and the churches maintain their control over us.

Our reservation was established in 1867 after the war with the whites in Minnesota in 1862. By that time the division among Dakotas had already become serious. The initial separation began when some of them cooperated with the intruding whites and intermarried with them, which was usually done for economic reasons. Relationships were established for government to government negotiations. The United States government wanted land for their clamoring white constituents and some of the earlier politicians on the local level astutely recognized that kinship was important to Dakotas. So with intermarriages, Indian agents were able to establish relationships, such as they were, between bands and tribes with officials in Washington, D.C. Some family members abhorred the mistreatment of Dakota women and their mixed-blood children that they observed, but kinship ties and protocol prevented them from acting in a decisive manner in response.

I believe the oppression here by white people was so intense that it sometimes meant choosing one's own safety and remaining alive instead of helping relatives. There is a story here about Solomon Two Stars having to shoot his own nephew in the aftermath of 1862 because the nephew had killed some white people in Minnesota. Solomon was stationed with other scouts in an area southwest of present-day Enemy Swim District. He was compelled to shoot his nephew because of the choices he was given by the United States Army. As an Army scout, he had to follow its orders just like the rest of the soldiers, which were to kill all hostiles. For Dakotas in leadership positions, their families would suffer the consequences if the Army and government, local and national, were defied. This wasn't new to Indians, because once white people had established themselves in large numbers, after having treacherously annihilated entire tribes in the east and southeast, they then began to assert their attitudes of superiority by forcing us to do what local politicians, businessmen, and individuals wanted. Too many times American Indians were at the mercy of ignorant uneducated men who were appointed Indian agents who didn't care about the well-being of a dark-skinned nation.

I grew up hearing negative stories about Gabriel Renville, a mixed-blood, and I was ashamed of him for many years. The most told story was that he was an Indian Scout for the American Army, but not only that: he was Chief of Scouts, too. This story contributed to the belief among Dakotas that he was a traitor. When I heard him called a traitor and why he was called that, I would wonder how someone could turn against his own people. But the history of 1862 and the years following were much more complicated than my childish understanding, and the true stories still need to be unraveled. The other story about my great-grandfather was that he was never elected or chosen by the people for the position of chief, but appointed by the federal government. I think the intention of this story was to make people believe that he was controlled by the ruling white people. This story created another crack in Dakota unity. But I did a little research and discovered that he was elected by the people at least one time.

Growing up I also heard that Indian dancing and white dancing were no good, at least for those who went to church regularly; they were "of the devil," it was said. I remember going to only one powwow. It was in the Enemy Swim District at a place called Shaker's Park. I was never exposed to anything about our traditional Dakota spiritual practices. In fact, throughout the years I was in school, I was led to believe that Dakotas had no religion, no culture, no values, until the white man came. Textbooks excluded accurate information about American Indian cultures here on this continent. We were even deprived of the information which early missionaries had recorded and documented about our histories, cultures, and spirituality. The values I was learning were from the Christian church and white society.

When we lived on the reservation, it was in an eighteen-by-twenty-four-foot two-room house with no running water and no electricity. It sat on a small knoll at the foot of the Coteau des Prairies, with no trees nearby. However, there was a coulee south of us where we went berry picking, and the creek there provided water for our needs. The dirt road which led up to our house was just off a Bureau of Indian Affairs' gravel road, which local people called "The Jones's Trail." Our dirt road was well trampled by our frequent walks on it to Grandma Jones's house—the place where we ran and played and felt free and safe. Grandma's house was where our mother had learned to cook and bake, can foods, and make butter and cottage cheese, and where she could wash our clothes in a gas washing machine. For us five older ones, this was a place where the sun always seemed to shine, where the days were always perfect! My sister Adrienne said Grandma must have loved us very much, because it seems like we came and went as we liked. Sometimes the smell of a small gas engine or the smell of fresh-baked bread stirs up memories of her house. With a few renovations over the years, the house we once lived in still stands and continues to be occupied.

Grandma Jones's house is situated on a knoll, too, and off and on her family members live there.

I can't remember a rainy day or a cloudy day during the times I played there, but I do remember playing with my cousin John "Skip" Wilson. He and I were born on the same day. Adrienne and I perceived him as being spoiled, but I wonder if that perception was influenced by his unwillingness to let us ride his new red tricycle. Anyway, the closest I came to riding it was when he generously allowed me or Adrienne to stand on the back while he pedaled. That must have satisfied us, because I don't remember fighting with him about it. We also liked to play down below the hill in the creek and at the natural spring which Grandma's second husband Sam Jones piped into a trough-like container. In this northeast corner of South Dakota, there are many such natural springs. Sica Hollow, a local state park, is known for its many springs, too.

Living with Grandma Jones were her two sons, Charlie Two Stars, still single at the time, and Elijah Two Stars, a widower, and Elijah's son Edmund. Like many other Dakota grandmothers, Grandma was also raising Skip, who was the son of her daughter Hildreth Two Stars Venegas, who didn't live there. Hildreth was considered by tribal people to be a career woman, which was extraordinary for the times. The Jones family had horses, milk cows, chickens, and guinea hens. The two-story, square farmhouse, with four bedrooms, a living room, and a kitchen, was like a mansion to me. There was even a piano in the living room that Charlie played while he sang bass along with whatever parts were being sung by Elijah, Edmund, and my brother Mandis and my sister Roberta. For many, many years, Charlie was the pianist/organist at St. Mary's Episcopal Church, the mission church, which we all attended.

In later years when Roberta was a teenager, my father would tease her about singing bass along with Charlie, which made us all laugh with her. Roberta is six years older than me, and Grandma Jones's house is where she learned to walk when she was eight months old. Our father and mother told us that because she was so little, she was able to walk under the dining room table. When I remember them telling that family story, I can see my parents' smiling, happy faces and hear the teasing tone in their voices, but there was also tenderness and pride. We didn't spend all of our time at Grandma's, but enough for all of us to have good memories of those early years on the reservation.

When my father spoke about his Aunt Jemima Jones, it was with much respect and love, because in the traditional Dakota manner, the mother's sisters are also regarded as mothers. His relationship with Grandma Jones became even more important when his mother died around 1950. My dad always said that Grandma Jones's home was open to whoever came and that she would welcome them to come in and eat something and drink some coffee. It probably made him happy to see my mother get along well with her and to learn so much about homemaking from her, too. It was those skills and that relationship that kept us fed when my father was away working and unable to send money home.

Our mother put in a huge garden that had to be weeded regularly by Mandis and Roberta. Our mother cooked lots of sweet corn and took it off the cob for drying, so we could have *waskuya*, corn soup, in the winter. In those days, and well into the 1970s, *waskuya* was served mainly for special occasions, like for a Christian holiday dinner. Although Dakotas eat corn soup more frequently today, it still remains a favorite food. We also have more opportunities for special occasions because not only has our population grown, but more and more tribal people are returning to traditional cultural practices which require serving food. So *waskuya* is almost always on the menu.

Drying corn is not a quick and easy method of food preservation, yet Mom allowed me to try taking the kernels off the cob like she did, and I was very little. Understanding my mother better today than in the past, I realize that must have been difficult for her, because she was a perfectionist and impatient. Things had to be done "just so," and be done the way she wanted them done, or be done over. After the corn was off the cob, she'd lay a large piece of canvas on the ground and spread the corn on it for drying. She also used the canvas for shaking dried beans out of their pods. Spreading the beans out on the canvas, my mother, brother, and sisters would pick up the corners and shake the beans out of their pods. I probably got in their way, but they allowed me to "help" them with their work. I realize now, after having learned about some of our cultural traditions, that we were behaving as a typically traditional Dakota family.

Mandis's memories of life on the reservation are good ones too, specifically before Indians became drinkers of alcohol when they were legally allowed to buy it. Recreation and entertainment for Dakotas were community social activities, such as functions at church, or going to play bingo, or going to *wasicu* dances. We used to have a building called the Community Hall located where the first agency buildings were built, and that's where the "white" dances were held. All the old buildings are gone now, and that place is now called the ceremonial grounds, and we have a permanent stone arena there for our annual powwow in July.

Life among Dakotas was still very communal in the 1940s and 1950s, despite attempts by whites to eradicate that from our lifestyles since before reservations were established. Mandis recalls that because almost everybody cooked and heated their homes with wood, the Episcopalian organizations, the BCU, Brotherhood of Christian Unity, and the St. Andrew men would go around to different homes on Saturdays and help cut wood. Mandis said, "I used to like that; nobody drank back then. Sometimes when we went to church or to Halloween (social), we went in a wagon pulled by a team of horses." He said respect for parents and others was still a real part of their lives yet, too. Although Mandis didn't like to sing, Mom and Dad would tell him and Berta that it was time for them to go over to Grandma Jones's and practice with their cousin Edmund while Charlie played the piano. They never thought of refusing; they just did it, he said, because of respect for their parents and relatives. His observations of today's tribal members is that we have become too individualistic; just what white people have always wanted, he said. It took many, many years for the missionaries and government to finally make an impact on our communal way of life, and we've only been attempting to be individualistic since the 1950s, so maybe we do have a chance to recover our traditional ways and once again be a whole people, instead of individuals.

When the school year started, Mandis and Roberta, and later Adrienne, had to walk about a half mile northeast of our house to a one-room building, which continued to be used by the township for a polling place until a few years ago, when it burned down. Our third to the oldest sister Naomi contracted tuberculosis when she was about five years old, so she didn't have a chance to start school until much later. Living in the back room of the schoolhouse was the white teacher, Daisy Anderson, who was very heavy-set, according to Roberta. Berta would sometimes spend the night there, because, she said, Mrs. Anderson seemed to be scared of everything—a sound, an unknown visitor, storms, fog. Berta couldn't have provided much protection; she was just nine or ten years old. One of her memories is of the two of them running for shelter to the school cellar during a thunderstorm. Another time, she recalled, they ran to our house for safety from something or someone, and spent the night. I can hardly imagine six people, or seven, if my dad was home, all spending the night together in our little house. We had only three beds in our two-room house, which consisted of a kitchen and a sleeping room. Sleeping on the floor wasn't unusual. That was where Adrienne and I frequently slept.

When I questioned my sisters about their school experiences at the "Jones School," as it was called, they said it was okay but that there were only two families of Indian children who went there—ours and Edward Crawford's, but there were even fewer white kids. Most other Indian children went to Old Agency Day School, Enemy Swim Day School, and Big Coulee Day School, which were all Indian, or to any one of the other one-room country schools that dotted the reservation. Mandis, Roberta, and Adrienne eventually switched to Old Agency Day School, because according to Mandis, there wasn't enough financial support to keep the Jones's School open. The white kids who went there moved on to a school in the small town of Peever five miles east.

I was puzzled for a while as to why our grandparents and parents were sent away to boarding schools when there were schools right here on the reservation. When our reservation was established, almost immediately churches and schools were built and in use. Yet they were sent away and most of us have suffered to some degree because of it. Because our grandparents, parents, and other relatives suffered emotionally, physically, and socially by being subjected to forced assimilation by the government, in conspiracy with the missionaries and officials of boarding schools, they didn't want their children to learn cultural traditions, spirituality, or language.

The government representatives and missionaries were devious in their approach to "civilizing" Indian people. If they couldn't make us into replicas of themselves through their education systems and by isolating our families, or by dispersing tribes and affiliated tribesmen to different parts of the country, then they had to revert to their original tactic, which was to attempt to annihilate us. Even after two hundred years of living with us, white people and their government were still expanding on their original plans to be rid of us. White governmental officials weren't ashamed of their greed for

Indian lands, and they didn't care who knew it. And neither were the devout Christian missionaries ashamed—they wanted the money that came to Indians as much as the traders did. They also argued over which denomination would get to establish a church among the Indians. They even documented all of their devious plans. I recently read this statement made by the Commissioner of Indian Affairs John Q. Smith in 1876:

> The civilization or the utter destruction of the Indians is inevitable. The next twenty-five years are to determine the fate of a race. If they cannot be taught very soon, to accept the necessities of their situation and begin in earnest to provide for their own wants by labor in civilized pursuits, they are destined to speedy extinction. (Gibson, p. 428)

White people's hatred, racism, and feelings of superiority were the underlying attitudes that led them to speculate falsely about us. They believed that if they confined us on reservations, denied us the annuities owed us, separated us from our families, and shipped us off to boarding schools, we would eventually physically die, or be assimilated into the white race. Although we didn't vanish as once expected, we did, however, suffer from the effects of their racism and their belief that they knew better what to do for us. Some Indian leaders eventually thought education would help us to be accepted and to be treated fairly, but there were never any guarantees from whites. Instead, education was used as a means to dominate and suppress. White education systems were designed to show us how ignorant we were, not only in the eyes of the larger society, but in our own eyes too. According to them, we had no history, made no contributions to the survival of the white race on this continent, had no heroes, didn't know how to survive unless the white people showed us how with their ingenuity and inventions, and had no spirituality. We were plain, blah, and brown—inconsequential.

We suffered through their education systems with their diseases, too. Many Indian families here on the Lake Traverse Reservation contracted tuberculosis well into the 1940s and 1950s, and today some still test positive. My father and mother both had sisters who died from TB. My sister Naomi, who is four years older than me, contracted it when she was five years old. She was confined to two sanitoriums for more than three years. Finally, my parents agreed to allow her to undergo experimental surgery that would remove one half of one of her lungs because it was her only chance of survival. Naomi knows that because there is a photo and news story about it in her medical file at the Indian Health Hospital in Sisseton. I don't remember Naomi being a part of our family until she was ten years old, which was after we moved to Minnesota.

In the spring of 1951, our family moved to Moorhead, Minnesota, one hundred miles north of our reservation and home. For our people, economic conditions in the past hundred years have almost always been bleak and economics were what caused us to move. At home, employment for my dad was working on small family farms for three dollars a day, or hitching a train to other towns and states to work in construction. Minneapolis was one of those other places where my dad worked for a while. He sent money home, but it didn't always reach my mother. They speculated that someone knew there was cash in the envelope and stole it.

Around the Fargo-Moorhead area were several large farms that grew produce which was shipped out to grocery stores. The larger towns of Fargo and Moorhead and the larger farms probably led my dad to believe that more work was available to keep him employed longer, enabling him to remain with his family. Also, my dad liked farming because his mother and father had owned a farm, as had other Indian people. Furthermore, "farmer Indians" is what the white government, missionaries, and settlers wanted us to become, so some of us did. Working on the vegetable farms was hard work, but neither Dad or Mom shied away from doing what was difficult. Both of them reminded us to never be afraid of doing hard work, and none of us were.

My first life-changing experience was entering a community that was entirely non-Indian and being the only Indian in my grade. I must have been a confident child before I entered that extreme environment that altered my self-concept. I believe I was a confident child because my father was involved with me. I can say that because my sisters have told me that he always held me on his lap, spoiled me, and taught me to say, "I'm boss woman," when I was first talking. Behavioral and family studies reveal that when fathers are in the homes and involved with their children, those children are better developed emotionally than are those without fathers in the homes. Also, according to studies, most girls develop confidence and a certain amount of fearlessness when their fathers are involved with raising them. I believe I exhibited that confidence because of some of the things my sisters say I got away with doing. But that all changed gradually as I spent more and more time among a people who disregarded my presence and who considered my race to be inferior.

White schools and textbooks have barely mentioned American Indians and their contributions to the progress this nation has made and the impact those contributions have had worldwide. White people, and now some Black Americans, take all the credit for making this an affluent and strong country. Consequently, when I was growing up, I thought I was part of a race of people who had nothing to contribute, who had nothing that others wanted or desired. Thus began my entrance into feelings of inferiority and shame. At first, my silence in the classroom was related to Dakota traditional behavior which dictated that children quietly observed and learned. They didn't have to be constantly asking questions, or trying to satisfy their curiosity. I think white people have an insatiable curiosity that isn't always healthy or good. As time went on, though, my silence became self-deprecating. I was never sure of myself, and I didn't think my contributions in the classroom could be valued or even acceptable.

White people's attitudes and behavior toward American Indians are totally contrary to the godly precepts upon which they claim they founded this democratic government. And even in their Penecostal churches, I experienced racism and ignorance.

When we first moved to Minnesota, it was to a farm outside of Moorhead with no living quarters. We had to live in tents until our father could find more permanent work and a house. That initial experience off the reservation was a very miserable one for all of us, and memorable too. The two tents we had to live in were made of canvas and weren't entirely waterproof, so when it rained, many things got wet. What I remember most was the steady downpour of rain, the mud, and the misery. Eventually, my dad found a job on one of the farms nearby that had a house we could live in. Sometimes we had family experiences that were good, but overall, the six or seven years that we lived in Minnesota weren't the best times. They weren't memorable like the times we spent at Grandma Jones's and living on the reservation among friends and relatives.

The job and house my dad found was at one of the vegetable farms in the area. The house we moved into was a one-room duplex with no running water, but it did have electricity—one light bulb hanging from a long cord in the middle of the ceiling. Near our house was a root cellar where some of the vegetables were stored when the temperatures turned colder. The root cellar's pitched roof was above the ground and the rest was underground. The roof was ideal for sliding when there was lots of snow on it. Our parents were always warning Adrienne and me to stay off it, probably because it was white man's property, more than for any other reason. But it was one of the few things that provided us with some fun, so we did it anyway despite the possible consequences of being caught. We didn't have sleds, and there were no hills, so we would slide down that roof whenever we thought no one was watching. Compared to the abundance of hills and valleys and trees that we were accustomed to at home on the reservation, the Fargo-Moorhead area was very flat, with the only trees in man-made shelterbelts or along the Red River.

We lived there for several months; then we moved into a quonset-type building behind a large warehouse. The warehouses looked just like the root cellars only they were much, much larger. The one near the house we moved into had dirt right up to the roof on one side, so Adrienne and I climbed up that, too. We couldn't slide down this one, though, because the roof was covered with corrugated steel and snow didn't stick to it. So this building, in the shadow of a huge warehouse, was the "house" we were living in when I started school in Dilworth, which was across some vegetable fields. Weather permitting, we walked across those fields, and crossed a large drainage ditch to get to school. In the fall there were still tomatoes on the vines in the fields, and while they lasted they were our after-school snacks.

We could no longer run freely and play wherever we wanted to like we could back on the reservation. There, even though our reservation Indian lands were interspersed with white-owned lands, we still experienced some freedom from the ever-present controlling white people. In the coulees and hills, we could still go to places where there were no white people. Now we had to remember that everything belonged to white men and that it was their property we were living on. There was no refuge, or place where we could feel totally at ease, comfortable, and accepted. Oh, we could play on the farm, but we couldn't go into white people's yards and homes. At least that's what we were told, but we weren't always obedient children. I don't know if we were defiant or just curious as children can be, but we dared to play where we weren't supposed to. Adrienne and I liked to make mudpies, so we stole eggs from the granary where some of the chickens had laid them. It never occurred to us that we could have sunk into the grain and suffocated. We were too intent on getting those coveted eggs.

One time Adrienne and I were playing in a windbreak of trees on the farm. We were deeply involved in making mudpies, so we didn't hear anything. Then one of us looked up and saw one of the men who co-owned the farm peering at us through the trees. It scared us so badly that we jumped up and ran home, leaving our muddy creations behind. I don't think we went back there too often after that, and if we did, we were watchful. When I remember that incident, I think about all the sexual molestations that are being reported on the news, especially those perpetrated by trusted persons. I don't know what this man was up to, but I can recall the look in his eyes and it makes me feel unclean.

School was another example of exposure to an all-white environment. In first grade at Dilworth, my teacher was the stereotypical image of a white spinsterly woman, stern-looking and mean. I was afraid of her. She was tall, slim, and gray-haired, and she wore those so-called sensible blacklaced shoes with chunky heels and wire-rimmed glasses. Her thin hair was always on top of her head in a bun. I witnessed the way she corrected other students, and I eventually had my day, too. I answered a question wrong, so she came over to me, and with her fingers bunched together, rapped me on top of the head repeatedly, like a woodpecker rapping on a tree. Perhaps she was "knocking some sense into me," as the saying goes. I don't remember any positive experiences that first year. I don't know if I was an angry child, but once when I was doing some homework at our kitchen table, I became frustrated and scribbled over the whole page. My mother quickly came over and made me erase all the scribblings and finish the work. It is from that time on that I recall my family saying I had a bad temper. Did the negative school experiences and others with the white world have something to do with it? Perhaps only my mother could answer that question.

Roberta was now about twelve years old, so she had to contribute to our family financially by sometimes baby-sitting the head owner's ("the Boss," as he was known by the male workers) children, doing household work there, and working in the fields. Adrienne and I would have been six and eight years old, and we had to work in the fields with the rest of the family. We even "cut" potatoes for spring planting. This meant sitting before a huge bin of potatoes with a knife blade sticking up on a ledge in front, the cutting edge pointed toward the small opening through which the potatoes came. We then quartered them and dropped them into a basket underneath. My mother could do this work very quickly, so I worked as fast as I could to try to keep up, even though I was afraid of knives. Just recently Adrienne asked if I remembered having to go back to the warehouse after supper to work until about 9 o'clock, although we had school the next day; I told her I did. My parents certainly didn't know anything about the 1938 Fair Labor Standards Act that Congress enacted to end oppressive child labor.

America's quest for more profits through cheap labor hasn't changed in the past sixty years when it involves Indians and migrants, legal or illegal workers. The law of 1938 was one of those spurts of conscience that rises and falls among the white population and Congress. In the December 19, 1997, issue of the Minneapolis *Star Tribune* was an Associated Press story about a recent five-month period of illegal child labor here in America. Reporters found that there were 165 kids working illegally in sixteen states. The reporters saw 104 children working illegally in agriculture in the five months. According to the story,

> Underage workers picked cucumbers in Michigan, green peppers in Tennessee and apples in upstate New York. Their grape-cutting knives flashed in the sunny vineyards of California, and their head lamps bobbed in the gloomy mushroom sheds of Pennsylvania. They packed peaches into crates in Illinois and hoed sorghum in Lubbock, Texas.
>
> On a hot July day near Bowling Green, Ohio, Pasqual Mares looked sadly at his 10-year-old daughter Laura, her back bent over a row of cucumbers. In a full week of harvest work, Mares said, he and his wife and their two working children had earned just $120—far below the normal minimum wage. "Someday, I want my children to be treated like human beings, not like animals," he said. "It's not right that the children work. But we have to do it." [1]

What was happening to us in the 1950s was not an anomaly—it has always been the norm for America in achieving its "greatness" as a world power. Early American white people came from England which was ruled by an aristocracy, as were other European countries. The royal courts and their families with their cruel treatment

---

[1] An Associated Press story printed in the Minneapolis Star Tribune, Dec. 19, 1997

of their subjects influenced the immigrants in how to treat others who had less than they had and were different than they were in religious belief, ethnic background, or race.

These former English subjects migrated here, bringing with them thoughts of subjugation. And that's what they, these ordinary people seeking a "better life," brought to this northern continent—an insatiable hunger and drive to have and be like those who had ruled them, to control others as they were once controlled. No one can deny that politics, business, and religion are about power and control. So there my family was on that farm in Minnesota, contributing to the power and wealth of a Scandinavian family.

There was other work that we did on the farm, too. Mandis and Roberta drove tractors when the vegetables were harvested, and except for Naomi and our baby sister Chyrel, we all spent time in the half-mile long fields hoeing weeds, topping onions, picking potatoes, and waxing and sacking the vegetables. Topping onions meant moving down rows of onions on our knees, bushel baskets in front of us, cutting off the tops of the onions with knives, two or three at a time, and dropping them into the basket. Picking potatoes was similar, only the plants were turned over by a machine, and we would maneuver along on our knees, pull the potatoes loose from the roots, and put them into the baskets we dragged with us. When the baskets were full, they would be dumped into gunny sacks. Once the hundred-pound gunny sacks were filled, they were left standing, and later a tractor pulling a trailer with two men on it and two walking along each side would load the potatoes onto the trailer. Then they would be taken to a warehouse to be stacked. It was all hard work. We just accepted the fact that we had to work, and we never asked our parents for the money we earned. Mandis was probably paid like the other male adults because I think that's how it was for the male Mexican migrants. If they were fifteen years old and older, they were paid their own wages, rather than having their pay included in their parents' checks.

Our parents were strict taskmasters, but they also expressed their love for us by saying, "we love you all the same," and then they would add that we should be satisfied that we had a home and food on the table. However, there were times when we didn't have food, or a place to call home, even once we were back on the reservation and among relatives. Despite that, I don't think I doubted my parents' love for me, although all of their actions didn't always indicate that love.

I can only imagine how it must have made my proud Dakota father and mother feel having us work with them, yet they knew we couldn't survive on just my father's earnings. There were times when we overheard our dad telling our mother how cheaply he was being paid for the hard work and long hours. Having heard such things and seeing the vast difference between our living conditions and the owners, had an impact on me. I disliked the farm owners and stayed away from them, although they had children who were close in age to Adrienne and me. I suppose we could have played with them, but we didn't. We preferred playing with one another.

Baby-sitting gave Roberta the opportunity to observe what went on in the Boss's household. One time she told us peaches and pears were purchased by the crate and were sometimes left on the steps leading into the house from the garage. It was probably our attitudes of disrespect and dislike that prompted Adrienne and me to try to steal some of the fruit. But besides our negative attitudes, I think we may have just wanted some fresh fruit because we rarely had anything sweet to eat. Or maybe we did it just to see if we could get away with doing something right under the Boss's nose. Exactly why we stole that fruit is not clear. We were taught not to steal, and we respected that value, but we stole anyway, and from a white man. Our motivation also may have been due to our having experienced our grandmothers' generous sharing with their families back home, done with kindness and happiness, without expectation of repayment. As a child in a white world, I rarely saw that happen. If these farm owners couldn't pay my father better wages, they still should have been urged by their own "Christian" consciences to give perhaps some groceries, or some crates of fruit to their workers' families. Seeing and hearing these farm owners profess to be Christians, but not seeing any evidence of it, was not lost to our understanding. Children see and measure life with their hearts more than adults do.

My father was probably pressured into attending the church that the farm owners were members of, which was a Pentecostal church. We attended for a short while, but we quit because of prejudicial treatment and lack of acceptance. Roberta recalled one of those incidents for me. She said that one Sunday when we got into the church, our father took us to the middle of the rows of pews and seated us. But a man soon came along and told us, in a curt condescending tone, to move because that was his pew, so we moved. Mandis had his own experience with the Boss and was turned against Christianity and church because of it.

Mandis had formed a friendship with the Boss's nephew, who was the same age. They used to go to movies together, until the uncle found out. Then he tried to force our father to stop Mandis from going to movies because they were "sinful and evil." When our father refused, the Boss threatened Mandis personally by saying that if he didn't stop, then his nephew could no longer be his friend. Like our father, Mandis cannot be bullied, and he refused. He could no longer pal around with the Boss's nephew on the farm, so they met elsewhere to continue doing things together. Mandis never forgot that man's self-righteous attitude and behavior. To him, this man was a representation of Christian hypocrisy, and that experience has kept him away from all forms of religion and spirituality to this day. In contrast, Dakotas have never coerced their own people or others into adhering to their spiritual practices, although these practices were the foundation of our strength.

This concept has almost always been difficult for white people to understand, because most of them come from a historical background of being under the control of a king and royal family. Woven into their autocratic government was their religion which helped maintain control over the people; both used fear to subjugate. If those white governments and religions knew the Creator personally and intimately, as their Bible says they should, they would not have had to use fear to sway or to influence.

Historically, our Dakota leaders, spiritual and otherwise, valued individual independence as a strength, not as a threat. These leaders sought spiritual guidance and wisdom from our Creator and *led* our people, as opposed to controlling them. Dakotas observed natural things around them and knew that we were created last among all living things; that the plants and animals could live without us, but we couldn't live without them. This worldview is so unlike that of the white populace, which continues to believe that they are superior to all other living things and that they must be in control. That was the kind of control being practiced by the devout "born again" white men who owned the farm where we lived in Minnesota.

These same devout Christian men and their families allowed us and others to live in poor housing conditions. The quonset-type building that was our home had a rounded roof, with windows only on the west and east sides, and a cement floor in the two large rooms. We had a gas heater and electricity, but no inside plumbing. The gas heater was not provided by the owners either; my father purchased it. I don't know how he did that with the meager wages he earned and with having to provide for six dependents and a new baby. Besides the cold cement floors in our house, there was the added burden of inadequate winter clothing and having to work long hours in cold warehouses which were probably contributors to my father's bout with double pneumonia at the time. He seemed to be susceptible to pneumonia and double pneumonia (recently I learned that WWI veterans experienced lung problems because of their exposure to mustard gas).

Anyway, my father had just returned from the Fargo Veteran's Hospital when my sister Adrienne, who was eleven, became very sick from a ruptured appendix. No one at home knew what was wrong. We went to a hospital for vaccinations only, and then only if we were back on the reservation, and could go to Public Health. So the situation must have been grave, because my parents took Adrienne to St. Ansgar Hospital in Moorhead. It was discovered that she was very close to death and would have to stay for extended treatment. My sister's stay in the hospital stretched into one whole month! And we had no money to pay for the hospital bill. My father was a seasonal worker, and had just recovered from a serious illness, too, so we had little or no money even for food or other living expenses.

However, we did have a TV. My mother used to watch a local daily program called "Party Line." The male host so impressed my mother that she wrote a letter telling him about our dire circumstances. Then at the elementary school in Moorhead, my fourth-grade classmates began to "notice" me, and they started bringing foodstuffs to the classroom. Finally one day I asked someone what was going on, and I was told that the food was for some needy people, but no one said who. I wanted to help those needy people, too; however, I was discouraged from helping. That puzzled me, but I remained quiet and just accepted their explanation. My mother had appeared on "Party Line," but it was aired during school hours, so the rest of us didn't know anything about the events taking place. So sometime before Christmas, or at Christmas, the male host of the television show and some other white people came to our house and presented us with all the food that had been collected, and someone paid the hospital bill. Each of our family members was also treated to a new set of clothes at the W. T. Grant Store in downtown Fargo. It was one of the most exciting Christmases we ever experienced, although we didn't even have a tree set up.

However, things soon turned sour. When my father's boss discovered the publicity about our situation, he was angry—perhaps because of the perceived discredit or dishonor it would bring to him and his brothers—devout as they were supposed to be in their Christianity. I don't remember the incident; however, my oldest sister does, and she has related her memories to me. The Boss first came to "talk" to our mother about our family's situation and how it had made the local news on TV; he didn't like that. She defended what she had done, and he reminded her that he, too, had helped by buying our family a washing machine. However, it wasn't as generous as he made it sound. Our father had earned a bonus, but unlike the other white male workers who received cash bonuses, the Boss chose to give our father a washing machine. So our mother told him he could take it back, although that meant washing clothes by hand again for a family of eight, two adults and six children ages three to sixteen. But he didn't take it back. Our mother was 5'2", but she wasn't afraid of anything or anybody. She always stood up for herself, and she was stubborn and independent. I remember our father getting frustrated with her at times and calling her "bullheaded."

Next, my father had an explosive argument with the Boss about our televised situation. The argument was explosive because no one crossed this boss, but my father had a temper, too. His boss was about 5'10", broad-shouldered, powerful-looking, with cold, pale blue eyes. My father was powerfully built too, though. He was 6', broad-shouldered, and had large hands that made huge fists. Besides, my father wasn't afraid of anybody—he'd had his share of drinking and fistfights back on the reservation and other places. His bumpy looking nose was a result of some of those fights. My mother told me about one of the times he had come home with a broken nose, and how the sight had shaken her up. In later years my two brothers would follow in his footsteps—they drank and fought fearlessly whoever challenged them.

When I remember my dad's boss at that vegetable farm, I can still see his scowling unsmiling face. It was like he wanted everyone who looked at him to fear him. When he smiled, it never reached his eyes. Many of the male workers on the farm had been the brunt of this boss's coldness and cruelty. But according to my older brother's and sister's recollections, the Boss had never tried to do to our dad what they had observed him do to others. I vaguely remember having witnessed some of those scenes. Mandis and Roberta were able to observe them because they had to work near our dad sometimes. We all did occasionally. Maybe it was because my dad was just as broad and as strong as his boss was, or because we went to his church once in a while. Anyway, I'm not sure why he didn't try to make our father fear him like he did with the other men.

Seemingly for the pure enjoyment of doing it, the Boss would bend a man's thumb backwards until the man cried out in pain. One time a male relative from the reservation came to stay and work on the farm for a while. His name was Tom Quinn and he was a large man! He was six foot plus, with broad shoulders and huge hands. He probably weighed two hundred pounds or more, and like my father, there was no fat on him. According to Mandis and Roberta, the Boss tried to intimidate Tom by bending his thumb backwards like he had done to other men. But Tom didn't cry out in pain; he endured it and then bent the Boss' thumb backwards, causing him to cry out in pain instead. Needless to say, the Boss didn't try to intimidate Tom anymore either.

At other times the Boss would compete with the workers. Other men couldn't beat him when he challenged them to throw hundred-pound sacks of potatoes on top of stacks that were higher than themselves, but Tom did. In fact, he stacked the hundred-pound sacks of potatoes higher than the Boss could! Maybe it's because of observing things like that that I learned not to show emotions, or to not let anybody see my weaknesses, and above all not to show fear. I'm not sure, because I think some of those characteristics are part of being Indian, too.

In the four years on the vegetable farm, we experienced poverty without Dakota relatives nearby to help, isolation, racism, and finally, an outpouring of help from the white community when we were in dire need of it. I couldn't understand these two sides of white people—the Boss and his family's pious Christian hypocrisy, and the charitable giving of people we didn't know. No wonder many Indians continue to disagree about their relationships with white people. Their treatment of us and their opinion of us is mixed and confusing. Some see that charitable side of them and decide they are really okay and want to "live" with us, but others continue to distrust them; they believe that the giving is only temporary, spur-of-the-moment giving.

Following the confrontation between Dad and his boss, and despite our material impoverishment, my proud independent Dakota father and mother decided to move us the next spring. But before we moved, Mandis left for the Air Force, with our parents' signed permission, because he was not yet seventeen. Our last home in Minnesota was a small four-room house that we moved into on the outskirts of Dilworth, a short distance from the vegetable farm.

Reflecting about white people's isolated instances of charitableness toward our family makes me contemplate their motives. Studies show that this country is noted as one of the most giving to charities, but why? Is it based on guilt? Perhaps it is an historical, sometimes unconscious guilt about the so-called founding of this country, its government, and all its wealth that is falsely viewed as having been earned and fought for honorably. Dakotas believe there is memory in all living things, and there is a belief among some that there is memory in the blood. Is it that historical memory in the blood about how this country was really established that haunts white people? Is that why they are compelled to give so charitably? Yet, I don't believe their charity is often extended to American Indians. White people have a long way to go when it comes to giving to Indians.

True, heartfelt kindness to us, without expectations of a return, is not a normal occurrence. I remember only two teachers who acted kindly toward me and they taught in the elementary school in Moorhead. Mr. Gronfore taught third and fourth grades, and Mrs. Collins taught fifth and sixth. Adrienne and I both consider these two teachers to be memorable. They didn't do anything special, but they smiled at us and talked to us, not at us. As many children can, we sensed something good in these two teachers. They didn't display the superior attitude that we sensed in most white people. One time when a severe snowstorm occurred and we couldn't get home, Mrs. Collins took us into her home and cared for us until we could go home. Then there were times during class when Mr. Gronfore would call upon me to read or give an answer to a question. And he did that despite the other students' clamoring to be recognized with their arms waving in the air. Although I would answer quietly, he didn't dismiss me as a student who was unable to answer. Instead, he gently coaxed me to be a part of the class even though I wasn't a participant in the other students' play groups.

There are few good memories of my school days and other experiences in Minnesota. I now know why white teachers and white schoolmates looked past me and through me, but I don't understand it. I made efforts to join their little play groups, but I was never welcome. In fact, I was ignored. I was even less than "those kids from across the tracks," who were considered to be white trash. At least those children were allowed into the play groups once in a while, but I wasn't, unless it was a game that the teacher oversaw. Then the other students were forced to play "with" me. One of the times that happened was when we played softball. Even though I was good at it, and better than all the other girls and some of the boys, I was almost always the last one chosen for a team. I didn't have one friend throughout my first six years of school during which I was always the only Indian in my class. Consequently, my memories of "school days" are not of what "my friends and I" did.

Throughout my grade school years, I was exposed to what the dominant society thought of Dakota people, and Indians in general. But I was still a good student and obtained good grades. I used to think that if I did whatever the teacher told me to do, and did it well, then I would receive praise, encouragement, and acceptance like some of the other students, but that rarely happened. There were only two memorable times in elementary school, once in fourth grade, and once in fifth grade. The first time was when my fourth grade class and others collected food for our family. Then in fifth grade, the teacher asked us to draw something out of one of our books. So I chose to draw a deer standing in a creek. I did it so well that the teacher actually praised me out loud in front of everybody, but first she had to ask if I had done the drawing myself before she held it up for the rest of the class to see. Evidently she thought I had traced the picture, although she specifically told us to draw it freehand.

Grade-wise and behaviorally, I did very well in school, yet that didn't keep some of the teachers from having negative perceptions of me. This teacher *knew* I listened and understood instructions, so why did she double check? In my opinion it was because of the prevailing misconceptions of American Indians—we couldn't learn higher academics; we were only good with our hands, not our heads. No matter how good teachers were, or how unbiased they were in their attitudes toward other races, the 1950s were years when Americans didn't do extraordinary things for other races of people in this country. So I think that although there were two teachers who were memorable that doesn't necessarily mean that they wanted to change their society. Most white people were satisfied with society as it was, even though it was unfair to other races.

Childhood is supposed to be a time for making memories, ones that you enjoy recalling and sharing with others. However, that wasn't my experience going to school in western Minnesota. For most of my adult years, I would wonder why I couldn't remember too many things about my elementary school days. It wasn't until I took some child development classes that I began to understand why there were so few memories. I learned that during development, children need interaction with others for learning to occur and memories to be made. For me, there was a definite lack of involvement with other kids once I entered public school in this northern plains state that was full of Indians, on reservations that is. A few years ago I would occasionally watch a television series about a young man who told stories about his experiences when in school, and he could recall many very specific things that he was involved in or that he did with other kids. As I watched some of those weekly episodes, I would try to remember similar occurrences, but I couldn't. The memories just weren't there, and I believe it was because I had been too isolated during those early years in elementary school.

In those early school days, there were no friends to do memorable things with—no sleepovers, no playing house, and no playing with dolls. I didn't like dolls anyway and I wasn't interested in them, but children need friends. I had only one doll during my childhood, and I don't even know why my mother got that one for me. I didn't like dolls because I perceived that playing with them was acting like a sissy. Because my dad spoiled me, I must have cried to get my way, so my family teased me and called me "crybaby," which I hated. I think that partly contributed to my becoming a tomboy. I never wanted to do anything that looked like a girl activity, so I played catch by myself by throwing the ball up in the air and catching it, climbed whatever I could, threw rocks, and went on "adventurous" walks with my dog Major. When we still lived on the vegetable farm, Mandis, Roberta, Adrienne, and I played softball or "500" until it became absolutely too dark to see the softball, and then we played "Kick the Can." When Adrienne turned eleven or twelve, she suddenly became too old to play with me, so I had to find things to do by myself. The one thing that I loved doing was climbing, but there wasn't much to climb near the house we moved to outside of

Dilworth. So one day I decided to climb the T-shaped poles that held up our clothesline. Balancing precariously at the top, I stood up straight, and fell off right on my head. If my brother Mandis had seen that, he would have said, "good thing it was your head, or you might have broken something."

When I went walking, it was only to places where I dared to go, which were the fields across the drainage ditch, or the road, at the end of which was a small tree for me to climb. I would climb as high as I could, and then, leaning on the small branches, I would daydream as the wind gently swayed me. I daydreamed about what it would be like to have a tree house in a great big tree, one that I could live in. Or I would dream about being an animal that could climb trees and sleep in them while the trees swayed gently in the breeze. I really hated having to come down out of "my" tree to go home.

There were four other homes near ours which had trees, but I couldn't go near them. My mother was adamant about staying off white people's property. We had to be absolutely respectful of them and their property. Consequently, I was always extremely careful about how I behaved when in white people's homes or within their boundaries. I never touched anything that was theirs. I still feel uncomfortable in white people's homes, and I only look and do not touch.

One of my most vivid memories of living in Minnesota was seeing our mother's reaction to white people staring at us when we were in town somewhere, and experiencing the shame they made me feel for being different, for being Indian. Wherever we went, most white people stared at us like we were aliens, two-headed monsters. My mother withstood it for about four years, but her patience and tolerance diminished finally. When she would catch them staring at us, anger would contort her pleasant, cheerful, unwrinkled round face, and she would lash out verbally by saying, "What are you staring at?" And then she would say to us kids, but loud enough for the whites to hear, "They act just like cows; look at them staring!" My mother always told us not to stare; that it wasn't nice, so we obeyed. If the word "rude" had been in her vocabulary, I'm sure she would have used that, too. The white parents, of course, never admonished their children, probably because they couldn't keep from staring themselves.

Other things my mother taught us were to share whatever we had and to play with kids who others didn't want to play with. This was not true of the white kids I went to school with. They always picked and chose who they were going to play with, and a dark-skinned Indian was usually not one of the chosen ones. Despite those early negative experiences with white people, my mother's teachings stuck with me, and practicing those values made me wonder why white people didn't behave the same way, although they attended church piously and faithfully. My mother made us behave at home as well as in public. She wasn't afraid of what others would think when she corrected and disciplined us. She wanted us to be well-behaved, and we were.

In my opinion, I was never accepted by white children because I was a dark-skinned American Indian. According to all that they had been taught, Indians were not equal. That's my perception because there were dark-skinned Italians living in Dilworth, but they weren't treated the way I was treated. Mandis, Roberta, and Adrienne are lighter-skinned than me, and they didn't experience what I experienced, although they remember certain individuals looking down on them, too, because they knew they were Indians. I think those early experiences of being considered "less than" others contributed to my lifelong tendency to side with the underdog. I have done that as an adult, and I did it when I was in high school, too. For example, one of my high school classmates was extremely shy and quiet, and no one seemed to want to become friends with her, so I did, as I did with her younger sister years later. Because I observe people's behavior and their interactions with others, I have noticed how Indian children normally don't avoid or taunt other Indians because they may be poorer or handicapped, or just different in some way, like white children do.

Despite the isolation in Minnesota, we were able to establish a fairly stable family life for a while. On those occasions when we went to church, we would go home, have Sunday dinner, and go for a ride in our car. Many times our dad took us to the airport to watch the planes land or take off. Sometimes he would take us to A & W for ice cream or root beer, or he would go and bring back a gallon of root beer and ice cream for root beer floats. For me, those experiences formed a pattern of living, with my family almost always sitting down to have supper together.

My fondest and favorite memory is of my dad cooking breakfast on Saturday mornings. This began after we moved to Dilworth. He would be standing in the kitchen dressed in his khaki pants with his tank style undershirt on, whistling a tuneless tune while stirring up the batter for his "panny cakes," as he called them. And there would be the smell of freshly made coffee, too. Pancakes and eggs were his favorite breakfast foods. I love this memory. He recreated it in each of the different houses we lived in. I also love the smell of coffee when its aroma wafts out of a newly opened can or package. That reminds me of my mother.

My father had a good physique, and he never developed a pot belly until he was in his seventies. He was strong and worked hard to provide for his large family. He looked many years younger than he was, and he had a good mind that was inquisitive, thoughtful, active. He listened faithfully to the daily news on the radio and later watched it on television. The Friday night fights was the other time he watched TV. A favorite memory of my familys is of when we sat down to eat supper, and we couldn't talk if the six o'clock news was on. If we did, our father, who was a stern-looking man, would scowl at us and say, "Listen!" emphasizing the "s." That's all it took, and we would become quiet. But sometimes it was hard to keep from laughing. We were normal kids and sometimes when adults want you to be quiet, that is the hardest time to remain quiet.

When I reflect on my parents and what they did to help us survive, there are many things I am thankful for. My mother was a hard worker, too, which my father said she learned from Grandma Keoke. He said that after Grandma's husband died, she worked hard by washing and ironing clothes for other people to help feed her family. She never drove or owned a car, so she walked wherever she had to go. Once in a while we would stay with Grandma Keoke, too. One of my special memories of her and her home place is of smelling and drinking her homemade raspberry tea, and eating her fry bread and potato soup.

Grandma was short and stocky and very healthy. I don't ever remember her being sick. Her coal black hair had a few strands of white in it and she wore it in two braids that hung down on each side of her head, or they would be fastened together on top of her head. She had two wood stoves in her house, one for cooking and one for heat. Sometimes she would take a blanket and set off walking into the woods to gather firewood. When she came back she would be carrying a bundle of wood on her back. When she washed clothes, it was in a large galvanized tub with a washboard. Her house was on the edge of a coulee and there was a large creek nearby that we played on when it froze and then again in the summer.

Adrienne and I and some of our cousins had a lot of fun in that creek when summer came. There was a large grapevine that hung over it that we used to swing across on—until Adrienne fell in. Then our Grandpa John went and cut the vine down, and that ended our vine-swinging adventures.

So our mother had good homemaking lessons from two Dakota women, her mother and my dad's aunt. They must have been good role models, because even while we lived in Minnesota, when our mother baked bread or was canning foods, she seemed to enjoy what she was doing. She gave us a sense that doing those things was not just doing menial tasks, but done for the family out of love. Consequently, my four sisters and I all love to bake and watch our families enjoy the fruits of that labor. We don't preserve foods on the scale that our mother had to, but some of us are able to do that, too. We all dry corn, and two of us like to make wild plum jam.

Our mother was also the one who tinkered mechanically with our car and sometimes with our radio. When something went wrong with the car, our mother was the one who checked it out to see what was needed, and then she fixed it. Roberta said that when Dad dismantled something and put it back together, he almost always ended up with extra bolts or screws. Mom drove the car frequently when we lived in Minnesota, too, but didn't do that as much once we were back on the reservation. Maybe because not too many women drove back then. When I married my husband, I was the only woman in my family and in my husband's family who drove regularly and had a driver's license.

Mom was artistic, too, and liked to create things through drawing, sewing clothes, or making jewelry. However, she couldn't do a lot of those things because she didn't always have the material she needed. Once I saw a baby's cap that was beaded entirely with turquoise beads, so I asked Roberta whose it was, and she said it had been mine. We think our mother beaded it, but we're not sure. We no longer have it because during one of our many moves, it got lost, just like all the family photographs. None of us five older siblings have pictures of when we were children, although at one time we had a lot of them, because our mother enjoyed using a camera.

It was when we were living in Dilworth that my mother became acquainted with the "born again" side of Christianity by watching television evangelist Oral Roberts, who claims to be part Indian. She must have corresponded with his ministry because she had a prayer cloth that she kept in the Bible. But I don't recall if her spiritual quest involved the whole family. I know we attended a tent meeting or a "crusade" near Fargo, where I saw a young boy using crutches go toward the front to be prayed for. When it was finished, he threw his crutches down and ran around the inside of the tent. I asked Roberta if what I remembered was correct and she confirmed it. But we didn't practice that kind of spirituality at home. Instead, each night we all knelt down and prayed the Lord's Prayer together and then said good night to everybody and went to bed. We always said grace at the table before we ate, and we were admonished by our parents to never take God's name in vain, and to live by the Ten Commandments. Our parents sometimes read the Bible for their own personal growth, but they didn't force us to do the same. When we went to the white churches, Adrienne and I had to attend Sunday School. Even then I wondered why Indians were excluded from the stories about people and their involvement with God, the Creator. Now I conclude that it is because of ignorance and intolerance of other spiritual beliefs.

We eventually began to attend an Episcopalian church, the Fargo Gethsemane Cathedral, where Roberta, Naomi, and Adrienne were confirmed together. I was confirmed there later. Mandis enlisted in the Air Force before we moved to Dilworth and started attending this church, so he was never confirmed. His opinion of Christianity and its followers was already tainted by his prior experience with a "devout man," so he probably wouldn't have gone to church anyway. I don't know how regular our attendance was, but we became acquainted with two of the ministers who worked there, Dean Baker (Dean was his title) and Reverend Harry Vere. As usual, we were the only Indian family in an all-white church. I remember some of these things much better than others, I think because of Reverend Vere's involvement in my life when I was twelve years old. By this time, we had three new additions to our family, too.

In 1952 Chyrel, a sister six years younger than me, was born, and then three years later, Byron was born. Lastly, my brother Merle was born, in 1958. He was killed in a car accident on the reservation when he was two years old.

My mom and dad started drinking frequently on weekends when Byron was about two years old. I was back in Dilworth School for the fifth and sixth grades. I can't recall ever seeing my mother drink before this. I saw my father so infrequently when we lived on the reservation that I can't remember actually knowing that he drank, although Roberta said she knew that he did, but she had never seen him drunk. So for all of us, seeing our mother and father drink and get drunk was a new experience. It wasn't unusual for us to see white people get drunk, though, because we saw that frequently on weekends.

We lived across the road from an American Legion Club where white people ate and drank, and danced and partied. Sometimes late at night some of their drunken noisiness would wake us up and we would sneak to a window to watch them. Usually Mom and Dad didn't want us watching those kinds of things, so when they caught us, they would send us back to bed with a stern admonishment.

During the last two years we spent in Minnesota, our stable family life fell apart right in front of our eyes. Roberta was sixteen and in the tenth grade when Mom and Dad made her drop out of school by saying she was needed at home. Adrienne and I continued, and Naomi didn't go to school at all. We had once had strict parents, but now it seemed that they didn't care anymore. Roberta and Naomi started dating, but I don't recall them drinking. Their boyfriends were Mexicans who came with their families from Texas as migrant farm workers. Then Roberta married Robert Trevino, who was one of the migrant workers, and ten years older. She moved with him to a small town north of Moorhead. Although our lives were being disrupted by circumstances that were beyond our control, we still enjoyed our new baby brother and one younger brother Byron.

I can only speculate about why our parents began to drink so frequently. It may have had something to do with our economic situation. I don't think my father worked regularly anymore, and there were so many mouths to feed, with no Dakota relatives to turn to. Then there was the isolation and racism, too. Maybe they just got tired of it all and tried to forget, or maybe the only place they were accepted, seemingly, was in a bar among other drinkers. Whatever the reason, we became a "broken" family and we didn't begin to experience healing and togetherness until many years later on the reservation. Our parents' absorption with their drinking led to neglect and a pattern of fluctuating between sobriety and drunkenness for many years.

Once, when we were still living near Dilworth, my parents took me with them to Moorhead, which was unusual because we didn't often get to go to town, and rarely did just one of us kids go at a time. I don't remember all the details of that day, but I do know that they left me in the car while they went into a bar to drink. It was daylight yet when they parked the car across the street a half block away. Although I was about nine years old, I don't remember them coming out to check on me during the long hours that I waited for them in the car. Finally it was dark and very late, probably midnight, because the bar was closing. I saw my parents coming out with some other people, and I was glad because I thought we were going to go home. Instead, without looking toward our car and me, they left with their friends. While I was waiting in the car I would hide every time I saw a cop car because Minnesota curfew laws were very strict. So, although I saw my parents leaving, I didn't dare get out of the car and chase after them.

I stayed there in the car until there was almost no more traffic, and then I got out and began the four- or five-mile walk home. Whenever I saw headlights or heard a car, I would hide in the shadows of buildings, bushes, or other objects. My sisters used to call me "scaredy cat," because I was so afraid of the dark, and there I was walking home alone. I was more afraid of the police than I was of the dark. Recently I heard Jackie Bird sing a song entitled, "Mr. Angel," from her most recent tape titled "Generation to Generation," and the experience that's sung about is similar to mine, only I didn't almost die. The song brought memories rushing back, and I cried, but I don't know why. Maybe I was feeling the loss of my parents again, and wishing they were here to answer the many questions that I have about our lives. I dislike the feeling of unresolved issues, and I know there are a lot of those, especially from when I was a minor. There is also the feeling that I never really got to know my mother, and I feel that loss also.

Then Mom and Dad began to drink at home, too, and bring people home with them from the bars to continue their drinking at our house. By this time, two other Indian families from our reservation had moved into Fargo and they would sometimes drink with our parents. One night before Roberta moved out of our home, she, Adrienne, and I went to a movie in Fargo. By the time the movie was over, curfew was drawing nearer, and there we were standing on one of the street corners waiting for Mom and Dad to come and get us. Finally, a cop car pulled up beside us and a cop asked us what we were doing there past curfew. After we explained, they apparently didn't think our parents were coming so they loaded us up and took us to a detention hall. And that's where we spent the night. The next day they took us home. When we walked into the house, we knew why Mom and Dad hadn't come to pick us up. They had been drinking. Things continued to worsen.

Finally, one night when I was twelve, I was in a car with Naomi, her boyfriend, Adrienne, and one other boy, who was driving. Naomi and her boyfriend were in the backseat while Adrienne and I were in the front. She was in the middle, and I was on the outside. We were riding around listening to the radio and singing along. I don't think the driver knew where he was going, and to make matters worse, we were driving near a new housing development area on the southeast side of Moorhead. Suddenly, without any warning signs, we drove into some kind of ditch, which made us stop abruptly. Adrienne's head hit the windshield, cutting it from the back to the front of her forehead. Blood was gushing out all over her face and she was moaning, not fully conscious. We were all scared, but we knew it was serious, and knew enough to take her to the hospital. Naomi's face was bruised pretty badly, too, and I almost bit a hole through my tongue. I don't think the car was damaged too badly, because the driver drove it to the hospital. They all went inside, but I remained in the car in the dark. The police were called and I think Naomi and Adrienne stayed overnight in the hospital. I don't remember what happened to the two guys, but I went home. Eventually we appeared in court with our mom and dad, and we three sisters were removed from our parents' custody. Naomi and Adrienne were sentenced—sent to reform school in Sauk Centre, Minnesota, until they reached eighteen years of age. Naomi was sixteen and Adrienne was fourteen. No one knew what to do with me.

One thing was definite: the officials in charge did not want to send me home. But I had two younger brothers and a younger sister there. If our parents were unfit, then they should have been removed, too, but they weren't. We three sisters must have been considered juvenile delinquents by the Minnesota court, so we were sent away. The only law we had broken that I am aware of was the 10 o'clock curfew. I learned later that if I hadn't been so young, I would have gone to Sauk Centre, too.

It was finally decided that I should be placed in a home other than my parents' home until a "proper" place could be found. When the court decided to send Adrienne and Naomi to reform school, they were immediately placed, not in a juvenile hall or a detention center, but in jail. Today I am amazed about that. I am amazed and outraged by the way white people continually manipulate their own legislated laws to serve the opinion that they know best what to do with Indians, and that they can ignore their laws when it comes to how they treat Indians. A detention center for juveniles was available, and it must have been there to keep minors separate from adult law-breakers, yet they deposited my sisters in the county jail.

I was temporarily put into an Indian couple's home in Fargo. They were somehow associated with the Gethsemane Cathedral Church, where we used to go to church. Reverend Vere knew us, and that's how I think he may have intervened. But I was unhappy there, so I tried to find a way to get home.

The day before Adrienne and Naomi were going to leave, I asked if I could spend the night with them before they left, and I was allowed to. I stayed overnight in the jail cell with them and saw them leave the next morning with a feeling of great loss. I felt badly, too, about their physical appearance. Naomi's face was noticeably bruised and Adrienne's right eye was black and blue and swollen shut. Her hair had been shaven so the severe cut could be stitched together. Our parents didn't even get to say goodbye. The last time they saw Naomi and Adrienne was when we were all in court together. And no one came for me until after school was out. A school was somewhere nearby, because I watched kids talking and laughing as they walked home with friends. I felt an ache in my heart and I wanted to cry, but I wouldn't allow myself to. I wished with my whole being that things were normal for my family. I wished it was me walking home from school. From that day on I think I had a hole in my heart, a feeling of emptiness that's still there in a small measure because I never had the chance to resolve some of these things with my mother. I don't understand why I was left in that jail cell all day, unless it was to teach me a lesson. Somebody eventually came and took me back to the Indian family's home, but I didn't want to stay, and I told them that.

I was angry and I wanted to lash out at somebody and make them hurt the way I was hurting. So I behaved badly and was uncooperative while in their home. Then I ran away. I told the people that I wanted to go visit a friend who lived in Fargo, so they trusted me and dropped me off there. I did stay and visit, but I was also trying to come up with a plan that would get me away and keep me away. I was naive enough to believe that I could do that on my own. I was desperate. I had never stayed at anyone else's home before, and I felt so alone and helpless. I felt abandoned and wondered why my parents couldn't do something. When night came I left there, looking for someone I might know.

I headed for Main Avenue in Fargo where my sisters went to "hang out." It was like everybody I knew had disappeared; I didn't see any familiar or friendly faces. I ended up with an older white girl who my sisters knew, and we rode around all night with a guy she barely knew. At daylight, he asked me where I wanted to go, so I told him to my parents' house. When I walked in, Mom and Dad had just gotten up and they were surprised, but glad to see me. They were actually relieved. When I wasn't at my friend's place where I was supposed to be visiting, the police had been notified. The first place they had looked for me was at my parents' home, but I wasn't there, so they had gone looking elsewhere. My parents were frightened and my father said that all he could think of was that I might have fallen into the Red River. I don't remember what happened next, but eventually I found myself back with the Indian family. And I ran away again.

I don't know how much time had passed from when my world began to disintegrate starting with my parents' drinking and the car accident; there was no contact between me and my parents or with my sister Roberta. I had such an ache in my heart and I was so lonesome. Although I was with an Indian family, they acted and lived like white people. This time I don't remember all the details of what I did or where I went when I ran away again. For the second time I was back at my parents' place in Dilworth, and it was daylight when I arrived. As I walked up to the house, there was such quietness that I wondered if they had gone to town. The door was unlocked, so I walked in. I was surprised to see everything in disarray. Pictures and clothes were scattered all over the living room floor. I could see that Mom and Dad had hurriedly packed up what they could and left. I wasn't sure, but I guessed they must have gone back home to South Dakota. Never had I felt so alone. Disheartened and dejected, I called Reverend Vere from the pay phone in the American Legion Club across the road and told him where I was. He came and picked me up.

I vaguely remember later that week Reverend Vere and other

white people discussing me and the predicament that I felt I had created. It's not hard for me to understand now who made the decision to send me to boarding school. The churches and federal government have always conspired together about how to deal with the "Indian problem," and my situation was no different. Again I felt abandoned and isolated, wishing for my parents, my family, a home life. I think it must be only white people who can make Indians feel so unwanted, even when they are trying to be "helpful." To me they weren't being helpful, though; they were only trying to take care of a situation that they perceived as not having been created by them—just like many other Indian problems. I ended up at Reverend Vere's until it was time to leave for St. Mary's School for Indian girls in Springfield, South Dakota, that was an Episcopalian Church-sponsored school. I don't think I knew what a boarding school was, but I soon found out.

Before I left Reverend Vere's, clothes had to be found for me. I don't think it crossed anybody's mind to buy me some clothes. Instead, a white woman came to see me with some clothes she had probably collected from church members. She seemed to have fun going through the clothes and picking out what she thought suited me best. The only piece of clothing I specifically remember was a red coat. She held it up and exclaimed about how pretty I looked in red with my black hair and brown skin. From that time on I hated the color red, until just a few years ago. I did, however, wear the coat, since it was all I had for warmth. The experience made me feel like I wasn't worth more than white people's discarded clothes. Which is what I believe they were. I know because I've been to their rummage sales, to the Salvation Army, and seen their secondhand junk. Another example is when white people donate clothing to reservations; their donations are castoffs that are outdated and from another era. They somehow think that Indians don't or shouldn't care because these things are free. They seem to think that we are like them, if it's free, take it, whether or not you need it—I've observed them doing this also. White people aren't known for giving their best to Indians, so why would they behave any differently for a little Indian kid?

This behavior is the opposite of Dakota behavior. When Dakotas give, they usually give their best—clothing, food, whatever it is; it's their best, because they know it will always reflect back on them and/or who they are. Just go to an Indian memorial, or ceremony where there is food served and a giveaway, and you will observe our generosity. When white people first observed and recorded this custom, they said we gave to a fault and that they knew it wasn't good for us.

Then I was on my way to a place I hadn't heard of. In the space of about two years, my family had gone from being happy and fairly stable to being dysfunctional and separated. We stayed separated for many years too. I think that the first time we were all on the reservation at the same time again was in 1971, thirteen years later.

So I spent the seventh and eighth grades in a boarding school on the extreme southern border of South Dakota. When I arrived at St. Mary's, it was dark. I didn't know where I was and I didn't know what to think. I just steeled myself to accept whatever was going to happen next in my life. Immediately I was introduced to Mr. and Mrs. Kenyon Cull, the headmaster and his wife. He looked British. He was slim and almost always wore tweedish-looking suits. He had reddish hair and a mustache, and wore thick black horn-rimmed glasses. His wife was from the Middle East somewhere, Turkey, perhaps. She was short and heavyset with dark eyes that had dark rings around them. Her hair was shoulder length and black with gray streaks in it. They had one child, a daughter. When I arrived, school had been in session for about a month or more. After introductions, I was taken to the dormitory and a room that I would be sharing with two other girls. That wasn't bad; I was used to sharing a bed with a sister or sisters. I then settled into boarding school life.

I don't remember what the enrollment was at St. Mary's. It was somewhere between sixty to one hundred Indian girls in grades five through twelve. When I remember some of the girls, I am surprised at the distances some of them traveled to attend school there. They came from states that were mainly west of the Mississippi River. The farthest anyone came may have been the girl who came from California. It was quite an experience for me to get acquainted with Indian girls who lived in other states. I enjoyed the friendships I formed there and I especially liked being with all Indian students. However, I also felt like I was being molded into a brown-skinned white individual.

For example, when we sat down to eat a meal, we had to pay attention to strict table manners. A senior student or staff member sat at each table to make sure we sat correctly, used our utensils appropriately, and conducted ourselves in a ladylike manner. We were even taught how to butter our bread. The bread had to be torn into quarters before we could butter it or eat it. Our whole day was scheduled, except for one hour after school when we could check out some money and go uptown. We could have at the most twenty cents for the younger ones, and maybe thirty cents for the older girls. Before we left the school, we had to check out, too. That meant that we had to sign our names on a piece of paper indicating what time we had left and what time we came back. When we got uptown, most of us just bought ice cream cones and went right back to the school. The most unusual thing about our daily walks uptown was that we were instructed to go into only one or two stores on the south side of Main Street. We were forbidden to cross over to the other side of the street. I found that strange and didn't understand it. I wonder if some of the white townspeople were afraid of so many Indians being in such close proximity to them and their children.

Parents or guardians were informed that those in grades five through seven could receive a monthly allowance of $3 from their families, and all others were allowed $5 a month. When I first received my allowance, I knew it didn't come from my parents; Reverend Vere had sent it. When any money was received from home, it had to be deposited in an individual account within the school, and then it was doled out to us and kept track of by one of the school staff members. It was a rule that no one was allowed to keep any money at all. The allowances had to be used for not only school supplies and personal needs, but for the snacks we might buy at the school store, or when we went downtown. If a girl spent all of her money before the next month, tough luck, she had to do without. As far as I knew, the school did not provide allowances or personal items for anyone. Thursday night was free night, meaning we didn't have to go to study hall, which we had every other night, I think, but Saturday night. I don't remember what we did on Saturday and Sunday nights. Knowing the philosophy of boarding schools and their religious background, I don't think we were allowed to be idle.

We could wear our own clothes to school and on weekends, except for special occasions and Sundays. When we went to church across the street, we had to wear our uniforms and white scarves on our heads. Wearing something to cover a female's head must be a male-instituted church and religious law, because the Bible states that hair is a woman's covering. Some of these laws and rules supposedly being followed by white people seem to be ones made to control rather than to contribute to the well-being of a whole people. When we had special visitors, like someone who had given financially to the school, or a church or school official, we wore our uniforms. We also had chapel every night after supper.

Disciplinary action sometimes meant spending a half hour or an hour alone in the chapel praying for forgiveness for our souls. Some of the offenses that demanded discipline that I recall were students physically fighting with one another, which happened once in a while, talking back to teachers, stealing, lying, and running away. Attempting to run away was the offense that caused Marie, my friend from North Dakota, and me to be campused for a month, which included sitting in the chapel alone, repenting and praying. I don't remember doing any kind of praying or repenting, because I didn't believe I'd committed a sin. In my eyes I was only trying to get away from a place where it wasn't my choice to be. I really didn't know, and still don't, how sitting in a chapel alone could profoundly alter one's behavior. The dominant society's fundamental Christian laws and mores are constricting and attempt to lead people to think that all people need to adhere to those standards in order to live well.

In contrast, Dakota custom expected the individual to choose for himself or herself how life was to be lived. If certain persons couldn't live within the boundaries of what was acceptable and good for the rest of the band or tribe, then relationships and interaction with them were severed. If you chose to be lazy, then you and your family suffered the consequences of that choice when hard times came. However, most Dakotas were industrious and resourceful, never wasteful or wanton in their behavior. One custom among Dakotas was that a son-in-law couldn't talk to or look right at his mother-in-law; instead, he had to make his observations or comments known to her through his wife or father-in-law. The basic premise was that this custom avoided conflicts between in-laws, which is so unlike white society and their disrespect for mothers-in-law and in-laws in general, which is shown by their continual jokes and jabs at them. Among Dakotas, kinship ties, established through marriages, were important. But I didn't learn some of these Dakota traditions until I was in my late thirties. And when I observed some of these traditional behaviors being practiced by our people, I thought wrongly and ignorantly that they were heathenistic and backward. I've been so wrong about many Dakota customs, but I've forgiven myself because I realize that I didn't have any control over how I was being educated.

As students at St. Mary's, we all had "details," or chores that were our responsibility for a month at a time. The two I remember having to do were kitchen detail and working in the laundry room. Not too many liked kitchen detail because of having to get up at 6:00 or 6:30 to help out the cook, set tables, and clean up afterward before going to class. On Saturdays it was major cleanup, which meant mopping and buffing the floors. I didn't like working in the laundry because of having to iron others' clothes. I was always scared of scorching or burning something because I'd once burned a favorite taffeta skirt when I thought I knew how to iron. We also had to sort and fold clothes and put them into the individual bins that each student had her name on. The only thing fun about this detail was getting out of class earlier than everybody else in the afternoon.

When Christmas came, I was allowed to go home for about two weeks. That was the only time anybody was allowed to go home besides summer, and then only if you weren't sent to a white family's home through the "summer home program." By this time, my mom and dad had been back on the reservation for a while. I didn't know where they were living, because I was unfamiliar with the reservation except for where my grandmothers' homes were and where Sisseton was. I was sent home in a car with one other girl from our reservation. Apparently the driver had received instructions as to where to take us, because I didn't know where I was going until we turned onto the road that led to my Grandma Keoke's. That's not where my parents lived, but it's where they met me.

When we pulled up to the front of the house, they both came out of the house quickly and hugged me, and I could tell they were very happy to see me. We then got into another car to go "home," or at least to our temporary home. The house we went to was about one and a half miles straight north of my grandma's on a dirt road. Again, it was just a small two-room house and in very poor condition. The walls had cracks in them through which the wind and snow blew in. There was no electricity or running water except in the creek west of the house in the trees. While there, I helped my dad gather wood which was used not only for heat, but to cook with, too. And on Christmas Eve, we all walked to St. Mary's Church, which was about a half mile to three-quarters of a mile across the creek, through the trees, and up a hill.

During this time at home, I took interest in our language and I began to study the Dakota alphabet in my mother's hymnal. That's how I learned to read Dakota. My younger sister Chyrel was now six years old; Byron was three, and Merle was seven months old. My father had no job, so I don't know what they lived on. Although I was glad to see my family again, I felt relieved, I guess, to be going back to St. Mary's where there was heat, indoor plumbing, electricity, three meals a day, and some kind of stability and structure.

Meanwhile, my mom and dad continued to drink off and on, which I learned much later. As for Roberta, she and her husband Robert Trevino moved to Belle Fourche, South Dakota, and then to Texas. My brother Mandis, who was still in the Air Force, stayed away for four to six years. He came home on leave once, while we were still living in Dilworth, when his basic training was finished. The next time he saw me, I was fourteen.

I wasn't unhappy at St. Mary's, because I finally had friends with whom I did things like playing jacks, going for walks on campus, and learning about each other's families and reservations. One requirement that most of us disliked was having to write our quarterly or annual "thank you" letters to people in the east and to the D.A.R.—Daughters of the American Revolution. I guess the school received some kind of support from them. I do know a lot of clothes were received and stored in a quonset on campus. Sometimes we were allowed to go pick an item of clothing out of there, but I remember doing that just once. I heard from other girls that some of the seniors were allowed to go get whatever they wanted. I don't know how true that story was. So I've wondered what was done with all those clothes that weren't used, and why those clothes weren't used more effectively. Many of us came from poor families who sometimes couldn't afford clothes, allowances, or packages. In my opinion, it would have been most appropriate to allow the needy students to pick out at least two or three sets of clothes from the stockpile. After all, that's why those kinds of donations were made. But these authoritarian people behaved as most others have toward Indians; they thought that they knew what was best for us. If they did allow some of the girls who had "favored" status to get more than others could, then I think it was unfair and points to white people's unchanging attitudes toward Indians, and how they pitted us against one another, consciously or unconsciously.

The St. Mary's situation and behavior is very similar to the times when annuities were promised to tribes who signed treaties. White agents were responsible for getting them distributed, but it wasn't done according to what was stipulated in the signed treaties. Instead, agents became conscious of how much power they had over Indians and misused it. They also realized they had access to material things that they may not have been able to afford themselves. Annuities were withheld if the agent thought it was necessary, sometimes to the point of creating confrontations between soldiers and Indians and also creating jealousy between relatives and between members of bands. Divisive tactics are still being used today by white people to turn Indian against Indian, and some of us are still too gullible to see through white people's wily ways.

For example, the permanent head doctor in Sisseton had been trying to solve some of the financial problems the Indian Health Service was experiencing because of government appropriation reductions. He was trying to improvise and provide more services with the reduced amount of money. One of those improvisations was to establish a dialysis center here at the local facililty to avoid having to transport diabetes patients forty-five miles one way to a Watertown hospital. During the winter of 1997 there were life-threatening weather conditions, yet those patients had to be taken care of. So during blizzard conditions the Tribal Roads Department, Bureau of Indian Affairs Roads Department, and Tribal Police had to risk their lives to save those patients' lives. The proposed dialysis center was to be situated in a space that was the kitchen in the Indian Health Hospital. But this plan was a cause for concern to some Indians because they were misinformed.

The Indian Health doctor was trying to alleviate the stress of grappling with our winter weather conditions and help avoid prejudicial treatment by non-Indian staff at other hospitals by developing a plan to keep tribal people here who need dialysis. But trouble was created between tribal members when they heard a skewed story about the plans for closing the IHS kitchen to make room for the dialysis equipment. The story was started by tribal people employed by Indian Health. They did not know all of the facts about the situation but they had been influenced over the years by the controlling white bureaucrats with their negative opinions of American Indians. These tribal people had become suspicious of change and wondered if it was in their best interest. They chose to believe the opinions of non-Indians rather than their own tribal members who sit on governing boards. Some of them even supported non-Indians in opposition to supporting a tribal member. That attitude has evolved from years of being brainwashed through the education system that believed we aren't able to govern or control our own lives.

The IHS kitchen probably prepared meals for only ten patients a month, if that many. But the story was told in such a way that it had some tribal members so concerned that they began calling the IHS doctor, Service Unit Director, and others involved with health care to voice their fears and objections. The Human Services Board is made up of all tribal members and they help conceive these ideas and try to implement them to make the IHS hospital and clinic a place that can deal with all of the health problems that we have. Yet here was a case of tribal people being pitted against one another again. The problem appeared to be totally our own fault, but it's not.

For far too many years, bureaucrats have been rumbling and threatening us about closing this facility. They say we don't have enough inpatient occupancy. For those same reasons, white bureaucrats and white-influenced Indian bureaucrats have been able to reduce services to tribal people here. Our health services used to include delivery, surgery, intensive care, an emergency room and a nursery besides a clinic and dental clinic. Now most of the patients are sent to one of three hospitals, Sisseton, Watertown, or Fargo, with veterans being sent to Minneapolis, Sioux Falls, or Fargo. Our population has grown tremedously in the past twenty or twenty-five years, with more than half of our people being younger than thirty years old. Yet the Aberdeen Area Office, the regional office for the Bureau of Indian Affairs and Indian Health Service, and the bureaucrats in Washington, D.C., decided that we didn't need all those services, so funding was cut and we no longer have full health services. And now tribal members who have insurance must rely on that for much of their medical expenses. There just isn't enough money anymore to take care of all of the tribal members. Aren't the rivers still flowing and isn't the grass still growing? That's how long the treaties were supposed to last—"as long as the rivers run and the grass grows."

And to think I used to want to emulate white people. Well, not anymore! Since learning a few things about Dakota cultural traditions and spirituality, I try not to look at other Indians judgmentally like I used to. Instead, I recall our shared history with white people, our shared losses, our shared grief, our shared anger, hostility, and resentment. Then, I can look beyond the present behavior and understand better, although not totally, and I am a little more compassionate. When I was at St. Mary's, I didn't yet understand the division among Indian people, although I'd heard adult family members talk about it.

One of the most special things that I learned while at St. Mary's was playing the piano when I was an eighth grader. I progressed so well that my friend Marie and I played a duet for a music concert held at the school. But my ability to play eventually diminished, because once I got home, there was no piano on which I could practice. I also enjoyed the school Christmas pageant that we all had to participate in. The whole Christmas story was acted out in song, with selections sung by our choir. We were invited to present our pageant in Sioux Falls. It was exciting to actually be able to go on a trip to Sioux Falls and perform at a cathedral there. I think those were opportunities I wouldn't have had at home. As for academics, St. Mary's was like most other boarding schools; it wasn't on the same level as public schools. I didn't learn anything about Dakota people there either, nor did I when I re-entered public school in Peever, back on the reservation.

We weren't supposed to get extra money or packages from home, but some of the girls had parents who were able to afford to do that. So, one time my friend Marie received a package from home. When she opened it, she shared some of its contents with me and our other friend, Dottie. For the first time in my life I ate a traditional Indian food, a cornball, which is what Marie called it. What an enjoyable eating experience! It was made with pounded parched corn, dried chokecherries, *wasna* (dried meat), and rendered fat. I envied those who received packages like that from home. It was like their parents and relatives were showing them that they were cherished and missed. I knew enough about our home situation to understand that my parents were financially unable to send me things, but I still couldn't help wishing.

The routines at boarding school were much like being in the military. We had to be up at a certain time, and our beds and rooms had to be fixed and cleaned before breakfast. There were two dormitories on campus, each with a sick room. One was a large two-story house for the fifth and sixth graders, and the other was a new H-shaped dorm, which was named after Bishop Hare, for the rest of us. Seventh through ninth grade girls had rooms on the south side and the tenth through twelfth grade girls had the north side. Those of us on the south side could never go over to the other side. Every night, the dorm mother checked each room to see that we were all in our own beds. The building where classes were held was built in the 1800s and all of its wooden floors creaked. I hated having to go down to its basement where the kitchen and dining room was. It was so dark and scary, especially during the winter months when there was still darkness in the early morning hours, and there were no other lights on in the building except in the dimly-lit hallways. The second year I was at St. Mary's, a new dining room and kitchen building was built which had a basement where we could play basketball, but it wasn't a full court. But at least there was no more ugly dark basement dining room and kitchen. The new one had plenty of big windows for light and sunshine.

The school campus was located on the south edge of Springfield on the bluffs of the Missouri River. Sometimes we could walk out there and watch the river. A park on the east side of the new dormitory was part of the school's property, but it was separated from us by a chain link fence and we were told it was off-limits. The town, however, had a ninety-nine-year lease on it and used it. When the Veres brought me back for my second year there, we came back through Nebraska and stopped at Niobrara so we could cross the river on the ferry. It was quite an experience riding the ferry while sitting in the car. If we hadn't taken the ferry, it would have meant going a number of miles to get to a bridge spanning the river that cars could cross on.

Despite my family's poor living conditions, I was looking forward to going home for the summer after my first year at boarding school. I thought I had "served" my time and would be allowed to return to my family. However, Minnesota authorities somehow still had control over my life and wouldn't allow that to happen. Instead, I was taken back to Fargo and Reverend Vere's home. When I think about all of this, I am surprised at how cooperatively three states worked together—Minnesota, North Dakota, and South Dakota—for the sake of one little Indian girl. To those who were in control, they were probably "killing the Indian, and saving the man." After I settled in at the Vere's house, it wasn't so bad. At least I wasn't in a totally strange place; the area was familiar to me, and so was the minister.

Reverend Vere was of average height, slim, and he had a pleasant face, but I didn't see him as much as I saw the rest of the family. Mrs. Vere was a petite woman, like my mother and my sister Naomi. She was cheerful, smiled easily, and tried to make me feel comfortable in their home. Their oldest daughter Virginia, "Ginny," was sixteen, and to me, she was sophisticated. She had her own room that she had to share with me, regular baby-sitting jobs, and her own money, and could go out with her friends, although she had a curfew. Tommy, eight or ten years old, was their adopted son. I didn't wonder or think about it at the time, but I think he may have been Italian. He had tan-colored skin and dark curly hair. He resembled some of the Italian kids who lived in Dilworth. Their house was a two-story, with four bedrooms, a kitchen, a dining room, a living room, and a sun porch. The fourth bedroom was downstairs, but I couldn't have that room because it was a guest room. I eventually settled in and even baby-sat for the neighbors across the street.

I also continued to correspond with my two sisters in Sauk Centre, Minnesota. Their lives were much more constrained than mine. Naomi and Adrienne described their guarded lives and routines in their letters. However, they eventually proved themselves to be trustworthy teenage girls and were allowed to work outside the reform school facility. I was completely surprised when Adrienne called me at the Veres. The call caused excitement, because she said she was coming to visit me very soon. Oh, how I looked forward to that. I really missed her. Besides fighting with one another, Adrienne and I had spent a lot of good times together, and she seemed to always be looking out for me. Although we hadn't "played" with one another for a long time, she seemed to miss me, too. I was now a thirteen-year-old teenager.

Innocently, I made plans with her and told the Veres about her intended visit. On the day she was supposed to arrive by bus, they had to be somewhere else, so I was home alone. One of their neighbors offered to drive me down to the bus depot to wait for Adrienne's arrival. The bus came, but she wasn't on it. I waited for the next bus, too, but she wasn't on that one either. Again, I felt like the only Indian in an all-white world with no hope of being reunited with my family. When the Veres found out what had happened, they made some phone calls. We discovered that Adrienne had indeed been working in a home outside of the facility premises, and had schemed with a friend to run away. They were coming to Fargo.

Just as they were getting on the bus, they were caught. For a time after that she couldn't correspond or receive correspondence. But I was able to continue writing to Naomi and let her know what was happening in my life, and find out about Adrienne.

The end of June was approaching and the Veres informed me that they spent July and August back in their home state of New York at their lake cabin. So, now, they were wondering what to do with me. I can't remember anything specific being said, but I was able to sense and overhear some things that led me to believe that I had created another "situation" for these people. Although I may have felt like someone who was cast about, I had settled into this home and liked the family. They treated me well and accepted my presence by trying to make me feel like a family member. So I was getting apprehensive about what lay ahead for me again. Just a short while before they were to leave for New York, they told me I was going with them. I was relieved, but afraid. To me, New York sounded like a foreign place, and it was so far away from my home and my family.

On the way to New York, we went up through Canada and crossed on a suspension bridge into Erie, Pennsylvania, where Mrs. Vere's mother lived. From there we went on to Jamestown, New York, where Reverend Vere's father lived in the country. I enjoyed the visit there because of his fruit trees and grapes, and we were allowed to go into the orchard and pick some miniature pears. Lake Chautauqua, where the Vere's cabin was, was our destination, so we continued on. As we were approaching Chautauqua, I was expecting to see scattered homes, but there was an entire community of cabins along the lake. We three kids were immediately enrolled in "day camp," which meant we went in the morning, and came home sometime in the afternoon. I had a new stereotypical experience at the camp when we had archery. Because I was American Indian, the rest of the kids, who were all white, expected me to hit a bullseye! Man, I sure disappointed them! I had to learn how to use a bow just like they did. Upon reflection, I believe I was treated very well, like an equal, and I enjoyed being there with the Vere family. At the end of August, we headed back for South Dakota and St. Mary's.

One of the strange things I remember about my eighth grade year at St. Mary's was having to learn the "Maypole Dance," which we did at our eighth grade and high school graduation ceremonies. My understanding of this dance is that it is a European celebration of spring. About eight or ten girls would each hold onto a streamer hanging from the top of a pole and while moving clockwise each would lift her streamer over one girl and under the next. I don't know what the significance of it was, and I don't recall having a choice about participating.

Normally, I don't get too excited about upcoming events, but I was excited as my eighth grade graduation date approached. Not only was I excited about entering high school the next year, but my parents and Adrienne were coming for my graduation. I was also expecting to go home with them for the summer. After the formalities were completed, we all had refreshments, and then my dad said we had better get going. However, Mr. Cull had other plans that neither my parents nor I had been informed about. He said I couldn't go home with my parents. He told us that I was participating in the "summer home program" and being sent to Council Bluffs, Iowa. My dad challenged him, but Mr. Cull said that if my father didn't leave, he was going to call the sheriff. I guess when he heard that, my father must have thought it was futile to continue, so they left without me. Hurt and confused and frustrated, I cried and expected my dad to do something, but he couldn't. It seemed like a replay of a couple of years before when we were at the mercy of a Minnesota court. So, once again I was angry and feeling defiant.

Once I was an adult and knew a little more about the law and jurisdiction, I'd go over and over that episode in my mind, trying to understand how my dad could allow those people to have so much control over us. I also wondered how a Minnesota court order could carry weight in South Dakota, and what would have happened if my dad had known the law. I have finally concluded that Indians, at the mercy of the federal government and its self-serving laws, were "damned if they did, and damned if they didn't." Indians honored, respected, and trusted those in positions of leadership despite all the wrongs that whites had inflicted on us. Those trusting attitudes and behavior are still alive today. Perhaps some would call it gullibility. Maybe it is, but some Indians still have faith that perhaps this time the whites can be trusted.

So, there I was again, feeling helpless and apprehensive about the kind of home I would be going to. The family I was sent to had two very blond and white-skinned little girls. One was six and the other was about ten months old. One of my first experiences with that family was being showed off to other neighborhood children. One day I was sitting in the backyard, wanting to be alone, when along the side of the house I heard footsteps and a voice. It was the six-year-old saying, "Come on, and see my Indian." Rising up inside of me was a feeling of pure hatred and anger, not for the little girl per se, but because of the ignorance—it's very tiring. So when they came around to look at me, I glared at them. It must have scared them, because they never came back to see "the Indian," or "her Indian." I didn't feel like a part of this family. Unlike the Veres, they were distant and not very friendly or affectionate. The only bright spot was getting to know two Mexican girls who were adopted by a couple up the street from where I was staying. We became friends and I spent a lot time there, which seemed to bother the couple I was living with. They said I had to curtail the amount of time I spent there. I think they were offended that I preferred to spend my time there rather than be in their home. The adoptive parents of the two Mexican girls were much more easy-going and accepting of me and of who I was than the couple I lived with. Their invitation to come and spend time at their home whenever I wanted to was an indication to me that they liked me. And I sensed it in their demeanor.

Then August came, and it was finally time for me to actually go home. The couple drove me back to South Dakota. I wasn't sure where to go, but we were given directions, and that's how we found where my family was living. I don't know what the white couple thought, because my parents were then living in the middle of some cornfields. The house had fields on the north, east, south, and west sides. The two roads leading to the house from the north and south were dirt. The house was an unpainted clapboard with two rooms, no running water, and no electricity. There wasn't even a creek nearby this time; instead, we had to haul our water with old cream cans from our relatives who lived a half mile south of us. But at least we had a car for the hauling. The house belonged to our Grandma Jenny Renville Thompson, the only living daughter of Gabriel Renville.

I learned a long time ago that Indians weren't the only people in America who lived the way some of us had to, but that there were whites, too, who were just as destitute. Yet, from all the propaganda in the white-controlled media and education systems, Indians were the ones depicted as the only poor people on earth, and it was believed. By all the information that was disseminated to the public after the Korean War, American white people were the ones who should be emulated. They had jobs, material goods, and money to spend. In grade school I recall having to watch movies on the industrialization of this country, its hard-working people, their inventiveness, and their ingenuity. The white people were portrayed as the perfect people, and anybody outside of that picture was unacceptable.

I can't recall the chain of events that led up to all that happened next. What I remember is my mother drinking and having our youngest brother Merle with her. The car she was in went off the road down a steep ditch and hit an embankment, throwing her out. Our two-year-old brother's skull was crushed and he was killed; our mother's right leg was badly broken. She ended up being in the hospital for nine months, during which time my father drank almost constantly. He eventually moved us to his sister's home in Peever, I suppose because he knew he couldn't care for us properly. Also, by this time my mother and father had gotten my sister Naomi's little boy Kevin back from our sister Roberta, who was still in Texas with a child of her own. So there we were, my dad, Chyrel, Byron, Kevin, and me, living with our Auntie Laura Bird and her husband Sam in their two-story house. They also had four children in the household, as well as an older daughter with her family living in part of the upstairs. It was a very unhappy time for me. I felt like we were unwanted intruders. My dad continued to drink the whole time we lived there, while I took care of the younger children when I wasn't in school. My two-year-old nephew eventually began to call me "Mama," which really embarrassed me because I was aware of the prevailing attitude about unwed mothers and illegitimate children. When my sister and parents were forced by Social Services to give him up for adoption two years later, I regretted having felt embarrassed about his calling me "Mama."

So that's where we were living when I started my freshman year at Peever School. I went through high school there and graduated with three other Indian students. During those years some of my experiences were emotionally harmful, but I believe God "kept" me through those times and caused some good to come from them. One of those experiences was frequently encountering the obvious white attitude of superiority and the attitude that we all drank and were no good. It seemed like we were always under suspicion. Indian students had their own truant officer. I don't know what else to call him, but I do know his office was at the Bureau of Indian Affairs. It kind of reminds me of when there were Indians who served in the United States calvary. Any time one of us Indian students didn't go to school for some reason, this man was called immediately. He would then check to see why an Indian student was absent from school. Back then those things were still looked at with suspicion by Indian people. We didn't view it as being helpful, but as yet more controlling behavior by a white-controlled system.

Developing individual strength because of having to be alone, although surrounded by other Indian students, is another way that I believe God "kept" me. Some of the other Indian kids had more freedom than me once my mother came home and both my parents remained sober. My father was very strict with me. Even if I had a ride to go to any of the basketball games or other school functions, he wouldn't let me go. I hated it at the time, but with hindsight I can see how it prevented me from getting into alcoholism the way some of my friends and relatives did later in life. Remaining apart from classmates made it difficult to get to know them. I didn't start school on the reservation or at Peever as most of them did, so they already had ties with one another. Some of them knew each other since first grade and I envied that. When my family moved back to the reservation, it was almost like they hadn't left, because my mom and dad seemed to be able to pick up where they had left off in their relationships with other Dakotas. But I never seemed to be able to be a part of that familiarity, or whatever it was, with other people in my home area for many years. Still, despite their alcoholism, my mother and father were strong individuals and some of that was passed on to me. But I also believe that God was there, too, to enable me to go through some tough teenage and young adult years and stay away from alcoholism. Because of the aloneness of those years, there are still times now when I prefer quiet and solitude to being with other people.

I was fourteen when I returned to the reservation, three years after my family had returned. In those nine years of being educated in Minnesota and in a boarding school, I had been subjected to white history, culture, and language, and had learned nothing to help me establish an identity, gain self-esteem, or develop confidence. Instead I had learned to be ashamed of being Indian and to be ashamed of our cultural traditions.

Through the 1950s and 1960s, there were ever-present westerns on television and in the movies through which I learned to be ashamed of being American Indian. The school systems were at fault too. The only good said about Indian people in Minnesota was that they helped the fur traders find their way through the wilderness, and helped them establish relationships with other Indian people. By sixth grade, I had begun to believe that Indians were ignorant and heathenistic, and I was almost completely unaware of the existence of other American Indian tribes. I thought there were Sioux and Navajos, and whatever other tribes were the villains in the movies, and that we were all just Indians. Comic books also strengthened my stereotypical beliefs about Indians. If I was influenced by all of the mentioned sources, then so were other children.

So, through the selective information about native peoples in schools, and specifically through some of the portrayals of Indians on TV and in movies, I was afraid of my own people. Indians were always on the warpath riding "painted horses," their faces contorted in rage and ugliness, yipping like animals, arms uplifted with hatchets or tomahawks, ready to strike the kind, compassionate, beautiful white people. But now that I think about it, I am amused, because those ugly faces were probably all white actors made up to look Indian. As a child I could never quite understand how those Indians could be so wild and cruel when I knew I wasn't, nor were any of my family members. Why then are there people who say television does not have negative effects on children? I believe that it can have deep, lifelong effects.

So as a child who had been exposed to stereotypes presented through white people's perceptions, my being afraid of Dakota people was understandable. One time when I showed fear of Dakotas was when we still lived in Minnesota. On occasion my family would return to the reservation for visits. For my parents, the visits probably provided some comfort, reassurance, and acceptance from extended family members. Close friendships and relationships weren't offered to us in white society. On one of those visits, we were parked on main street in Sisseton. Adrienne and I were alone in the car when we spotted an Indian man walking up the street toward us. I'm sure that our faces must have registered fear to one another, because we both rolled up the windows and threw ourselves down on the floor, hiding from him. We were probably afraid he was going to scalp us, since that was a prevailing perception that had never been dispelled by education and textbooks.

We did this one time when our mother left us in the car in Moorhead, too. Adrienne and I saw a Mexican man coming down the street where our car was, and we got so scared that we locked all the doors, rolled up the windows, despite the 80 to 90 degree heat, and hid down on the floor. And you know, we never once behaved in fear when we saw a white man or white men coming toward us on the street. Once I was back on the reservation and among Indian people again, I would think about our actions and wonder why my sister and I reacted that way. It wasn't until I was in my forties that I began to understand why I reacted in such a shameful way in response to another Indian person, and perhaps even to a relative, since the Renvilles are a large family among the Sisseton-Wahpetons.

Growing up, I had formed no identity to give me a sense of place and a feeling of ownership of this land. I felt like an immigrant, a transplanted native. I couldn't identify with white people because the differences were too obvious, such as skin color, foods, culture. Confusion was inevitable. Was my existence valuable? I never used to think so. Consequently, I thought about death and suicide off and on throughout my childhood. I really thought this country belonged to white people.

It wasn't only movies and television, either. Textbooks, too, lacked accurate and complete information about this continent's indigenous people. The lack of education about us was apparently prevalent in college, too. Once when I was in a tenth grade English class, the teacher, who I liked and had great respect for, made a very racist comment. I don't recall the topic of discussion, but she eventually said, "Well, what do you think this country would be like if it was left to just the Indians? There would be no scientific discoveries, and no technology; we would still be living in tipis." I was so insulted, but I had nothing to draw on to make a reply. I believed it, too. Even if I had sufficient knowledge, I probably wouldn't have made a reply. I was too shy. The only time I spoke in school was when I was asked a question or when I was called upon to read something, which was, oh, so embarrassing.

Despite the prevailing attitude and ignorance about Indians, I continued to strive to do better than was expected of me. However, I didn't start my senior year right after Labor Day like everybody else. To a certain extent, some Indian families continued to defy compulsory education for their children, and would allow them to start school later. Another reason that Indian children didn't start school when they were supposed to was because they didn't have adequate clothing. So the parents would wait until they had enough money to buy maybe a pair of shoes or one set of clothes, and then the children would start school. The Bureau of Indian Affairs day schools understood that and knew that the children would return, even catch up in the school work. But the principal at the Peever School didn't encourage me because he thought I would be too far behind, unable to catch up. I may have missed the first three to four weeks of school my senior year. Finally, though, because of my older sister Roberta's persistence, he relented and I was allowed to return. I was angry with the principal and his perception of Indians, so I worked hard to show him that I was better than what he thought I was.

The irony of the principal's perception is that it's now the opposite. He must have read about my college accomplishments, such as my grade point average and scholarship awards, in the Sisseton newspaper. When he saw me recently at the Tribal Elderly Nutrition Center where both Indians and non-Indians are fed a daily nutritious meal, he surprised me by saying, "Oh, there's my star student." I was puzzled by that until I thought more about it. I can only speculate that he was acknowledging me as his good student because of what he had read about me in the paper. I don't recall ever being called one of his star students while I was in school or at any other time. I don't have any contact with him or with most of the white classmates I went to school with, and I haven't gone to any class reunions either, so this former principal's comments are otherwise unexplainable.

Although I was a shy senior, I forced myself to participate in our class play, tried out for chorus and sang in it for graduation, was an alternate to Girls' State, and was on the A honor roll. Despite those accomplishments, no one counseled me, or told me about college. Consequently, I thought only white people had the privilege of doing that. My dad was always telling me that education was the way for me and others to go, but I eventually concluded that meant only a high school education. So I got married to Owen German, who is still my husband. But there was always an empty feeling, a wistful feeling, a dream that I could someday prove to myself and to white people that I was able to attend college and succeed. I think my wish was to prove to white people that Indians could go to college, could enter an academic setting, and achieve high scholastic goals. Almost all Indians, at some time, have heard the same stereotypical comments from white people, like counselors and teachers, who could have helped, but didn't. The most notable comment was, "You know, your people are good with their hands. They have difficulty with math and science concepts, maybe you should think about going into the military, or to a vocational school."

We are in the twenty-first century and ignorance about American Indians is still rampant. American schools, and the whites who control the curriculum and textbooks, are more willing to acknowledge the contributions, histories, languages, and cultures of American Blacks and Hispanics than those of American Indians. Why? Is it guilt? Is it shame? We are not unapproachable, but I don't see those who are in power lining up to help fix what their ancestors broke; instead, they continue to contribute to the brokenness. Recently I heard a white female telling a TV journalist in reference to AIDS that "Americans can't tolerate what they can't fix." I think she hit the nail on the head—white Americans created an intolerable problem when they used alcohol to steal everything from the Indians, and now, they don't know what to do. Many Indian people in their writings and in their speeches have been telling educators to fix the school systems by educating students about American Indians, and by rewriting history books, social studies books, astronomy books, science books, etc., to include tribal contributions to world knowledge. Small efforts have been made, but they remain small.

When I went to school at South Dakota State University for four years, I never felt like I belonged there. Because it was the 1990s, I had high expectations of white people and their attitudes and treatment of Indian people, specifically because this was a higher educational setting. Here, I thought, surely the people are on a higher level in their perceptions of us, but that is not what I encountered. White students looked through me and past me, just like when I was in grade school. There were times when I would be walking across the campus or be in the Student Union when I'd recognize a fellow student. I'd look directly at her or him to make eye contact and smile, but they never saw me. I was invisible. When you are the only dark-skinned person in a classroom, you can't keep from being noticed. But when they saw me, they chose not to acknowledge knowing me. Their arrogance, that they had a right to belong and I didn't, infuriated me, and it made me want to run back to the reservation and home where I was accepted and belonged.

It was rare to have a white student talk to me. I am very sensitive to body language and can perceive attitudes of people toward me, and I observed their arrogance and attitudes of superiority. Even most of the instructors, some of whom are committed to lifelong learning, are ignorant of Dakotas and American Indians in general. What does that say about education systems in South Dakota? What an indictment against this institution of higher learning and a university that prides itself in turning out well-educated graduates sought after by businesses nationwide!

Once, for an assignment, I had to go to the library for some information on Dakotas. I found only two books about us and none about Nakotas. Not even the book *History of the Santee Sioux* was in their collection, and here we are the dominant minority east of the Missouri! Granted, the university has been trying to address the ignorance problem, but their efforts need to be more aggressive. Students don't have a choice about whether they can take general studies courses and I don't think they should have a choice in learning about the "Sioux," and other indigenous peoples here in America. Recently I read a newspaper story about a class being offered in a Minnesota university which teaches tolerance. Some of the students' comments were that they didn't realize they were intolerant to other races or minorities until this class was taken. Sometimes those kinds of things have to happen in people's lives in order for them to realize where they are on such issues. It is too easy to say verbally that one isn't racist, and it is another thing to be confronted with a situation that may challenge that ethnocentric and egocentric perception.

Higher learning institutions aren't the least of places where racism and ignorance about American Indians exists. Having attended all-white churches most of my life, I know about the ignorance and intolerance firsthand. Once I became more knowledgeable about the churches and the people who call themselves "born again," I began to observe them with a more critical eye. I became familiar with the Bible; I could quote it and use it when I needed it as I was instructed to use it, I was a good pupil. Memorizing verses is stressed in these churches so that you can fall back on its teachings and its strength when your own human weakness prevents you from "loving as Jesus first loved you," or "doing unto others as you would have them do unto you." Experiencing racism is an extreme test of one's faith. Still, I was seeking a deeper spirituality, something that was meant for me, an Indian. I never found it there because I didn't feel completely accepted. I couldn't belong because my skin color made me different, and being different here in America is intolerable.

I moved from the Indian mission churches on my reservation to white churches in my search for spirituality. Of course, when my family was living off the reservation, we had no choice about what race made up the majority in the churches we went to. So I decided as an adult, that if I wasn't satisfied, I was going to try out other white churches to see if they were better, to see if I could find what I was looking for. In my own personal relationship with God, I was stable, but Christianity teaches that a body of believers is needed in order for one to gain spiritual wisdom. And by their example, you need a building to commune with God. But when I went to those beautiful buildings filled with so-called enlightened, charismatic white people decked out in their Sunday best, I found limited spiritual wisdom. My gosh, these were places where people vied to be the best musician, the best vocalist, the best teacher, the best dressed. There were few who were sincerely committed to growing spiritually unless it was according to their guidelines or according to what they thought was acceptable. There was a lot of behavior that was learned and practiced superficially. Such as lifting their hands and praising the Lord in adoration of him and loving him, or being filled with the Holy Spirit, "loving as Christ first loved you." I saw examples of their behavior outside the walls of their beautiful church, in the community in casual settings, and they did not practice loving everybody or being kind to everybody. They were very selective about who they would "bless" with their loving kindness.

It is much too easy for Christian white people to love another race a world away who are being oppressed and suppressed and not even see what is happening right under their noses to indigenous people. And it is worse when they ignore what is happening in their own country to American Indians. What makes me the angriest is how ministers use their pulpits to preach to their congregations about abortion, the right-to-life, and how they must vote into Congress Christians who follow God, yet they never preach to them about taking an active roll in changing what continues to happen to Indians nationwide. The cheating and stealing are still going on wherever there is American Indian land and property and the ministers and their churches in America turn blind eyes to it.

One occurrence that made me leave a church was when my

daughter Gabrielle was two years old. Once the morning services began, the minister would tell the people to greet one another with a hug or a handshake. For the most part I hated having to participate in this ritual because I never felt comfortable doing it, because I believed that these white people were insincere and pretentious, but I did it anyway. I know in my heart when people are sincere or insincere in their encounters with Indian people. My daughter had seen these greetings since she was a baby, so it was natural for her to follow her parents' example. When she turned around and extended her hand to one of the persons behind us, she was ignored. So I turned away, endured the service, and never went back. Not once did anyone come to see why my family wasn't going to church there anymore, not even the minister. We changed churches and when we left that church, too, it didn't make much of a difference to them either because no one came from there to inquire if there was something wrong.

And one time at that last church I went to, a visiting speaker was featured for a special service. I was looking forward to hearing him because our church friends were telling me about how much he loved God and that he had such a tender heart toward people, very compassionate and understanding. On his first or second night there, he was speaking about this country being founded on godly principles, and then referred to the Indians by saying, "all that was here when we first came were savages." Of course I withstood it with pained silence, but I never forgot it. What made me the angriest was that the "godly" white people sitting there never caught it. They behaved just like the rest of the white people in this country—unaffected by all that happens to American Indians. Now, who are the ignorant ones? They have never risen above their own prejudices although they believe they are good and devout people, and above all the most intelligent. In this "religious, spiritual" environment, I learned to distrust most the born-again Christians, those who consider themselves to be the most enlightened above the more traditional churchgoers.

I am ashamed that I once believed that these white Christians were right and Indians were wrong when it came to spirituality and wisdom. Although I am one of the younger ones in my family, I feel like one of the oldest because of my spiritual and emotional maturity. I know my sisters and brothers respect me and are influenced by what I believe and say, so I carry a heavy burden knowing that I influenced most of them to follow me into these white churches. What I am most ashamed about is having once believed that Dakota spirituality was evil and not good for us. I am grateful that the Creator didn't allow me to be satisfied in those churches. Instead, I was stimulated to continue on in my spiritual search and I began to listen to Dakotas when they spoke about their traditional spiritual practices; at one time I had dismissed them and what they said. But eventually I began to learn that we had a deep spiritual relationship with the Creator and with all living things until the federal government forced change upon us. Currently, my family and I don't attend any church regularly and we don't practice traditional spirituality either. But I am content knowing that I have a personal relationship with my Creator God and that he is wherever I am.

My oldest son is a Sundancer and is the chief Firekeeper of that group. I have gone to their Sundances and experienced a spiritual oneness with other Dakotas while there, but I am not compelled to join myself to them exclusively. Despite the racism and ignorance I experienced in the white churches I attended, I did become a spiritually strong individual through some of their teachings and through reading the Bible. And I have become stronger spiritually by learning some of the traditional spiritual practices too.

I think that it is wonderful and amazing that our spirituality was so strong that we couldn't be persuaded to convert by white Christian missionary efforts alone. It took the federal government's involvement to cause us to move toward changing our spiritual practices, but even then, changing us has never been completely successful.

There were many Dakotas who refused to change, or if they did attend church, they also continued in some of the traditional ways. And there are more Dakotas today than ever before who are blending both spiritual practices and making it work. The suppression and oppression we endured and continue to endure are incapable of stripping us of what is deeply rooted within us, of what we are born with, of what flows through our veins. Hallelujah! Can anybody say "amen"? Writing that makes me chuckle because it causes me to compare the white Christians to Dakota people in their spiritual practices. Whites seem to need to hear from their listeners during their sermons and exhortations that there is agreement. Yet among the Dakota, the people listened quietly, and most of the time with their eyes averted or closed, until the speaker was finished.

Then the only acknowledgement was a *"Hau"* from the men, and a *"Han"* from the women. That is why many non-Indians didn't believe that Indians heard or understood what was being said.

I have much to learn about Dakota spirituality, but I am not discouraged because there are many like me who are endeavoring to re-learn their traditions. The most important thing is that my people did not reject me when I was seen at traditional ceremonies. I was accepted and my ignorance was tolerated. They knew I would eventually learn. That is so unlike white people's behavior. With Indians, I can progress at my own desired pace. No one hurries me by telling me that I should attend this ceremony or that ceremony so I can learn and grow. But in the Christian churches, if it was discovered that you didn't know very much about the Bible or what it meant to be "born again," you were "encouraged" to attend as many prayer meetings and church as possible. In fact, if you didn't attend Wednesday night and Sunday night services in addition to Sunday School and Sunday morning services, you were considered to be an immature Christian and your sincerity was questioned.

Now I seem to be on a mission to educate and inform as many white people as possible about Dakotas. Sometimes I wonder if it's worth it. Sometimes I wish we could just close ourselves off from all contact with white people. Sometimes I daydream about a time before white people intruded into our world. The waves of white people who beached on our shores seem to be resistant to our endeavors to educate them about our cultures, or maybe it is fear "that we will do to them what they have done to us," as one non-Indian friend said to me, that keeps them from us. But I am a Dakota, and we have never been the kind of people to "roll over and die." We are survivors because of our industriousness, our resourcefulness, and our spirituality, and because of our ability to adapt. And few people outside of the Indian communities acknowledge that or appreciate it. Tolerance and patience seem to be our downfall, though, when it comes to dealing with injustices that this white society has dealt to American Indians. Most white people seemingly are unreachable, Dakotas are not. What I mean is that we continue to strive to educate Euro-Americans about our societies even though we experience lack of acceptance and lack of interest.

Our culture and spirituality are inherent. The younger generations are searching for something that will give them a purpose for being here, and our cultural heritage and spirituality can provide that. When they acknowledge the validity of the Dakota lifestyle, there will be a tremendous movement among them to once again be a part of a lifestyle that was created for them. I do not feel discouraged or hopeless about our young people, because I can look at my children and know that there is memory in the blood.

Although my children were raised in Christian churches, they all respect traditional Dakota spirituality. My oldest son DelRay is a Sundancer, a Pipe Carrier, and the chief Firekeeper. My middle child Scott is devoted to politics and to trying to make the reservation a better place for other Dakotas. Scott, at twenty-four years of age, was the youngest councilman to be voted into the Tribal Council, serving one two-year term. DelRay was the first tribal member to become manager of the Sisseton-Wahpeton Sioux Federal Credit Union, and Scott was the first Tax Director to bring in millions of dollars in taxes to the tribe. Both continue to serve our people by sitting on various tribal committees. Gabrielle is my youngest and loves Dakota traditions, especially powwows, because she is a fancy shawl dancer. I regret, however, that they didn't grow up hearing the Dakota language spoken like their parents did. But I do what I can to help them understand some basics of the language.

I feel that I have to say that it isn't culturally appropriate to speak of or otherwise call attention to oneself in Dakota society, and because I was raised that way, I don't enjoy writing or talking about myself. However, I feel compelled to do it so white people will know that the society and education systems they have created here in America do everyone a disservice, even their own children. From the beginning, information about the relevance and contributions of indigenous people on this continent has been deliberately omitted because white people have thought we Indians are the "vanishing race." Whites were also motivated by the desire to destroy all evidence of Indian ownership. This country waves a banner of freedom, proclaims equality for all, and boasts of having been founded upon Christian precepts, yet its people have committed the great sin of omission, excluding accurate information about American Indian people from their education systems. The Bible that I have read emphasized that there are sins of omission as well as commission. It also says that if a Christian knows that he should do good and doesn't, then it is a sin.

White America has not only sinned against its own children by denying them their right to know about other cultures, but has broken their own fundamental spiritual law by not doing what is good and right to American Indians. White people, in their failure to obey their own religious laws, and through their fear, intolerance, and ignorance, are largely responsible for American Indians' dysfunctional lifestyles, not only in white society, but within our reservation cultures, too.

For most of the Europeans that poured into this country in droves, their intent was to eliminate, assimilate, acculturate, or control the native people. Despite their attempts, we endured! We endured starvation, diseases, massacres, separations, racism, ignorance, and missionaries. Why? Perhaps so we could teach the world something about tolerance, patience, endurance, generosity, and about overcoming almost insurmountable odds. I believe it is because we have been spiritual people from the beginning. This helped us live in balance with all creation; it helped us recognize and acknowledge that all living things had a place on this earth. We tried not to take things for granted, but instead we were grateful to the Creator for all that He had given to us. I am not romanticizing about our race because we had some among us who had hearts that weren't right toward the Creator or toward others. But I believe that we had a deep respect for who the Creator was that made us acutely aware that we were small creatures in comparison to the rest of creation. From reading early recorded sayings of Native Americans, I have a picture in my mind of a people who regarded the spiritual world as important as the world that we can see, hear, and smell; therefore, we lived fearless of death, unlike many white people.

Chapter 4

Memories

Lydia Whirlwind Soldier

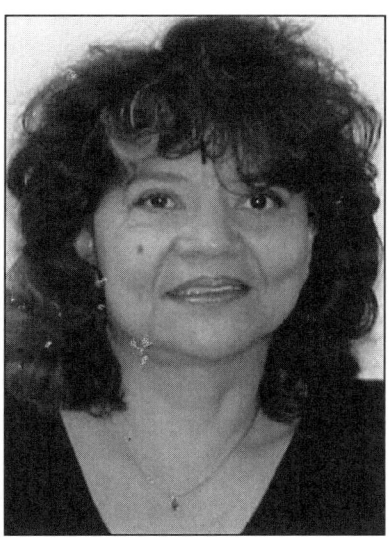

Lydia Whirlwind Soldier is an enrolled member of the Rosebud Sioux Tribe. She was born and raised in Bad Nation, a Lakota community in south central South Dakota.
After receiving a B.S. in education from Sinte Gleska University on her reservation and a M.Ed. from Penn State, she taught at Sinte Gleska. Since 1986 she has been Indian Studies Coordinator for the Todd County School District.
Her articles, book reviews, and poetry have been published in the *Journal of American Indian Higher Education, Wicazo Sa*, and the *Sioux Falls Argus Leader*. Her book of poems, *Memory Songs*, was recently published by the Center for Western Studies in Sioux Falls. The essay below is part of a longer work in progress.

I have wrestled with telling my story because of the repercussions I expect from the Catholic community here on the Rosebud Reservation, but I have resolved not to spare the worse because I am writing my story for the children who suffered in the boarding schools. I speak for those children whose stories will never be told, for those of us who still suffer from post-traumatic stress, for the lost generations who stand on the street corners and dig in trash for aluminum cans to sell, for those who deaden their pain with alcohol and drugs, and for their families who have suffered from generational grief and invisible scars. Finally, I speak for those who have lost their culture and heritage and have not seen it as a loss.

My story begins on a summer day when I was four years old. My memories have never faded. The events of my story flash by me every fall. I was living in the only place I had known, in the remote Lakota community of Bad Nation on the Rosebud Reservation, seventy-some miles northeast of Rosebud Agency in south-central South Dakota. I had been raised in a Lakota Tiospaye, which means I had daily exposure to all of my blood relatives, my extended family. Unlike most Lakota families whose maternal extended families were the most influential in child rearing, my paternal great-grandparents and grandparents raised me, and were an ever-present influence in my life.

It was late August. I had spent a carefree summer riding horses over the rolling hills, swimming in the creeks and dams lined with scrub oak, elms, and giant cottonwoods, and picking and eating chokecherries, plums, and buffalo berries along the ravines that led to the Big White River. My playmates were my four brothers, my four male cousins, an uncle who was about six years older than I, and one female cousin who would come to spend time with us.

The day began as all days did that summer, with a hearty breakfast of pancakes with chokecherry syrup, peanut butter, and milk. We put away our beds, helped straighten up the house, and went out to do our share of the gardening. My job was to pick potato bugs off the remaining potato plants. I carried a small can of kerosene into which I put the potato bugs I collected. My brother and uncle hoed the weeds between the potato plants that were still producing, and between the melon and squash plants, and they hauled water from the well. After our chores were done, we played in the nearby creek, wading in the water, splashing each other, and watching the sandy mud ooze up between our toes. Then I thought I heard someone call my name and turned, looked up, and saw my grandmother standing on the high bank above us. Her eyes told me something was wrong. She quietly told us to come back to the house.

We ran barefoot to the house, carrying our shoes. In the yard a dark dusty car idled noisily. I would later find out it was from the Bureau of Indian Affairs. An Indian man stood by the car, nervously smoking, raking his fingers through his short dark hair. I wondered about the car and the stranger who stood outside, not coming into the house. We ran into the house excited about the visitor. Then I looked at the worried faces of my grandmother and mother and knew that something was wrong. I asked, "Wicasa he tuwe he? Who is that man outside? Takuwe hi he? Why is he here?" My grandmother said, "Hiyonihib, he has come for you." We all asked, "Takuwe," "Why?" My mother hushed us and hurriedly washed our faces and muddy legs and feet, combed our hair, and slipped on our shoes. We were told again that we had to go with this man; he was taking us to school. My mother walked with us to the car; the man told her to put us into the back seat. I heard my mother say, "She's only four years old," but he gruffly said something and my mother said no more. We climbed into the back seat, not certain of what was happening.

Today, when my uncle talks about that day, he talks about being kidnapped. My grandparents had managed to keep my ten-year-old uncle from being sent to boarding school up to this time. My brother was six years old, my cousin was five, and I was four. Fortunately for my other cousins, my aunt had taken them to visit my maternal grandmother that day and they had escaped the round-up.

None of us had state birth certificates because we had all been born at home. My great-grandparents had enrolled us into the tribe and had gotten our birth certificates from the Bureau of Indian Affairs, but somehow we had been overlooked in the round-up of children who were supposed to go to school. Under the threat of a jail term, some parents and grandparents still hid their children. I remember hearing the story of one grandmother who carried her grandson on her back, running and hiding in the ravines, until the Bureau of Indian Affairs police thought they had gathered all of the children in the community. The BIA had come to Bad Nation after my uncle and they had found a nest of small children, children who spoke only Lakota.

Boarding schools for Native American children according to the United States government were established to "remove the children from the demoralizing influence of their families to the boarding school, the more distant the better." The churches, working with the government, did their best to destroy Lakota culture and religion. Under the guise of helping the Lakota people make the transition from their "savage" lifestyle to Christianity, the churches came onto the reservations. Christianity was well-established on the reservation by the time I was born. All of my relatives had joined the Catholic Church and most had gone to school at St. Francis Mission.

Before we left, the man asked my mother where they wanted us to go to school. My mother told him that since my father and grandfather had gone to St. Francis Mission, it would be better if we were taken to a school my parents were familiar with. As we drove away, I looked back. My mother and my grandmother stood by the house looking after us through the dust as the car sped up the hill on the gravel road.

Once our home was out of sight, we quietly watched the passing scenery out of the car windows. I watched the yellow-breasted meadow larks open their wings and fly up in protest at the sound of the rattling car as we drove by, and land on the fence posts further up the road. I asked my brother, "Did you hear that? The meadowlark asked us, 'Tokiyalapi he? Tokiyalapi he?' 'Where are you going? Where are you going?' My brother said. "Shhh!" So I quietly sat looking at the corn fields, farm houses, and cattle. Little did I know that for the next nine months I would not see the wind sweeping the silver sage and the tall grasses across the open plains of Bad Nation, or our horses trotting across the pastures to gently nuzzle our hands, waiting to be fed. I would miss the creek with its little stream of flowing water, shadowed by the great fallen cottonwood which we used as a foot bridge when we didn't want to get our feet wet, and the cool willows with their strings of leaves swaying in the breeze along the marshy areas where I sometimes went to watch the redwing blackbirds flit on the cottontails, and listen to the sweetness of their hinge-squeaking songs.

As we got further from home, I became afraid and began to worry. We whispered in the back seat, and my brother said, "Don't be a crybaby." I had always admired my brother Clement's confident adventurous outlook on life. He had heard Lakota men's stories all of his life. This was his chance to go on a "wazuya," an odyssey and an adventure. I sat and looked at the back of the man's head, wondering who he was, and why he had come after us. Why didn't he speak to us or even look at us? We traveled for hours over dusty gravel roads, and we all fell asleep. When we woke up, we were at St. Francis Mission.

My cousin and I were taken to the two-story girls' building. I never imagined I would be housed and educated in this huge rectangular gray stucco building for the next eight years. After a time of knocking, someone finally came to the door. I cannot remember the name of the Catholic nun who opened the door to take us into the building, but I will never forget her grim lips and her hardened narrow blue eyes. My cousin and I huddled together when we saw the stern expression on her face. I looked hopefully for a smile that would suggest that I was in a safe place. When she realized that we might cry, an insincere smile that was nowhere near her eyes forewarned us of the trouble we would experience in the coming months.

We had seen people like her before; they had come to Bad Nation with their "charitable" attempts to save us. We didn't know if this was a man or woman. We assumed a woman because of the long black dress, "but men who come out to Bad Nation also wear long black dresses," I whispered to my cousin in Lakota as I giggled behind my hand. A black veil covered her head, above a now empty expressionless face. Her face was tightly wrapped in white material that seemed to cut into it. She wore a bib type white cloth over the top front of her body. I remember looking up at this person as her mouth moved, enunciating words directly at me, words I did not understand. Her voice was cold, harsh, and deprecating. She looked at me with distaste and impatiently asked, "They don't understand English?" We understood enough to recognize the disapproval in her voice. We understood the directions she gave us by the way she pointed here and there. Her disapproval activated my senses. I knew I was in trouble.

This was only the beginning. In the next few years, until I learned to speak English correctly, I would be treated as if I were retarded or hard of hearing. The people who ran the school thought that the louder they spoke, the better I would understand, so at times all communication was conducted in shouting voices.

I remember a recurring nightmare I had for many years. A nun shrouded in a dark habit roared at me in the middle of a large field with groups of unidentifiable people on each side of the field. They joined in, their relentless voices accumulating into a roar. When one side had finished roaring at me, the other side would start. I tried to escape but was unable to. I cupped my hands over my ears to block out the roar as I lay curled up on the ground.

After the nun finished talking to the man who had brought us to the school, she opened the door and shoved us inside. She guided us to a room with two large pillars and a winding staircase to the right. Every time the nun moved, a large ring of keys jingled against a long rope of beads and a cross that hung at her waist. I later found out it was called a rosary. She used her keys to open the double doors leading into a very large playroom, pushed us in, and slammed the door. I heard the keys jingle and turn as she locked the door behind us. This was my first experience with locked doors.

The large playroom was empty of furniture except for a potbelly stove in the middle of the room. Long benches lined one side of the institutional green wall. On the northwest end of the room were student lockers which would remain empty most of the time. A long green ping-pong table was pushed against one of the walls. The floors were bare hardwood, and the tall gray windows covered with heavy metal mesh let in light on the east and west walls. There were no curtains. Dust and soot mixed with rain permanently stained the window panes, making the glass look dingy and dark. Later I would experience the high ceiling echoing back the sounds of children talking and laughing. It would take me a while to get used to the sounds bouncing back at me, especially the angry disapproving voices of the nuns and the sound of the whistle they used to signal us to line up. The three doors that led into the playroom would always remain locked.

We didn't cry, but we clung together, not saying a word. Other children, all girls with short hair dressed in identical uniforms, were in the playroom. They looked at us and smiled. Some played tag, while others sat on the benches talking. Still others slept on their stomachs, stretched out on the benches with their arms hanging over the sides. There were no toys or books, nothing to entertain the children. We stood by the door for maybe fifteen to twenty minutes, not knowing what to do, not knowing at what to expect. At last, we walked quietly to one of the benches and sat down, still clinging to each other's hands.

Finally, two older girls and a nun came to get us. We were taken back into the room we had come through earlier, but this time we turned left and were taken down dark musky concrete steps, down into a washroom that smelled stale and humid. Bathtubs lined one side of a long narrow room. There were benches along the other wall and showers down at the other end. Bare light bulbs hung from the ceiling, glaring down on the drains in the concrete floor caked with dirt and hair, culturing mold.

The older girls ran hot water into a long white porcelain tub with a dark ring about waist high. We were told to undress and get into the tub, and then we were given a large bar of yellow soap that stung my skin. Later, we would find out it was lye soap. It sucked the oil and moisture out of the skin, causing it to dry out and crack. By mid-year, most of the children had chapped, cracked, and bleeding hands.

Then we were given clean clothes, underwear, socks, and uniforms. The uniforms were made from a cotton canvas-type material, olive green with matching print blouses. Each grade wore the same type of uniform but in different colors. Little did I know that in the sixth and seventh grades I would be working in the sewing room, cutting and sewing these uniforms for the little girls.

I stubbornly and quietly clung to my clothes as they tried to pry them from my hands. These clothes were my last connection to home and I struggled to keep them, but rather than cry, I let them go. We were not allowed to keep any personal items. All connections to our former lives would be severed until the following summer when we were allowed to return home. Meanwhile, we would live in a sterile environment where feelings were not expressed, an empty place in which to reshape our minds. A place where we would be "assimilated."

Once we dressed, we were placed on stools while our hair was cut in a blunt Dutch boy style. As I watched my long hair fall to the floor, I wondered what my relatives would think when they saw my short hair. My hair had never been cut. Short hair was a sign of mourning. Our people cut their hair only when a loved one died. I reached up to touch my short hair and a harsh voice sounded. I instinctively knew that if I reacted more, I would be punished. After our haircuts, white powder was sprinkled on our heads. We later found out that it was DDT for head lice. I had never seen head lice, but we would all eventually catch them. Our heads would be sprinkled with the white powder or soaked with kerosene, which was not washed out until a week later.

We were then taken back into the playroom. I do not remember if we ate an evening meal, but I do remember that in the evening we were assigned beds in a large dormitory. At this time, my cousin and I were separated. We whispered to each other as a loud scolding voice sounded. We were determined that they were not going to separate us. I gritted my teeth, tightly closed my eyes, and hung on to her hand as tightly as I could. But my cousin was shoved away from me and given a bed several aisles away. Still it was a comfort to know that at least I could still see her.

The mattresses on the beds were stuffed with corn husks and covered with blue and white striped cotton material. We were each given a pillow, white cotton sheets, and an olive green woolen army blanket. An older girl showed me how to make my bed. I would later feel that my bed was the only place where I could find privacy and peace.

I watched the other children kneel. I stood there until I saw the nun walk quickly and briskly toward me, her long black skirt and veil swishing, her keys jingling against her rosary. Then I quickly knelt down. I watched and followed the other children's actions. They knelt by their beds, and bowed their heads, their lips moving with the bedtime prayer. At that time I didn't know the prayers, but I would find out over the years that we prayed because we were "heathen sinners." Many times I did not know what offense I had committed; nevertheless, we had to get on our knees often to pray so that the unseen demon would not take us to a fiery place below. I was not familiar with the concept of hell until I was taken away to school.

After the prayers, I saw the girls climb into their beds, so I climbed into mine, and the lights were turned off. In the late summer evening, I lay watching the darkness creep across the ceiling until I could see no more. I looked at the windows in the dark and saw only the reflection of the moon through the heavy metal mesh screens. I realized that my mother and grandmother were not there, and my relatives were not there, and I didn't know where they had taken my brother and my uncle. I realized I was isolated in a strange place and I could not leave.

My grandmother had always spoken to us in Lakota about kindness, but the adults in this place showed no kindness. Their cold stares warned me I was not in a safe place. I could not speak my language and I did not understand most of theirs. I would learn that when they were not cold and harsh, they were completely indifferent. I would learn that if I were sick, if I had an earache or a leg ache, I would not receive any comfort, but would be told that I was exaggerating. I would be hospitalized for four days after having my tonsils removed; I would have a permanent tooth pulled, and my parents would not know until I told them the following summer.

The children at the school would learn to compete for affection or attention or simply to be recognized. A Lakota society that valued cooperation was losing its children to the teachings of competition, to the philosophy that one should strive to be better than her brothers and sisters. The concept of Mitakuye Oyasin, the Lakota philosophy of relationship, would lose its meaning for many of the children.

At last, I covered my head with my blanket and quietly thought about the events of the day. I had persevered. I pressed my fist to my mouth to keep from crying. I felt the tears flood my eyes. I tried to swallow my tears. I only sniffled at first, trying to be brave, but then I heard my cousin crying, and then other children crying, and finally I cried with them. The dorm seemed filled with the sound of weeping children. I longed for the warm loving comfort of my Uncicila, my great-grandmother. But there was no comfort for me, or for any of the crying children.

Decades later, when I attended Penn State University to receive a Master's degree, I met a woman who had been a matron at one of the boarding schools in South Dakota. She told me she never got accustomed to the little girls sobbing for their families at night after the lights were turned off. She told me it was heartbreaking, and it always brought tears to her eyes.

During that first night, I woke several times expecting to find that I had escaped from this bad dream. Behind closed eyelids I squeezed my great-grandmother's image into my memory, and thought of her soft gentle manner and voice, and of her kindly giving nature. "Uncicila, tokiya yaunhe? tokiya yaunhe? Great-grandmother, where are you, where are you?" I cried.

In the early hours of coming morning, I jumped up and ran to the window to look out into the courtyard below to see if my parents had come for me. I did this for at least a week or maybe even two and cried quiet tears each time, until I finally realized that I was there to stay. Nobody was coming after me. I did not register in my little four-year-old brain that my parents really did not have a choice; they had not abandoned me. And over the next months, I found that tears only worsened the situation. At their best, tears only provoked loud scolding voices and cold stares.

After those first weeks, I stopped wondering where I was when I awoke. I quit running to the window for a time. Finally I remembered what my great-grandmother had told me. She had pointed out the morning star, and told me that no matter where I was, no matter how far from home, we would both be able to see that star. Remembering those words, I began to look out the window again and to believe that my thoughts and my great-grandmother's thoughts mingled. I began to have hope that I was not alone. Sometimes I thought that if she knew how much I missed them all and knew how lonely I was, maybe she would come after me. I wondered if my great-grandmother and my other relatives were looking at the morning star. I knew they woke early each morning to pray, asking for help and health for the family. Many mornings I looked at that star brightly shining in the east above the dawning sky. But as its light slowly faded, so did my hope.

Then my prayers were answered one day, when I saw my great-grandmother coming through the playroom. Her gentle face beamed. She wore her homemade long dark blue calico dress, and a brooch held together her collar under her chin. She wore her dress moccasins, called hanmikceka, with simple designs on the toes and a purple shawl. Her long thin braids were held together with a leather thong and covered by a beaded hair net. She leaned on her cane with every step she took. It was the first time I had seen my great-grandmother since I had come to St. Francis and my hair had been cut. I ran to her, tears streaming down my face. Seeing her sparked my feelings of abandonment and grief. Her eyes filled with tears as I wailed, and she put me on her lap and held me to her, "Sika, sika, poor, poor, little one," she cried. I felt my heart had been squeezed and wrung out as I wept. She told me everything would be all right as I struggled to swallow my tears. I tried to tell her what happened to my hair, but I sat there hiccupping, unable to talk. Grief sucked the oxygen from my lungs.

This strong matriarch of our family tried to keep the moisture from her eyes. "Are you being a good little girl?" she asked. I nodded, saying "I try to be, Uncicila." She nodded, smoothing my short hair, satisfied with my answer. She removed her handkerchief, gently wiped my wet cheeks, wiped her eyes, and blew her nose. I held her hand all the while she was there. When she finally got ready to leave, my cousin and I would not let her go, clinging to her, quietly sobbing and crying out, "Uncicila." The nuns pried our fingers open, as we clung to her clothes. She stayed longer trying to reassure us that we would soon get to go home. She talked to us until we calmed down. But she never came to see us at the school again. It was too difficult for her to leave us behind. I spent only two more summers with my great-grandmother, only six months, before she passed into the spirit world.

After my great-grandmother's only visit, I looked down into the courtyard every morning, but it was always empty. The tall fence around the school could keep out our loved ones, but it couldn't contain the sadness and the loneliness of the children of St. Francis Mission. What kind of place was this where the barking of dogs or even the calls of the owl and other night birds could not be heard? Some nights my dreams were of other times and places. The magic of those dreams would unfold and seem more real than life. I dreamed of riding my horse between the scrub oaks along the creek. We rode quickly under some trees to keep the ticks from falling on us. I saw the wildflowers, tiny white and yellow blossoms, blue bell-like flowers and sage that bobbed in the prairie wind. I felt the fresh breath of wind that carried their delicate scent. I heard the rattling of the large cottonwood leaves and I remembered how we climbed those giant trees near our dam and how we played in the small stream of water near our garden. The reality was that for the next eight years, from kindergarten through seventh grade, I would be locked in at St. Francis Mission.

I was the third generation of Whirlwind Soldiers who had attended St. Francis; none had graduated. We did not thrive in this Catholic domain. It was another world, a nightmare, and it left me with terrible dreams that gnawed on me for decades. When I think of St. Francis, I think of windows covered with thick metal mesh screens, of cold stiff canvas uniforms, of kneeling in prayer on hardwood floors, of marching in quiet straight lines, and of asking forgiveness for our sins.

The teaching of the church became a prelude to one little girl's nightmare. One night we were awakened by her screams. The nun rushed out of her room to the little girl's side, shaking her, asking her what was wrong. The little girl pointed at the burning potbelly stove with flames licking the cracks around the door, and said the devil had come out of the stove and was trying to take her. The nun told her to get back to sleep, that she was keeping the other children awake and scaring them with her foolishness. After this happened several times, the girl convinced us that there was a devil in that stove. Knowing that we were afraid, one night the nun pretended to chase the devil around the stove with a poker. Cornering him, she opened the door, and made him get into the burning stove. After that, none of the girls wanted to sleep near the stove, no matter how cold it was.

Later, the nun told us that the little girl was possessed by the devil. We became even more afraid and avoided her. She seemed to interpret this as rejection and became angry, hitting us with a hair brush when we passed by her bed to line up in the morning or pinching us when the nun was not looking. Later in life she ended up drinking on the streets of Rapid City and finally ended up being killed by a hit and run driver.

We lived by the sounds of the bell and whistle. The bell woke us every morning, and the whistle signaled us to quietly line up in straight lines. We marched to every activity: class, meals, and church, twice on Sundays. We kneeled and sat to the sound of the bell and the whistle. I even learned to make my bed "army regulation."

Order, obedience, and silence were important; they never explained why. I wondered if it was to keep us from sin, to keep us out of hell. If this was not hell, it certainly was purgatory. I remember the atmosphere of uncertainty. I was ruled by the fear of retaliation for speaking Lakota, and I unintentionally got others in trouble by talking to them in Lakota. My punishment was kneeling in corners, my knuckles smacked raw with a ruler. Whippings raised welts on my legs. My hair was cut, and I was jerked around by my hair. I was slapped in the mouth and I had bruises on my cheeks from being pinched and shaken. We would learn over the years that raw knuckles and cracked hands were not something that one cried over. I willed myself to endure. I counted the months, weeks, and days until summer vacation. I would never get used to the mistreatment nor the resentment I felt. All the while the nuns tried to impart their "kind" religious knowledge and "wisdom."

As I got older I became more and more determined that the nuns would not break my spirit. I thought about the times when my brothers and cousins would try to make each other flinch or blink. I would not flinch, or blink. I would think, "I am a Lakota! I am Lakota! First and foremost! I am! I am! Nothing will ever change that!"

A typical day at St. Francis Mission began around six A.M. We were awakened by a nun clanging a bell as she walked through the dormitory. I remember the anger and impatience etched on her face as she deliberately rang the bell in someone's ear. We were fortunate if her attitude toward us was cool and impersonal. It seemed a daily ritual to have a child in tears. If we didn't get out of bed before the nun reached the end of the dormitory, we were jerked out, sometimes by the hair. It quickly became a habit to sit up and begin moving around to avoid her retaliation. We also got into trouble if we did not make our beds properly. The nun tore apart the improperly made bed and the offender would have to make it over. Sometimes the bed was torn apart several times before she was satisfied with the way it was made.

The only source of heat was the potbelly stove that stood in the middle of the dorm. Our breath steamed into the cold air as we dressed quickly under the army blankets to keep warm. A line of little girls waited to go into the bathroom; another line waited in front of the sinks to wash. The icy water made the room feel warmer as we washed our hands and faces. The only time hot water was available was on bath days, once a week.

Today, images of boot camp come to my mind when I think of the little girls' dormitory: neatly arranged pillows at the head of each bed, beds in neat rows, tops of sheets turned down over army blankets tucked in tightly with neat regulation square corners. After I grew up, these experiences transformed into a comedy. We laughed at the many jokes told about how easy boot camp was for our relatives who went from the boarding schools to the armed services. The boys talked about the discipline, of having to do push ups, of "hitting the deck," "giving ten," of standing at attention for hours at a time; they talked about "chow time" and "running laps." They understood military jargon long before they were shipped off to Vietnam.

After we washed our hands and faces, combed our hair, and made our beds, we were in neat little lines quietly marching to church. Every door that we went through was locked, and securely locked after we passed through. I often wondered how my relatives would get in if they came to visit me. Were those locks to keep us in, or to keep our relatives out? I went to church every day for eight years, and twice on Sundays. The church was always warmer than the dormitory. I sometimes wondered if God was ever cold. The value and relevance of Christianity did not last for me after those eight years, for I never went to church again after I left St. Francis Mission. It took many years for my heart to warm.

We filed into the aisles and quietly knelt on the cold hardwood pews, and before long the familiar numb feeling began to creep into my knees. To this day, my knees ache when I kneel on them. We sat in the pews according to grade level, the youngest in front, the older students in the back. The boys sat on one side of the church and the girls on the other. We were not allowed to talk to each other or to look at the boys. The threat of a sharp finger jab in the back or a quick jerk of the hair kept us vigilant.

Our stomachs grumbled hungrily as we quietly watched the altar boys dressed in white vestments over black robes came out and light the candles. Some of the boys aspired to become altar boys, while some of the girls believed it was a privilege or an advantage to be chosen to clean the church. After all, this could mean a treat, a few kind words, a pat on the head, or maybe even a promise that one might go to heaven. During Easter, lines of unfortunate little girls spent many hours on their hands and knees, with small cans of gasoline and little square pieces of cloth, cleaning the wax and dirt off the church floor.

Although I never aspired to this privilege, I was chosen when I was in fifth grade. For several days after I suffered with severe headaches and with an upset stomach. To this day the scent of gasoline gives me a horrible headache and a queasy stomach.

Eventually, mass was finally ready to begin, and the priest came in wearing a long white gown over a black robe, with a very unusual black cap covering his head. As a child, I thought the priests shaved spots on the tops of their heads and the caps were worn to cover those spots. The mass, which seemed to last for hours, was said in Latin. We did not understand what was being said or know what was going on, but we bowed our heads and folded our hands in front of us. All we knew was that we had to be silent and act respectfully humble. We knew that somewhere behind us sat a nun who would swiftly dispense punishment if we didn't mimic the nun in front of us, kneel when she knelt, stand when she stood. I often wondered what would happen if the nun laughed. An infectious laugh, the kind that would sweep through and make everyone happy. Of course, it never happened.

On Friday evenings, two priests listened to confessions. I remember one of my older cousins telling about a priest who was a strict disciplinarian. He treated the Indian people with a paternalistic air, most often like naughty children. He especially seemed to delight in thumping the boys on the head, leaving welts on their foreheads.

On confession days, two confessionals were available, but no one wanted to go into this priest's confessional. A nun seeing the long line at one of the confessionals divided the lines into equal groups. Loud comments such as, "You didn't! You beast! You dog!" came from this priest's confessional. Then a very embarrassed child with a sheepish grin would emerge while the other children would cover their mouths to stop their fits of laughter. The confessional wasn't the only place where people avoided this priest. When he believed some were misbehaving, they felt his authoritarian wrath. Most often it was the little boys on the receiving end. When this priest died, the boys were allowed to file by for viewing. My cousin told me that when the adults were not looking, some of the little boys thumped the dead priest on the head.

As I got older, I tried to avoid going to confession. I still remember the prayers, "bless me father for I have sinned. . . ." I could not think of the sins I had committed, so I told the priest I had bad thoughts. I was thinking about how I felt about the nuns' cruel behaviors. He persisted in questioning me about my bad thoughts. Were these bad thoughts about boys? Did I want boys to touch my body? I could not answer because I did not know what he was talking about. Overcome with shame, I never mentioned bad thoughts in the confessional again.

Hunger made some of the children faint in church. Dropping here and there, they were picked up, shaken by the nun, and sat on the benches until mass was over. The children who passed out from hunger were helped to their feet by other children. Then we all marched quietly back to the playroom. Once in the playroom, we quietly lined up for breakfast. We became experts in marching in straight lines. We filed into the dining room and lined up along the long tables. Everyone knew where they were supposed to be; the smaller girls followed the example of the older girls. We stood by the table until a nun blew a whistle and then we said the meal prayer together. "Bless us oh Lord, and these thy gifts. . . ." Then she blew the whistle again and we sat down to eat.

The meals were very sparse at St. Francis. Every morning big bowls of mush, milk, and bread were placed on each table by the older girls. Some mornings we got soup that was left over from the day before. At lunch time we had a variety of foods, and every evening we had some type of watery soup with barley or vegetables and a few slivers of meat. Bread, butter, and milk were passed around the table. To insure that everyone got something to eat, older students sat at the end of each table. There were times when older children took more than their share, so the smaller children did without. Hunger made us appreciate whatever we got. I remember one time finding worms in my soup. I pushed them aside and ate the soup anyway.

Those of us who spoke only Lakota were especially cautious. Not knowing what to do, we learned to always wait and watch before we did anything. We often tried to guess what was expected of us, but if we did the wrong thing, we were punished.

Only a certain amount of time was allowed for the meal; everyone ate quickly and quietly. Then the whistle was blown again. We stood up and said another prayer, "We give thee thanks, Almighty God, for all your benefits. . . ." Then the nun blew the whistle one last time and we quietly marched out.

The older girls stayed to clean the dining room, clearing and wiping the tables, mopping the floors, and washing dishes. The little girls went back to the play room. Without toys, we became very creative. We played tag and hopscotch. If we had paper and pencils or crayons, we drew dolls and designed clothes for our paper dolls.

During my first year, I also missed my brother and uncle terribly. I had not seen them since the beginning of the school year. I searched for their faces in every group of boys I saw. I searched as we waited in line to leave the dining room. When I finally spotted them in a sea of faces, they seemed glad to see me. I was so relieved. I forgot myself and waved to them. I was promptly jabbed in the back, but I at least knew they were still there and okay.

By eight o'clock we were in the classrooms studying. Boys and girls were taught by the nuns from first to third or fourth grade. The priests taught the older boys, while the nuns taught the older girls. The lessons were presented in a very rigid and cold way, setting the tone for the day. I imagine this was their way of discouraging us from speaking Lakota.

Children were afraid to ask to go to the bathroom. Sometimes the nuns ridiculed us or sometimes they accused us of finding excuses to leave the classroom. I didn't know which was worse, being punished for an accident or being ridiculed and accused of dishonesty. I certainly didn't think going to an outdoor bathroom in the middle of winter was fun. Once in first grade I was afraid to ask to go to the bathroom, so I waited until the last possible moment. When I finally had the courage to ask, I ran all the way but I did not make it. I sat in the bathroom quietly crying, not knowing what to do, until an older cousin accidentally found me. She somehow got into the building, found clean underwear, and cleaned me up. She sent me back to the classroom, warning me not to say anything to the nun because I would be punished.

Eventually I felt totally isolated. I was afraid to speak. If I spoke Lakota I was punished; if I spoke broken English I was ridiculed; and if I was too quiet I was called "buck Indian." "Buck Indian" could mean stupidity for not understanding English, it could mean having poor hygiene. Being too quiet or shy meant being "backward." I do not know where the term "buck Indian" originated, but even today some Lakota people use that term. Not realizing they internalized their oppression, they ridicule others by calling them "bucky" or "buck Indian."

The afternoon was class time for the younger students. For older students afternoon was a time to learn different skills. The boys worked at the dairy barn, or the shoe shop, carpenter shop, or the greenhouse which was right next to the girls' playground. For the girls, it was the laundry room, the dining room, the kitchen, or the sewing room.

Today, when boarding school survivors get together, we talk about the many things that happened during this time. These discussions either validate what we experienced or invoke memories which grow more vivid. One person saying, "Oh, I remember when that happened," or "That happened to me too." I will write only about the things I personally experienced or know about. No matter where we were, it seems we were constantly watched and controlled. One incident sticks in my mind. Even while on kitchen detail we were reminded of the cruelty some people are capable of committing. This incident occurred in the kitchen and was devastating to the girls involved. Apparently the nun who supervised the kitchen detail sent two girls into the cellar to bring up potatoes for the next meal. While there, they discovered a litter of kittens. When the nun found the girls cuddling the kittens, she placed the kittens into a gunny sack and drowned them in a bucket of water. The girls became hysterical. These girls came from very devout assimilated families who visited them during church holidays. The nuns transferred these girls to other work areas. Had these girls come from traditional Lakota families they would have been kept in the kitchen. The nuns knew that if this incident became known by the tribe there would have been strong criticism. The nun who drowned the kittens was transferred out the following year.

Assimilated families were generally those who had long-standing family ties with Christianity and the Bureau of Indian Affairs. They were free from old allegiances to the tribe and more open to new ideas and opinions. They believed strongly that in order to succeed they had to distance themselves from their Lakota heritage, culture, and language; most claimed to be more French than Indian. They were quiet to the severe discipline and abuse administered by the Catholic church and government to the traditionalists. The progressive traditionalists were those Lakota such as Chief Spotted Tail, who realized that in order for the children to succeed they must learn to read, write, and speak English, but they also believed the children would be able to adapt Lakota culture and language to mainstream society and vice versa. At the other end of the spectrum were the traditionalists who deliberately tried to keep their children out of school. However, the progressive traditionalist and traditionalist traveled a difficult road because educational materials and methods were not adapted to give them a realistic chance for school success. In fact, many of the concepts taught, such as competition and materialism, were a direct contradiction to Lakota beliefs and culture. Rivalries between the traditionalists and progressive traditionalists and assimilated progressives surfaced in the political arena as well as in other areas. The progressive assimilated had an advantage over the traditionalists because of their willingness to cooperate with the assimilation policies. Because of the attitude in the schools toward traditional children, they had a more difficult time adjusting and staying in school.

Getting back to my story, St. Francis grew most of the food needed for the children. Every fall the potato fields were plowed up before we rode rattling flat bed trucks into the fields. Teams of three to four children competed against each other, dragging and filling the heavy gunny sacks with potatoes. The team that picked the most potatoes received candy bars. As we picked the last of the potatoes, boys raked the dead plants into piles and set them on fire. As we passed by we tossed potatoes into the fire hoping that they would be baked by the time we passed through again. Eventually we learned that eating too many nearly raw potatoes caused us to suffer from gas pains. After a day of picking potatoes, we were exhausted and fell into bed each night. In the spring, teams of children cut the potatoes for planting, again competing for candy.

It seemed we were constantly hungry. I remember one time, a

Brother, who was in charge of the greenhouse, came out into the girls' playground carrying a bushel basket of carrots, throwing them on the ground like he was feeding chickens. We scrambled for this treat. Days later one of my friends and I played close to the greenhouse, hoping he would again come out with the carrots. When we saw him working around the vegetable garden, my friend said, "Let's go over and see him; he'll give us candy if we sit on his lap." When we approached, I saw the look on his face and decided it was not safe to be around him. Later, when she came back with candy and offered me some, I refused. Somehow I knew something was wrong.

Of the many images and memories from this time in my life, one remains that affected my love of music. Free time began after class until supper time. For several years, this free time was when I had piano lessons. My father, who was a talented musician, wanted his children to learn about music. He managed to pay for piano lessons for me. He had no idea he had condemned me to outright torture. I started out by playing the scales. A ruler across my knuckles drew blood with every wrong note I played. The punishment gradually got worse. Sometimes the ruler ended up making welts on the top of my head. I returned to the playroom with swollen eyes from crying. Finally, I decided I had enough. I wanted to escape, to insulate myself. I wanted to hide from all things cruel and hard, fit into the smallest places, behind . . . underneath . . . or maybe inside. . . . So I hid out on the playground, but I was discovered and punished more severely for being sneaky. Another time I went to the music room early, I sat and worried about the coming lesson and punishment. I became so afraid I hid behind the piano when I heard her steps echo through the vacant hall. I held my breath hoping she would not hear the rapid beating of my heart. I heard her open the door and grumble as she went looking for me. I fell asleep as I waited behind the piano. When I finally woke up I had missed the lesson and supper, and I could not get back into the playroom, because of the locked door. I was punished again. I was relieved when my father could no longer afford the lessons.

We were allowed to go out on the playground on warm days. It was a wonderful break from the dingy atmosphere of the playroom. The playground was a place where there were no locked doors. Usually we played, drawing pictures of our homes and families in the dirt with sticks and telling stories. Other times we made little altars with small stones among the weeds, pretending to pray. There was a brief free time after supper for the younger students; then it was bedtime. Some evenings there was Bible study. The older students had a study period every evening. All lights were out by nine.

There were times we got away with speaking Lakota. We sat underneath the ping-pong table in the playroom and spoke Lakota to each other. Other times we sat along the fence on the playground as far as possible from the buildings so we would not get caught. However, the nuns were watchful: they would appear soundlessly and punish us. Once I was jerked out from underneath the table by the hair. I especially liked to sit out on the playground when the south wind blew. I had been taught that the south wind carried a spiritual message. The sound created a live force, my ancestors whispered to me in the wind. I knew that if I listened closely enough, spiritual messengers would tell me that I was not alone. After my great-grandmother died, I imagined that I heard her voice in the wind, singing a lullaby as she did to comfort me when I was troubled or when I could not sleep. Then I felt even more strongly that the south wind brought me spirit allies and this made me more determined to endure this test of mind and spirit. It kept me from settling into a pattern of resignation. Of course, I never spoke of such things to anyone. What my captors did know about me constituted a mere fraction of my Lakota world. What really mattered to them was the success of their acculturation policy.

During these times on the playground, we thought we could detect a nun approaching by listening for the jingle of her keys as she walked. Sometimes she outmaneuvered us by holding her keys. We learned to be ever vigilant, because the consequences of being caught were cracks on the knuckles with a ruler that drew blood, and sore knees from kneeling in corners. After a time, some of the girls I played with were afraid to speak to me. We had already been caught speaking Lakota under the ping-pong table, and on the playground. Even if we whispered to one another, the nuns thought we were speaking Lakota.

In second grade, I was taken to the Mother Superior's office by my teacher who thought I was not trying hard enough to pronounce English words correctly. She wanted me to pronounce the word "little" for the Mother Superior. Mother Superior glanced up from her writing as we entered her office. She seemed irritated to see me again. Her cold eyes and hard mouth caused me to shudder. I recall her angry voice rising as she solemnly waited for me to pronounce the word "little," pursing her lips in stern disapproval. I was so afraid that I stood there trembling, feeling guilty. I already knew that I was going to disappoint her. With a hesitant tremulous voice, I tried, pronouncing each syllable of the word like a word itself. I pronounced it "lit-tool." She slammed her heavy hands down on the desk, startling me, causing me to shrink back. She stood towering over me, her face red with rage. She saw me as an unteachable and willful child. She caught my cheek in a pinch hold and her furious tongue lashing began. She said, "This is why you get into trouble; you can't even pronounce a simple word like little. If you are brought to me one more time, young lady, you will be sorry!" I willed myself to endure, and my expressionless face hid my fear. I didn't know what the punishment would be but I knew it would be worse than a pinch hold that left a bruise on my cheek.

Almost every afternoon around 3:30 a ringing bell signaled us that it was "bun time." The smell of freshly-baked bread always delighted the children. They scampered into line with excited cries, swarming, hoping there would be enough for all. When there was not enough, the children happily shared. Fortunate children who received jam or peanut butter in care packages from home shared with their many friends. We devoured the buns and we licked our fingers, wanting to eat every last crumb. I never received peanut butter or jam from home, but one time, my great-grandmother sent wasna, a mixture of dried meat and dried chokecherries or berries. We felt very special as we shared our long journey food. Wasna is a compact and nutritious food carried when people travel on a long journey.

In the spring, we were allowed to go to the boys' playground on Sundays to see our brothers. We saved our buns for them because we knew they were hungry. My older brother and uncle came over to see how we were faring and then they would go off to play. I carried a comb and combed my little brother's hair while he ate his bun. The only other time we saw our brothers and other male relatives was when our parents came to visit us.

I knew when my great-grandparents came to St. Francis Mission. I recognized my great-grandfather's cough in church. I would turn and quickly look to see if my great-grandmother was with him, but she never was. Although there were times when I didn't see or hear him, I knew he had been there to check on us because he left a quarter for each of us at the school store. That meant that we could buy a candy bar for a nickel. The nuns kept a record of the money the parents and relatives left for the children. Other than combs, peanut butter and jam, crayons, pencils and paper, we were not allowed to have any personal possessions and this included money.

As time passed we knew what the nuns expected of us. Corporal punishment seemed to be next to kneeling as a favorite punishment. It was a common sight to see children kneeling in the corners of the playroom or dormitory. If the nuns didn't have time to punish children during the day, they were punished at bedtime. This gave students time to reflect on their infractions. However, many students didn't remember what they had done wrong by the time the punishment was administered. There were times when the nuns forgot about the children kneeling in the corners. I remember waking up in the middle of the night seeing children curled up in a fetal position sleeping on the cold hardwood floor. They did not dare leave their corners because of the threat of worsh punishments.

Corporal punishment was being slapped in the face, a twisting pinch on the cheek, having one's hair pulled, or a whipping with a strap or a paddle. There were two types of paddles. One was a ping-pong paddle, the other was a long rectangular board with holes on one end and a handle on the other end. The number of swats was determined by the infraction. Sometimes, we were made to watch the paddling. Other times it was done out of the room, but we could still hear the swats and the crying. Being paddled in front of other students was the most humiliating, therefore the most psychologically effective. For me, verbal inquisitions were the worst punishments, because I had never been spoken to by an adult in such a humiliating way.

One day I found out how the paddle with the holes worked. My cousin and I were playing in the playground and we decided to jump over the trench that was being dug for the outdoor bathroom. We were told to stay away from the trench, but when the whistle was blown, we jumped over the trench as we ran for the playroom. The nun grabbed us both, and told us we had disobeyed her. We had always been careful not to appear fearful. As early as I can remember we got subtle messages from our relatives that it was not Lakota to appear fearful. She asked my cousin how many swats she thought she deserved. My cousin not knowing what to say tried to prove her bravery; she said, "ten." I thought, "She really doesn't understand the question." When it came to me I was not as brave. I said "one." The rectangular paddle was used on me. The blow sent me flying across the room. The holes drilled in the board left blood blisters on the back of my thighs.

After so many infractions or demerits, we were not allowed to go to the Saturday night movie. The movies were usually about war between Hollywood cowboys and Indians, or the perils of immigrants traveling west in a wagon train led by a Bible-carrying wagon master. Stage coaches rattled across deserts and open prairies while being attacked by "wild savages." Usually, Indians with dirty matted braided wigs outnumbered cowboys with cool hats and boots who somehow managed to hold off the shrieking painted savages, as they charged and circled the stagecoaches or wagon trains. Whatever the theme of the movie, there was always a clear-cut message: it was battle between good and evil. The success of the indoctrination was evident when the Lakota children cheered the cavalry as they came charging over the hills just in time to save the innocent immigrant women and children.

While the good children were at the movie, the bad ones sat in a classroom copying pages out of the Bible. A certain number of pages was assigned to each student and no one was allowed to go to bed until all the pages were completed. Demerits were posted so everyone could read about the alleged misbehavior. I read the list often to see the reasons for punishment. One time "for whistling in the hallway" was written after my name. I never learned to whistle but I did try, mostly just blowing air. As the years passed, the only feelings I had toward these nuns were feelings of resentment and fear. How could I be expected to feel any warmth toward my captors.

In my seventh year, I felt like a captive in an alien society. I began to rebel. Their final answer to the problem of how to Christianize Lakota children was not the answer for me. I developed a callous on my finger from copying pages out of the Bible. I developed thick callouses on my knees from kneeling. I felt I lived in a Catholic continuum, from the brutal efficiency of the punishing nuns to the wrath of their God.

Christianity was an ever-present dimension in my life. I learned I was on the long road to the fiery pit of hell; I learned about sin and guilt; I learned about devils and purgatory. If I was good, I was told, I would go to heaven, a heaven with fluffy white clouds and little white angels and with golden gates that were guarded by a white man named Peter. I learned to fear the righteousness of God, a hostile God with harmful powers ready to strike out at a little heathen child who would not give up her language and her Lakota ways.

I became more and more determined to not to break under the trials and hardships I endured. My passive smile was a mask covering my inner thoughts. I concealed my disrespect and my fear. I was still Lakota and proud. Their superior attitude led them to believe there could not be any thoughts in my backward little mind. They had taken my freedom of choice, and my personal autonomy, and insisted on conformity. They had isolated and divided my peers with their favoritism, their regulations, and their religion.

Their religion dictated to us and gave us conflicting messages. They did not respect me as a Wakanyeja, a unique being and spirit; they did not even respect their God for creating me. They did not respect my individual worth and qualities as my grandparents and great-grandparents had done.

School and home were unconnected realities. At home I had been given the freedom to make my own mistakes, and learn from my experiences. I had been taught that when I made a mistake, it was my responsibility to set it right. I had not been burdened with guilt. I had not been threatened with punishment, here or in the afterlife. I had not been treated as a sinner. Hating might have come easily in this life of injustices and forced assimilation, but I tried to remember my Grandma Julie's words. "Being angry and hating is an individual decision but hating is wrong, hating will hurt no one but you."

When it was needed, my relatives spoke to me about my behavior. They quietly shaped my worldview and influenced my outlook on life. Coercion was not their way. They had faith and trust in me; they had patiently taught me right from wrong. However, the Lakota way was considered a permissive way of raising children by these apostles of the church.

In spite of all of this psychological warfare and abuse, I was resilient. I responded to this oppression with energy and will. Every year, September quickly passed into October, and then November, these months seemed to flash by, Christmas came with a two-week vacation. After Christmas the days dragged on and on; it felt like forever. I felt that spring would never come. I patiently waited for the meadow larks to return. Once I heard their songs and saw them on the playground fence, I knew my grandparents would come for me. My reality was the summer months with my relatives. The first few weeks at home, I stayed close to my grandmother. I walked and worked with her until I began to feel safe, and whole again. Until peace was restored in my mind, until my heart was renewed with the courage I needed to look at my situation as a challenge. The three months of tranquility ended too quickly. However, I somehow managed to cling to what I had learned about Lakota culture for the nine months I was separated from my relatives. I tried to act consistently with the values I had been taught at home: to be sensitive to others, to respect and to be respected, and to value the uniqueness of people. I tried.

As a small child, I had faith in the teachings of my relatives. In the summer months at family gatherings and at mealtimes, I heard of my ancestors' courage. Often my throat closed with emotion as I listened. I lived around the friable edges of those stories when I went back to school. I reminded myself often that the ultimate reality was that I had ancestors who were heroes and patriots. We intently listened as my grandfather told stories about the Lakota people. Weaving stories of how great Lakota leaders defended their way of life, their families, and the land that was rightfully theirs. I would hear about the values they lived by, about their generosity, fortitude, bravery, and wisdom. My grandfather knew what mattered most in this world. My role models at home demonstrated the goodness of these values.

Despite the boarding schools, there were students were taught and lived "Lakol Wicohan," Lakota culture and philosophy at home. There were also students who completely denied their heritage. Between these two extremes, there were students with varied degrees of acculturation. Many felt rejected by the white society, and yet they rejected their own heritage. They became shadows on the margins of both societies, and they didn't fit into either one. In truth, they didn't feel Indian anymore; they felt alone, and they tried to fit in the best they could. That was their way of surviving.

At school the students who refused to give up their heritage became a tightly knit group and developed a type of camaraderie, united against the enemy. These students were the dark-skinned ones who spoke Lakota in quiet voices. Later, many of them dropped out of school. Some of them stayed in school, while others returned after dropping out because their parents believed in the value of education and encouraged them to persist.

Meanwhile, the students who collaborated with those we considered to be the "enemy" learned the strategies of white society. As children, they didn't know the implications of the choice they had made or that their families had made for them. They were more successful in assimilating into mainstream society. These students came from strong Christianized families who idealized the teachings of the church. They reported us for speaking Lakota. They called us "buck Indians" and made fun of the way we spoke English. Many of these were the light-skinned mixed blood students who identified with and were favored by the nuns and priests. They denied their Indian heritage, saying "Oh, I'm very little Indian; I'm mostly French." They had been convinced that being Lakota and bilingual made them inferior. Many times these students didn't know they were oppressed. Today, they deny they were oppressed, and they deny their involvement in our oppression. They honor the silence of our pain, the pain that shaped us all. But we cannot focus blame on them, because they were only children then too.

I lived for the times when I would be allowed to go home. Home meant happiness, and acceptance, where trouble and harsh scolding voices were not heard. One of those special times was Christmas. The smell of cedar boughs, the golden glow of candles, and elders singing Christmas hymns in Lakota will always bring back happy childhood memories. Those loving memories will be told in stories to my grandchildren. These stories will contain the Christmas spirit I remember from my childhood because the Christmas spirit is parallel to Lakota teachings and values in many ways.

As a small child, I was fortunate to grow up in a community where the first language was Lakota. The Lakota language is the heart of Lakota culture and creates a sense of security and continuity in the relationship among tribal members. In traditional Lakota society, it was disrespectful to speak to an elder without addressing that person in kinship terms. These kinship customs held together our Oyate Sica tiospaye (Bad Nation community). Christmas was a joyful time that the whole community celebrated together. In the 1940s, most Lakota people traveled by horse-drawn wagons. I remember watching eagerly for the wagons to come to the little white church about half a mile from our house overlooking the valley where my great-grandparents still lived. Even the winter storms didn't stop the people. They arrived in their wagons, horses breathing white clouds of vapor. The men, warmly bundled from head to foot, quickly set up the tents and started the fires. Children tumbled out of the wagons where they had snuggled under blankets on the hay. Women quickly organized the campsite, hurriedly unpacking and cooking. Those not camping would carry their bedrolls into the community hall where they would bunk after the midnight festivities.

When I heard that my beloved Whirlwind Soldier great-grandparents had arrived at the church, I pestered my parents to walk over to the church with the menfolk, who went to greet the new arrivals and help them settle. My mother usually said that it was too cold for me to walk in the blowing snow. I would be disappointed; but I watched by the window, waiting patiently for my father to take us to the church.

Tents completely surrounded the church when we finally arrived. Smoke rose from the stove pipes sticking out of the top of the tents. My great-grandparents' white wall tent was always warm and cozy with a small wood stove in the center set into the ground to warm the ground as well as the tent. Folded colorful patchwork quilts and cushions were set up around the inside of the tent for seating. White canvas covered the ground. We carefully removed the snow from our shoes before we stepped into the tent.

My great-grandmother busily made "kabubu bread," sometimes called "cokin," a skillet bread. A large pot of coffee and a kettle of "papa" soup (dried meat) with "wastunkala" (dried corn) and "timpsila" (wild turnips) boiled on the stove. My great-grandmother offered these delicacies to all who entered. I remember the smells of the traditional foods, and the warmth and the happiness of that humble little shelter.

By evening, tinsel, candles, and cedar boughs decorated the church. A large pine Christmas tree decorated with a great assortment of homemade decorations stood in the center of the meeting room. Brightly wrapped presents and colorful homemade cotton sacks of candy and fruit surrounded the tree. Community members drew names to exchange presents. Tea, coffee, and soups simmered on the wood stove and boxes of cakes, pies, sandwiches, and homemade breads sat around it.

I never understood the Latin spoken during midnight mass, but the feeling of family togetherness was beautiful. The candles gave a warm golden glow to the face of my great-grandmother. I looked up at my tall great-grandfather, an olive green army surplus trench coat covering his broad shoulders. I tried to memorize his coppery colored high cheekbones, his square jaw, his eyes almost gray from cataracts, in preparation for the time when I would be separated from him again. His strong callused hands folded as he humbly bowed his head in prayer.

After mass, children happily accepted the bright candy and fruit snacks. Elders exchanged beautiful homemade pillows, aprons, scarves, and quilts. They made speeches and remembered those who had traveled southward to the spirit world with prayers. Then the Oyate Sica tiospaye ate their Christmas feast—happy to be together again for another Christmas.

That night I was allowed to spend the night with my great-grandparents. I remember being tucked into a warm bundle of blankets. I went to sleep listening to the brave heart stories of my ancestors. Sometime during the freezing night I heard my great-grandfather get up to add more wood to the fire.

The kindred Lakota spirits of my great-grandparents, George and Elizabeth Cook Whirlwind Soldier, shaped my beliefs and values. Their devotion to the children in the community set an example for me. We didn't know we were poor, but we did know we were loved, as shown by the gentleness, the hospitality, and generosity of all who lived around us.

The population of Oyate Sica dwindled slowly. One family at a time moved to find jobs and to keep their children from being sent away to boarding schools. Today, we all gather on Memorial Day at our cemetery. We remember the proud and independent people of Oyate Sica as we offer spirit food and reminisce about the happy days of our childhoods. The scent of cedar and the golden glow of candles on a cozy winter night will always bring back the memories of my tiospaye—the Oyate Sica.

In the fall of my seventh grade year, two important things happened that changed my life: my parents decided to separate, and I met a friend named May.

At that time, I did not actually know what divorce meant, but I was relieved that my mother would be happier. Because of the divorce, my parents were threatened with excommunication from the church. When my father returned from the Army, he began drinking. After my great-grandmother died, it seemed he did not care anymore and his drinking began to cause havoc in our family. The divorce meant that we would live with my paternal Whirlwind Soldier grandparents in the summers. I rejoiced when I found out that I would not be allowed to return to St. Francis Mission for my eighth grade year unless my parents reconsidered their decision to divorce.

It had been a struggle to keep my identity intact at St. Francis. I had felt that my roots were being torn from me. Yet I could not leave my ancient generational past behind. In fourth grade when we were learning American history, I waited for the nun to teach us the Lakota history I had heard at home, but in school we learned about the Pilgrims and how they brought Thanksgiving to the Americas.

American Indians were not mentioned after that. After several days of listening to the hardships of the immigrants and their westward migration, I finally asked about the Lakota. I asked where we fit into this scheme of history. Where was the history of my people? I got the distinct impression that in my teacher's opinion the land was empty, ready for the taking. According to her, the people who lived on this land were few and wandered aimlessly, not really using the land. So the nun was taken back by my question. She did not answer right away while she thought about it, but finally said, "Why Lydia, this is your history, this is American history." I knew this was not true. American history, the way it is taught in the schools, is not the history of my people. Even at that age, I began to feel that I was losing my place in the world. My people were not important enough to be mentioned or to be learned about.

Values I had been taught at home seemed not to apply at St. Francis. I had been taught to be respectful, and I had always been treated with respect. However, because of the treatment I received at St. Francis I had begun to settle into a pattern of disrespectfulness and defiance toward adults and toward the Catholic Church. At any rate, my seventh grade year would have probably been my last year at St. Francis because of my behavior. I did not care anymore.

I remember once telling my father about what happened to the "runaways," and how often I felt like running away from St. Francis Mission. When the runaways were caught, they were brought back. Their hair was cut with scissors, snipped here and there, chopped at different lengths in spiky disorder. Then they were dressed in rummage clothes sent by the "good Catholics" in the east—misshapen black crepe dresses, or dresses splashed with bright flowers, large and ugly, faded woolen sweaters shrunk with hot water and stretched out of shape, mismatched socks and high-heeled shoes. The runaways' faces were painted with exaggerated black eyebrows, and bright red lips and rouge on their cheeks. Signs hung around their necks that simply read, "I ran away." This was done to humiliate them, and to discourage the rest of us from running away. Then they were put on display: they stood in the halls as we marched through to the dining room, and we were told to look at them. They stood against the wall of the dining room eating so they could be seen. They had been locked in the attic for several days before they were brought down for viewing. One of my friends told me she had to carry food up to them at meal times.

One runaway had her natural curls chopped off, each section of her hair cut in different lengths, the longest being two inches. So she took a scissors and tried to straighten up the cut. To the disappointment of the nuns, the girls began telling her how cute her hair looked with her natural curls closely shaped around her face. When I told my father this, he said, "I don't ever want you to run away from anything; once you run, you will never have the courage to face difficult things in your life. Besides," he said, "I'll take you right back." But even if I had decided to run, I didn't know which direction to go. Bad Nation seemed so far away. All I could perceive of the distance was the long hours of driving it took my grandparents to come to St. Francis. We were told that if we ran away we would get lost in the canyons and would be eaten by the bobcats that lived in the area. I remember a boy who ran away at Christmas time during a winter storm. Search parties looked for him but they did not find him until the following spring. His skeleton was found and identified by a bag of marbles clutched in his hand.

In my seventh grade year I made friends with May. I don't remember when and how May came to be at St. Francis. I just noticed her one day and liked her. She was wearing a uniform like the rest of us, but there was something different about her. Her curly hair was brushed back from her friendly face. She seemed to be older than the rest of us. Actually, she picked my cousin and me as friends. I watched her fill out order forms from her collection of clothing catalogs. When she invited us to help her pick out clothes, we were thrilled. We looked at the catalogs, checking off the clothing and shoes in the colors she liked. Then she would fill out the order forms, saying she would mail them the next day. I don't remember that she ever received any of the clothes she ordered. All letters were given to the nuns to be censored before they were mailed. The nuns blacked out words and sentences they felt were inappropriate, and told us they would mail them. Although I wrote many letters when I learned to write, I never received any letters from home. Maybe it had something to do with the complaints I had about the treatment and the food.

May did receive packages from home. She got crayons, paper, and pencils. On Sundays we spent hours drawing paper dolls and designing clothes with matching shoes, coats, and gloves similar to the ones we saw in the catalogs. We dreamed of owning clothes that would be like the ones we designed. May also shared her peanut butter and jam with us at bun time. She opened cans of peaches and pears and shared them too. She combed and curled our hair. I can imagine how comical we must have looked sitting next to the potbelly stove with pin curls in our hair. She would take off our shoes and polish them. We knew we were not allowed to paint our nails as we looked at her collection of nail polish. But it felt wonderful to have someone caring for us. She was like an older sister I never had. I admired her and followed her around, imitating her haughtiness. She sat up late at night after the lights were turned off to curl her hair. She somehow avoided being caught and punished.

May kept her catalogs and other belongings in her locker. We were allowed to keep such things as crayons, coloring books, paper dolls, and jack stones in our lockers. However, we could not keep our own clothing that we had brought from home. These were taken from us at the beginning of the year when we were given uniforms and returned to us at the end of the year when we were allowed to go home. May had a padlock and wore the key on a string around her neck. I had never owned any of the things she had, so I thought it was a treat when she let me open her locker with her key.

The nuns didn't like May because she was not one of the willing flock and did not appear weak. They accused her of being a bad influence and punished her for infractions at every opportunity. "Sit straight," "Chew with your mouth closed," "Be quiet," "Keep your elbows off the table," they said. She didn't sit up straight enough in her desk and got five demerits for that. She didn't have her work in on time, five more demerits. She was late lining up for mass, more demerits. After a time, May was not allowed any privileges. I sympathized with her and started doing some of the same things she did, and each time I was also given demerits. Every Saturday night, May and I and other children were banished to a classroom where we were assigned to copy many pages out of the Bible. There we sat for hours writing while the other students went to a movie.

One Saturday night, we did not feel much like copying Bible verses. The letters seemed so small, and we knew it would take us hours to complete our punishment. We knew there would be trouble for us if we did not. So we sat writing, until May picked up the paper she was writing on, crumbled it up, and said, "I am not doing this anymore." She threw the paper at the supervising nun and it landed near her desk. The nun stood up. She was a tall woman, a good three inches taller than May. She came around the desk, grabbed May by the hair and said, "Now you pick that up!" Even though she dragged May around by the hair and pushed her face into the floor, she still could not make May pick up the paper. May was quick and fast on her feet, but she could not get away. She held up her left arm defensively close to her face and head, trying to protect herself. She tried to pull away from the nun and wipe the blood that trickled down between her nose and mouth with the back of her hand while the nun pulled her hair and struck her in the face. I stared at them, holding my breath in silence, wishing there was something I could do to help May. She struggled to free her hair and fought back. In the struggle she pulled the nun's veil to the side of her head. There was disbelief in the nun's eyes. She looked stunned by May's actions. "Idiot, how dare you lay a hand on me!" she screamed. Her weakness exposed, she was suddenly afraid of May and ran into the hallway.

May stood tall and strong. She had marks on her face that would soon turn to bruises, and blood dripped from her nose. The air in the room was muddled with fear, and the strained silence made me fearful as we quietly waited for the inevitable. Whatever the rules were in this game, May never learned to play and she didn't care. We looked at each other and smiled, almost laughed. I thought about the nun's veil. We had always wondered if the nuns were bald or if they shaved their heads. We had almost found out. We didn't know what was going to happen, but we knew we were all in trouble.

After twenty agonizing minutes, the nun returned with another nun. I saw the dull flush of anger on her face. They grabbed May, beating her to the floor as they dragged her into the hallway. I heard May cry out. The sounds frightened me. I imagined the thumping of feet against ribs, I heard the thuds against the wall and May's muffled cries. Finally, silence. I sat with my head down. Feeling a lump in my throat, I thought "I cannot cry now." Then the door opened and closed as the nun swiftly returned to the room breathing heavily, agitated, anger surging and filling her predatory eyes. She folded her arms in front of her and faced me. "Stand up," she shrieked. When I stood up, she again shrieked, "Do you want some of the same?" The room was absolutely quiet. Her palely lit menacing eyes flitted between me and the other girls' impassive faces. Although they sat quietly at their desks, we knew of guilt by association. Her words penetrated me and left me disturbed and fearful. The expression on her face warned everyone she would not put up with rebellion. She was determined to make an example of May.

I looked at the floor trying to detach myself from the fear and anger I felt. She wanted me to grovel. She stared at me, her arms folded in front of her, daring me to argue, daring me not to be afraid, fear would let her know that she had won. I felt my heart turn as cold as her heart. I gripped my hands tightly behind me, taking an involuntary step backwards. She knew I was afraid. My adrenaline was up, I braced for the blows. I resented the fear I felt. I knew she was looking for a reason to hit me. I sat down quietly in my desk, trying to appear unaffected. I wondered how and when I would experience the same beating. It would be nothing new to me. I thought of their hypocritical words, "Blessed are the meek, for they shall inherit the earth."

My Lakota teachings had more meaning to me than did their "theology." I believe in the great mystery called eternity. I was taught all creation, even Lakota children, are part of the great mystery. That great mystery is everywhere. This concept is Mitakuye Oyasin: we are related to all of creation. But the nuns discounted our Lakota philosophy and religion and wanted to beat it out of us. They called our philosophy "nature worship." We called it spirituality. They also called our rituals devil worship. But we know our rituals attract positive energy, reinforce Lakota teachings, and prevent violence, anger, and all other negative energies.

To my surprise, the nun told me to finish what I had been copying out of the Bible, read the Lord's Prayer, and then go to bed. She was now in command of the situation. I was not a challenge to her authority and she knew I was afraid. I was just a skinny little eleven-year-old, who had never fought or even hit another human being.

After I finished, I walked into the cold, gloomy hallway. All the doors along the hall were closed. I climbed to the head of the dark stairway and looked around for May, but I did not see her. I thought maybe she ran away and I didn't want her to leave me behind. I raced back down the stairs, two at a time, and rushed back down the hall, wanting to shout out her name. I forced myself to stop. I stood there until my heartbeat slowed down. Breathing heavily, I returned to the dark and silent dorm and to my bed. I felt like screaming, "I hate this place, I hate everything about this place, I hate the locked doors, I hate the nuns watching us every minute, waiting for us to do something wrong." Tears filled my eyes; I was angry enough to cry. I thought, "They always seemed to know what was bad and tainted and judged me as fitting into that pattern of thought."

Trembling with fear and anger, I crawled under my blanket. I knew I was locked in and that even if I wanted to run away, I could not. I stared out at the huge snowflakes that floated past the metal mesh and stuck to the window.

Under the flurry of snow, a road out there would take me home. By now I knew that I would have to go north and avoid the roads if I wanted to get home. The wind began picking up, driving the snowflakes steadily against the window, hurling them against the pine trees east of the dormitory. It blew the snow out of the trees where it had collected on the branches. I hoped May was not out there in the storm. I looked around the dorm and directly at the pot-belly stove. I felt they had tried to incinerate my Lakota spirit and my beliefs. Their diabolic agent who lived within that stove licked at the cracks near the door of the stove. I was glad I did not sleep close to it.

I lay in my bed and thought about the story my grandfather told, his face wet with tears, of his sister dying in the little girls' dorm during a flu epidemic. When my great-grandparents heard from a runaway that she was ill, it had been too late. My great-grandfather hired a car to bring him to St. Francis to check on his children. He pounded on the door until they finally let him in. He went through the dormitory, lifting the sheets off the faces of the dead children until he found his daughter. He wrapped her in a blanket and carried her out, with the nuns protesting. The Bureau of Indian Affairs police followed at a safe distance, afraid they would catch the flu. He brought her home and buried her in Bad Nation.

I thought of the spirits of those little children, most buried here in the Catholic cemetery, sometimes several in each grave. I thought about the tears that ran down my grandfather's face when he told this story, tears shed quietly and freely for an older sister whose tombstone faces the warm southern winds of summer. The only other time I saw tears on Grandfather's face was when his mother died.

I thought about the other separations. The first separation at St. Francis happened in my third grade year. That year, our teacher, a cruel charade of a woman, had been determined that all of us, but especially my cousin and I, would speak English correctly. Her erratic personality seemed to veer between fanatic intensity and cold distraction. The first day of school she had walked around with a red switch, whipping it in the air, telling us what she expected. It was a definite forecast of how my life would be changing from bad to even worse.

That year we had many welts on our faces and legs from that red switch. When things didn't go the way she planned, she stalked the room enraged. I learned to attach significance to the most subtle vocal inflection, and the most fleeting glance.

When there was a wild angry look on her face, we found out that switch could talk. It searched out all our misdeeds and it told us that we were evil children as it came down on our heads and across our faces. I often wished that she couldn't see me, but I knew that switch would find me. When one child was switched, it usually meant that other children would also get it. We learned to put our heads down to placate her when she started her ranting and raving. When she looked directly at me, her eyes were messengers of cruelty. I thought of switches and dark closets.

My spirit was beaten and tattered in the third grade. The first time she used the switch on me it caught me at an angle across my forehead and my eyelid. The swelling nearly closed my eye. I fought against being put into the closet, crying silent tears as I was overpowered and locked in. I struggled to breathe in the inky darkness; it was difficult because of the dusty chalk smell. I sank to the floor, and lay there trying to breathe. I put my nose next to the crack at the bottom of the door and drew shallow breaths trying not to draw the chalk dust into my lungs as I went to sleep. I knew that even if I prayed there was no one there to save me; my captors were representatives of God.

I wonder if any of the other nuns ever questioned where I got my injuries. I suspect that my injuries made perfect theological sense to the other nuns in this tight little world of Catholicism since I had been reported for speaking Lakota. This cleared their conscience.

I had hoped that the closet punishment would never happen to me. I remember walking by that closet to sharpen my pencil and hearing a child whimpering there. Years later, nightmares would jolt me awake from deep sleep, chalk suffocating me, closing my throat as I gasped for breath while my husband held me, telling me everything would be alright.

Our third grade teacher singled out my cousin to use as an example of what would happen when a child did not pronounce certain words correctly. She called on my cousin when she didn't even raise her hand, not that she ever would. When my cousin didn't answer she would call her to the front of the classroom. My cousin stood with innocent eyes, hoping for good will, her head lowered with her finger in her mouth. The nun asked her to pronounce certain words; each time she was unable to answer correctly the nun switched her across the face, berating her each time. The talking switch asked her why she could not answer correctly. When my cousin did not answer, the nun said she knew why. She said my cousin was still speaking that incoherent language. She switched my cousin's tear-flooded face, dragged her to the storage closet, and locked her in. This happened many times during the year, until my cousin did not speak Lakota anymore and she developed a habit of pulling little patches of hair from her scalp leaving bald spots on her head. The nun was determined to break her. When she could not, she held her back in third grade for another year. So I had to go onto fourth grade without her. I looked for her often during recess but she was usually kept from recess. It took many months before I adjusted to not having her in the same classroom with me. I worried about how she was being treated; I imagined her in the closet whimpering, with red welts on her face.

When I finally did see her, I anxiously asked how she was but she would not answer. When my cousin finally went on to fourth grade, her reputation for belligerence followed her. The fourth grade teacher did not hesitate to whip naughty children on their bare bottoms in front of the class and lock them in a closet. That summer at home, when I spoke to my cousin in Lakota, she answered only in English.

I lay in my bed thinking of all of these things, while wondering where May had gone. An hour later, May still had not returned. The children had come back from the movie. The sounds of children getting ready for bed, and the quiet talk about the movie, died away to silence. I tried to sleep, but I lay awake listening to the wind moaning through the mesh screens, thinking about May and how she had been like my big sister, taking care of me and comforting me in my illnesses and hurts.

I stayed awake most of the night waiting for May to return, but I never saw her again. I was told that her that parents had come after her. No one saw her leave, but her possessions disappeared overnight. In the weeks and months that followed, I asked about her many times. I often wondered what happened to her that night and I never forgot about her. The important lessons I learned from May was to enjoy the little things in life. I remember her positive outlook. I thought about the kind things she had done for me. She taught me that situations are never so bad that humor cannot be found. I thought about the fun we had, and about how we laughed, placing our hands over our mouths to control our fits of laughter so as not to get into trouble. She lived the values I had been taught. She left behind reminders of the importance of sharing, and kindness and lessons in fortitude.

Decades later, I asked a friend about May. She told me May had married and now lived with her husband and children on a reservation in a different state. I was glad to hear that she was well and happy.

After my seventh grade year in school, I left St. Francis in disgrace. My parents were divorced and excommunicated. The Catholics let us know in no uncertain terms that unless my mother and father reconsidered, we could not go to school at St. Francis. This was a reprieve for me. I was very happy about not going back, but I was afraid of the uncertainty of going to a new school.

Then my father remarried and signed up for the government relocation program. It was decided that we would go to Oakland, California. I was twelve years old and in the eighth grade. I spent the next half year in public school in California, entering into another world where I did not belong. I felt like a tangled tumbleweed blowing here and there. I did not belong anywhere, not in the world of the city, or in the schools at home. I didn't miss a day of school in California, but I felt completely alone. By the end of the semester, my father was ready to come home to the reservation. I was happy to come home, away from an abusive stepmother and back to the stability of my grandparents.

My mother had decided we were better off with my paternal grandparents because we had grown up in my father's "tiospaye" extended family. She knew we would be well taken care of and she had no home to take us to. I did not see her for the next two years. I did not hear her side of the story until after I was eighteen years old.

After we came home from California, my grandfather enrolled me into the government boarding school in Mission. In one school year, I had gone to two very different schools. I wondered what the Jesuits at St. Francis would think now. We were going to a school that didn't require us to go to church every morning. Meal prayers were not said, and we did not march to every activity. This was another cultural shock for me. Everything seemed so relaxed that I didn't know how to act.

I also could not believe the first breakfast at Rosebud Boarding School. We actually had pancakes, eggs, butter, bacon, orange juice, and milk. I carried my tray along a buffet style table while the servers filled my plate with food. I sat and stared at the food before I ate. We didn't eat this well at home. Lunch and dinner were just as good. It was not uncommon to have fried chicken, homemade bread, different stews thick with meat and vegetables, potatoes and gravy, salads, and meat loaf, food that we never had at St. Francis. They actually asked me if I had enough to eat, and told me that I could go for a second helping. Similar to St. Francis, we still had clean-up duties, but I did not mind because we were allowed to talk. I actually enjoyed the work. I wasn't hungry anymore, and I didn't have to worry about doing the wrong thing.

The matrons and my eighth grade teacher at the school were Native Americans. They spoke to us in quiet voices, and they laughed and talked with us. They knew many of our relatives. They let us choose our own beds for the year, next to our friends. We still had a curfew of 9:00 P.M., but we could bath or shower whenever we wanted to. The doors were locked only after curfew. I remember trying the doors many times during the day just to assure myself that I could walk through any door at any time. We were even allowed to wear our own clothes. We traded and borrowed each other's clothes, and we sat up nights visiting and curling each other's hair. We were even allowed to listen to records that some of the girls brought from home, and I learned how to dance.

That was a wonderful year for me. I had many friends and the freedom to do things that I had never done before. We went to town once a week, sometimes to a movie. When I didn't have money, one of the matrons let me iron clothes for her so I could earn spending money. We traveled on a bus to basketball games. I even tried wearing makeup. I had no idea my father would be upset when he saw me wearing lipstick. I quickly removed it when he told me I was too young and that he never wanted to see me wearing makeup again.

I was very embarrassed, especially because of the way my brothers looked at me. They agreed with my father. What he didn't know was my experimenting with cigarettes. I hung out with my friends in the smoke room. I thought I was in when I was given a cigarette. They told me suck in the smoke, take a deep breath, and inhale. It wasn't as fun as I thought it would be. I choked and coughed trying to catch my breath. The girls roared with laughter as one of them thumped me on the back as I gasped for breath. After that I pretended to inhale while I quickly blew the smoke out of my mouth.

The year came to a close with my eighth grade graduation. We were told about the man who had been selected to speak at our graduation, a well-known educated Native American. I was very excited when I saw a picture of him. He had accomplished much. He had a doctorate degree, and he had been elected to a powerful political position in the state. I was so proud and happy. Yes, my grandfather was right; Indian people could be successful in whatever they tried.

The day of graduation, I happily waited to hear the speaker. We were told he spoke fluent Lakota. I hoped he would speak to us in Lakota. I was so happy that I smiled at everyone. Soon my grandparents arrived, Homer Sr., and Julia Whirlwind Soldier. My grandfather wore a suit and tie. He had been on the tribal council many years and was anxious to hear the graduation speech. My beautiful petite grandmother's long braids encircled her fine delicate features, and her gentle smile acknowledged me as I waved at them. I sat with my class, excited and happy, waiting for the speech. I knew it was going to be inspirational, and I knew that if this man could be successful, I could be successful too. He started his speech, talking about his background, and his educational experiences. His final advice was, "Forget that you are Indian: being Indian will never get you anywhere." I sat there stunned. I put my head down as I blinked back tears. I didn't want to draw attention to my tears. I did not hear another word he spoke. I did not want to listen to this fraudulent Lakota. I had witnessed the power of Christianity over the Lakota and resented it. Now I saw the result of assimilation efforts, and I felt beaten.

After the graduation ceremony was over, I told my grandparents that I wanted to go home right away. Once we got home, I threw my eighth grade diploma on the table, with tears in my eyes. I said, "This is what you wanted me to do, I finished for you, but I will never go back." Then I cried. I had never spoken to my grandparents with such disrespect. I was ashamed. I never saw my diploma again. I did not want the reminder of my disappointment. My grandfather didn't say anything that day; he only looked at me. My grandmother sat down in her chair, also not saying anything.

That summer progressed the way of other summers in Bad Nation. I eventually put away my anger. We went horseback riding, hiking, and swimming. Some nights, we made our beds in the hay rack under a canopy of stars. My father's sister Grace told the soothing winter stories under the summer sky. These were the stories that had been told to Lakota children on cold winter nights for centuries. These stories fed my spirit with real life endings instead of the happily-ever-afters of the white school systems. They kept our language, culture, and history alive. Sometimes summer storms came up fast during the night, and then the thunder beings flashed their eyes across the night sky, woke us up and chased us into the house carrying our blankets and pillows.

I also helped my grandmother in the garden. We gathered chokecherries, grapes, plums, and buffalo berries and made the jams and syrups that we ate during our Thanksgiving and Christmas vacations. We also gathered plants and teas, washing and drying them to store for the winter.

I didn't think of school again, until about three weeks before it was to start. My grandfather talked about the importance of education. He said it was his dream to see all his grandchildren graduate from high school. He said he knew his grandchildren could be successful in anything they tried and he wanted them to have decent lives and be self-reliant. I did not say anything. I just listened.

At night I watched him read by the golden glow of the kerosene lamp. I can still see him today, he always wore a clean faded chambray shirt. Occasionally, he ran his hand through his thinning gray hair, his reading glasses resting on his thin Lakota nose. He had been the first vice president of the Rosebud Sioux Tribe after the Reorganization Act, and he had been a councilman most of his life. He had only finished eighth grade at St. Francis, yet he valued education. He studied the tribal laws, both civil and judicial. He studied the treaties, the Dawes Act, and the Reorganization Act, and he knew what the government had promised our people. He would be disappointed if I didn't finish school, yet he also wanted to give me a chance to make up my own mind. He talked about the importance of education. I agreed with him, but in my heart I did not know if I would survive if I went back. The graduation speech ran through my mind many times. I felt my spirit being attacked as I tried to hang on to my self-esteem and my identity.

That year I boarded at Rosebud Boarding School and attended the public school in Mission because the boarding school did not have a high school. The government built the new public school for the reservation children, but somehow the non-Indians on the reservation had control of the school. The school board was majority non-Indian. It was a definite example of apartheid. The majority was ruled by the minority. I was overwhelmed. My heart was not in going to school. The teachers knew nothing about me or my culture. The curriculum, a generic mainstream American curriculum, did not prepare me to work and live on the reservation. I was now going to school with many Lakota children who knew absolutely nothing about their culture and many of them did not care to know. I was just another backward Indian. I didn't do well that year, and I told my grandfather how unhappy I was. He knew I was not a child anymore and that I would probably drop out of school if something was not done. The following fall, he enrolled me in the Flandreau Indian School, a government boarding school located in eastern South Dakota. The students came from tribes from North Dakota, Wyoming, Montana, South Dakota, and Minnesota. I was thankful it wasn't another Christian boarding school.

When I thought about going away I worried about my little brothers and sister. I thought about my father and mother and how their actions affected my life. Every now and then they would reconcile for a brief time. I was glad that I would not have to listen to their arguments. Like any other child, I had hoped that they would work things out between them and that we would be a family again, but that didn't seem likely, because they were no longer consistently available to their children. They remembered every now and then that we needed clothes and winter coats, but my grandfather ended up being responsible for most of our needs. In the summer months my brothers and my sister and I lived with my grandparents, who were doing their best to raise us. I felt guilty that they had to raise six more children after raising their own. They never complained, but I still felt that I was a burden to them. So I did whatever I could to make life easier for my grandmother. I hauled water and helped her wash clothes. I tried my hand at cooking and washed dishes, and I helped take care of my brothers and my sister.

I went to Flandreau for the next three years, and time seemed to pass quickly. I tried to remember why I was there. I would think about what my grandfather said about education, yet I felt my heart was made of rawhide. By the end of that time, I had finally come to a point in my life when being away from my relatives was less painful. All my physical needs were being met. I had enough to eat; I was warm; I did not have to worry about anyone hitting me; and I had friends, both boys and girls. However, at times I retreated to my room and spent time alone, reading or sleeping. I realized that I had no respect for the white educational system firmly in place at Flandreau Indian School. I also had a belligerent attitude toward all clergy and anyone spouting verses from the Bible. I had no role models in a system that still seemed hell bent on changing me. The pressure for me to change was not as violent in Flandreau but still it was there, just more subtle and covert. For example, there were no activities that reflected the Indian student population. Even the Indian employees at the school held no pride in their identity; if they did, I never heard them speak of it. They didn't teach our own history and did not encourage us to speak our language.

One of the Indian matrons finally recommended that I see a counselor. I went to see him but I couldn't relate to him, so I decided not to go. He seemed distant and avoided looking at me in the eye. I eventually was told that I was depressed by this counselor. I know I had buried the emotional, verbal, and physical abuse at the bottom of a great deep pit; the pain inside that pit had been covered securely—I thought. But the grief had absolutely nowhere to go. I carried this heavy burden. I hoped that if I ignored it long enough, it would simply disappear.

I had taken my grandfather's advice. I knew he wanted what was best for me. I also knew that something was missing. I felt like a transient, displaced, and not belonging anywhere. It seemed there was no niche that I fit into, but I was still determined to make my grandparents proud of me. I thought I had to make up for the problems my father and mother had caused my grandparents.

Since my grandfather wanted me to be self-reliant I knew that I had to have some sort of training. The last year at Flandreau I went to see a career counselor. I told him that I had two first cousins who were registered nurses, both of whom spoke Lakota fluently. I thought I would like to become a nurse too. He asked me in a patronizing voice if I really thought I could become a nurse. "Perhaps it would be better if you became a hair stylist," he suggested. "But, if you have your heart set on the health field, maybe you could probably become a nurse's aid." I left his office without saying another word.

I finally graduated from Flandreau. I had at last accomplished what my grandfather wanted for me. But going to school in yet another system I had little faith in was very difficult for me. I had experienced institutional racism in every school I attended.

Even after graduation from Flandreau Indian School, the goals my grandfather had set for me still echoed in my mind. I wanted him to be proud of me, so I applied for a nursing program in Albuquerque, New Mexico, and was accepted. Instead of going on to school, I got married. Despite that change in plans, my grandfather was happy, because he thought I had chosen a good man to care for me.

My grandfather knew how I struggled to stay on the path he created for me. The stories he told me about our ancestors gave me something to hang on to. I thought of his words when I was completely discouraged. Today, when I visit my grandfather's grave, I tell him how much I appreciate the time he spent with me and the faith he had in me. He would not have been surprised that I ended up a teacher. I eventually admitted that I loved to read and I valued education as he did. When I graduated from Sinte Gleska University and went on to Pennsylvania State University, I felt his spirit was with me.

In 1994, I was relieved when I heard that the girls' dorm at St. Francis Mission was burning. Every time I passed through St. Francis, I looked at that building with haunting memories. Weeks later, I saw the clean up crew hauling away the rubble. No matter how deep those charred walls, rubble of tangled concrete, and rebar are buried, I know the ghosts of the abused will haunt the descendants of those who attended St. Francis Mission. The flames will not destroy the consequences of the injustices and abuse suffered by the children who attended that school. The lessons learned from the Jesuits and nuns will reverberate through our generations until a healing takes place.

Following the fire, a local newspaper published a letter of apology from the Jesuit Community of St. Francis Mission to the people of the Rosebud reservation concerning Jesuit treatment of Indian children. In my opinion this was a letter of excuses and justifications.

The Jesuits must face their responsibilities instead of justifying their abusive treatment of the children who attended St. Francis. Or blaming the government's assimilation policy and Chief Spotted Tail's "demand" for the Jesuits to come to the reservation and educate the Lakota children. (Educate us, yes, but not abuse us.)

Although the government did establish racist assimilation policies for the Native American tribes, people who live by the Christian doctrine still could not possibly justify the tactics they used against the Lakota people. They cannot be excused for zealously enforcing the government assimilation policy. Native American children suffered or died because of government policy enforced by the malevolent practices of the Christian churches. War criminals of World War II used the same excuses, blaming their superiors and their government's policies for killing six million Jews.

St. Francis Mission may have been only one cog in the machinery that enforced the assimilation policy for the Federal government. That one cog might be considered minor, but it was a very necessary part in the more complex process of destroying a nation of people. The machinery of assimilation or annihilation could not successfully function without that one cog.

We know that by the beginning of this century the number of Native Americans was reduced to fewer than one million. We were declared a "vanishing race" until the middle of this century. What humanitarian efforts did the Christian church use to protect us? Christians must have truly believed in destroying us, to be so successful in their attempts to acculturate us, to destroy our cultures and the children who were so trustfully put in their care.

Jesuits justified their church-affiliated school by stating that Chief Spotted Tail demanded that the churches educate the Lakota children. But Chief Spotted Tail was not in a position to demand anything from the government or the churches. He was a prisoner of war. He was never baptized or converted into Christianity. He asked. Asking is far different from demanding. He asked the churches to come to the reservation and establish their schools. He knew this was the only way he could keep the children at home. He saw how children were treated in the boarding schools when he visited his children and grandchildren at Carlisle Indian School in Pennsylvania.

He also believed in education. He knew that education would empower our people to run their own government. Spotted Tail realized that we as a "subjugated people" had no choice but to place our children in such institutions. He picked what he thought to be the lesser of two evils. If the children attended schools on the reservations, the parents would at least see their children occasionally and they would come home during the summer vacations. Native American students sent to schools in other states were not even allowed to come home. Many were placed in the homes of whites to work as servants during the summers, and after they finished school. Others were never seen again, because they were buried in distant graveyards. One of my maternal grandfathers was placed in a Quaker home in Pennsylvania, where he worked as a farm laborer for many years until he was finally allowed to returned home, speaking English with the "thee's" and "thou's" of the Quakers.

How ironic it was that this Jesuit letter of apology came out during the Christmas season. The literal teachings of Jesus Christ were literally the oppressive tools used to beat us into submission. We were expected to live by these teachings. However, the inconsistent behaviors of these pious Jesuits and nuns of St. Francis Mission confused the little children. We learned from the contradiction between how they expected us to live and how they demonstrated their righteous teachings. These were our first lessons: lie, never mean what you say, and only say what is expected of you.

The physical, mental, emotional, and sexual abuse that occurred within those walls were taught well by these apostles of St. Francis Mission. I saw a nun leading a little girl by the hand into her room in the middle of the night several times. I saw how a girl would be summoned by a priest or nun, returning withdrawn and with swollen eyes from crying, refusing to speak to anyone. The behaviors demonstrated were eventually emulated and have become family tradition for many. They spoke of kindness and patience, yet their behaviors were contrary to these teachings. Their voices still echo in the adults who verbally abuse their children. I will never forget how the nuns talked to us rudely and harshly, shaming us in public.

We were told that as the girls' building burned, many former students wept. I cannot imagine who would be weeping as the building burned. Were they weeping for the children who suffered and even died within those walls? Or were they weeping for the "good times" they had while living there? Truly, there are good and bad memories in all of our lives, but how do we identify what is good and bad? We were told one thing and the opposite was demonstrated. These hypocrisies confused the children of St. Francis Mission. We all know what happened in these boarding schools. We have heard it in many stories from our grandparents and parents. We experienced it. Those who saw me punished for speaking Lakota might have turned away and denied what was happening, but I know that I was severely punished. This denial behavior is similar to how some Jews identified with their oppressors and persecuted their own people in the concentration camps.

The psychological warfare of divide and conquer was used: favoritism toward the mixed bloods and discrimination against the full bloods still divides us today. The separation of children from their parents and siblings ravaged the family structure. Our contemporary disrespect for elders, parents, and authority in general are the results of the treatment children received in the boarding schools. The alcoholism, violence, domestic abuse, and sexual abuse of children are also the legacy of the malevolent practices of these God-fearing Christians, including the Jesuits and nuns.

The Christian churches are very wealthy organizations and much of this wealth is gained through exploitation and depiction of "those poor little Indian children" in their direct-mail advertising. These charitable resources should be used to restore the tribal cultures the Christians attempted to destroy. Solutions such as treatment centers for alcoholism, and counseling for depression or deviant behaviors such as child abuse and domestic abuse must be offered and must involve community input. Most importantly, those solutions must be culturally relevant. Their assimilationist ideology must be publicly declared as wrong. I hope their paternalistic attitudes, "we know what's best for you," or "we are going to do this for you," are also in the past.

Yes, some of the members of the Catholic Church may be trying to take responsibility for their role in the destruction of the Lakota Oyate. But one reason for their apology might be that they are losing their members. We can no longer be forced to attend their church. We no longer look with awe to their hollow teachings.

Still, I hope the Catholic Church is sincere in its apology. I hope it lives up to their teachings of loving and respecting its fellow man. In fact, the church should rejoice that we as a people can now recognize the destruction and oppression that plagues us so we can start healing as a nation.

Why did all of this happen? The major reason was government

policy. "Christianize and civilize these savages by sending them to boarding schools; separate them from the influence of their heathen parents," government officials said. Some chiefs in their wisdom wanted their children to be educated to the white man's ways. They believed that knowing the ways of the white man would help us protect our remaining land and natural resources. Some chiefs asked the churches to come in to educate their children, because they literally believed the Christians did live by their teachings. They thought the churches would be a buffer in the assimilation process, so the children would not be sent away to schools in eastern states. And finally, the chiefs truly lived according to their own values, so naturally they endorsed education. They thought of it as the process of seeking wisdom.

However, the trust our leaders placed in these schools and churches for the care of the Lakota Wakanyeja, these sacred and unique beings, was responded to with indifference, prejudice, discrimination, and intolerance. The unscrupulous methods used to acculturate us destroyed many of our children's lives. These schools, with their myopic attitudes and goals, created a lost generation floundering in alcoholism, drugs, domestic violence, child abuse, and sexual abuse. In the end, we all lost.

Today, the divide and conquer tactics used against us still affect how we all view our sometimes distorted and disoriented world. The foreign hierarchical system was forced on the Lakota and flourishes among many of our people today. Those who accepted their teachings have in turn become oppressors or sub-oppressors who model and see reality through the eyes of those who oppressed them and model that reality in their daily lives. They reinforce prejudices by devaluing and ridiculing anyone who may have tried to retain the Lakota language and culture. The belief that Lakota language was an impediment became the justification for exclusion and isolation of many Lakota people. These native oppressors have often carried the Bureau of Indian Affairs' and the churches' paternalism to extremes and used the Lakota way of non-interference and individualism to reach their personal goals of control and self-interest.

We all were victims of cultural chauvinism. The Christians did not choose to learn about or understand our emotions, our values, and our beliefs, or learn what motivates us. They did not understand that our way of life was completely based on kinship relationships. This kinship system was ridiculed, ignored, or considered insignificant. I remember a nun with a mocking smirk on her face saying, "Oh, you Indians are related to everyone." I did not know if we were supposed to be ashamed.

The Catholics did not believe that it took a whole village to raise a child. Instead they believed in force, intimidation, and threats of hell. They did not open their hearts and minds to the beauty of Mitakuye oyasin, the beauty of relationships, and Lakol Wicohan, the Lakota way of life. But despite their close-minded determination, they failed in their attempts to completely destroy Lakota culture for many families.

During the boarding school days, many traditional Lakota families took Lakota culture and religion underground. These families were persecuted and isolated. Despite that, some of them managed to keep their children out of the boarding schools, and trained them in the Lakota ways.

One tactic of church leaders was to focus special attention on the children of influential community leaders. They kept those children under the wings of selected denominations and attempted to train them as catechists and preachers. Ironically, some of these "educated" children grew up to record the history and culture of our people that might have been lost forever. I am grateful to all the families who were strong enough to stand up for their beliefs and maintain their pride in our cultural heritage.

As an adult, decades after I left St. Francis Mission School, I struggled through seasonal bouts of depression. Every fall a subtle change overcame me. The autumnal loveliness took on a different tone. Habits of the mind blew through me like gusts of icy wind. I took long lonely walks along the creek in the Grass Mountain valley, sometimes sitting for hours under cottonwood trees. I became somber, and melancholy. In the early morning hours, the fresh cool dew clinging to the spectacular array of bright and blazing colors displayed by the tree nation didn't lift my heart; instead I felt a kind of numbness. As days went by those colors resurrected sadness, anger, and despair.

When the meadow larks gathered on the fence lines and calls of migrating birds filled the air, I finally became aware of the nature of this pain. I thought of the times when I went back to the boarding school. Memories of harsh discipline, locked doors, isolation, and condemnation of my culture intermingled with the separation from loved ones. I had not allowed myself to grieve for my losses, instead I carried them with me and they were so ingrained in my mind that they ensnared me. I realized that being locked away had its consequences.

Real feeling were not encouraged at St. Francis. The first rule was "Forget about being who you are." Other messages were "Don't cry, because no one cares how you feel." My spiritual growth was stunted. I could not pray. I did not feel a part of nature's elements, the sun, the air, and the earth, anymore. My indomitable stubbornness had carried me this far, but I questioned my worth. Still, I was no longer willing to passively accept what had happened to me. It was as if I were standing on the edge of a bottomless chasm into which I was afraid I would fall. The path that my grandfather had cleared for me now seem muddled. I felt lost. My relatives had gone on and left me lost in a world I didn't want to be a part of. I felt I was merely an empty shell of life. I somehow had to find a way to free myself. I wanted to live harmoniously with all I had been taught by my relatives.

I would stand looking out into the oncoming night and I would examine my crippling losses. I felt loss at every hand. The magnitude of my losses imprisoned me. I had lost my self-esteem; I had lost fluency in my language; I had lost the opportunity to learn parenting skills because of physical separation from my parents; I had lost precious time with my great-grandparents. I had even lost my name. The Whirlwind was taken out of my name, so I became known as Lydia W. Soldier. I was told by the nuns it would be easier for me to write my name because my name was too long. But, I thought about my grandfather every time I wrote my name. He had said, "Remember who you are; remember where you got your name. Respect your name; be good and make us proud; don't bring shame to your name. Whirlwind Soldier is your name." These devastating losses initiated the anger, resentment, and mistrust I felt toward education, Christianity, and my parents.

I had left a vital part of myself behind in the boarding school. But worst of all, I had to admit that my parents had left me there. Years later, I visited my father in the Veterans hospital and as we sat talking I asked him if he remembered how old I was when I first went to school. After thinking about it for a moment, he said he didn't remember. I said, "Dad, I was four years old!" He sat looking down at his hands and when he finally looked at me, he had tears in his eyes; he said, "And we left you there!" Maybe they thought they had no choice. Maybe they thought that I would at least have enough to eat and a warm place to stay at the school.

Eventually, I began to go into deep grieving purges, but my losses were so devastating and so pervasive that I didn't know where my mourning began and where it ended. I was finally able to admit to the anger I hid and the gravity of the sorrow that pulled at me. I knew I had to understand what had happened to me and to my people before I could heal. I could not heal without inviting those boarding school memories that I had totally ignored. I have lived around the ragged edges of those memories. I finally realized that I had launched an offensive passive resistance, hiding my anger and hate. I quietly carried my wounds like trophies, but I was still rebellious. But those losses had a choke hold on me and began to guide my life onto a path I did not want. I had joined the occupation at Alcatraz Island in California, and the American Indian Movement. Then, when Wounded Knee II occurred, I took my children to my mother and told her I was going there; it was something I had to do. I was arrested for unlawful assembly in Kyle, South Dakota, when we tried to attend a ceremony held by the medicine man Fools Crow. The tribal Chairman of Pine Ridge passed an ordinance that stated more than two people gathering was unlawful assembly. After I was released from jail in Pine Ridge, my husband would not let me go back into Wounded Knee because I was nine months pregnant. But there were other ways I could help. I had put my life on the line. We had been arrested by the Oglala "goons," who prodded us with their guns, beating many of us. We had run a road block, traveling more than a hundred miles per hour, with the body of Clearwater who had been killed in Wounded Knee. Fear of death was behind me. Death, as my grandparents had known, was part of living. Until I could realize the truth of this, I would not gain peace in my heart. If I aspired to happiness, I had to find balance and harmony in my life. This was the reflection of Lakota philsophy—all a part of living—that my grandparents had been trying to teach me.

"I've made it!" I shouted in my mind, "I've made it!" I was one of the survivors of the boarding schools. I was not an alcoholic, I was not one of the walking dead. I had refused to shed my identity like the dead scales of a reptile. But I still denied my emptiness of heart. I was empty of faith. I had not prayed since I left St. Francis Mission, even in my own way. My faith had died at St. Francis, my world had been shaped by this loss. I was losing the ability to cope, the ability to look at life as a challenge. Words I had read reverberated in my mind. They were the words of a Cheyenne prophet, who foretold what would happen to the children if they were sent away to the boarding schools: "They will ask for your flesh, those that go will forget their Indian ways," he said. And Pratt, who established the Carlisle Indian School in Pennsylvania, justified assimilation policies by saying: "the Indian had to die, in order for him to live as a man." And then finally, there were General Sherman's words, "The only good Indian is a dead Indian."

The chipping away process of the Catholic church had destroyed many children's lives. Their attempts to destroy innocent children seemed unreal, yet I knew I had experienced their destructiveness. These experiences were far behind me, but they haunted me and returned to me every fall and in nightmares. There were the recurring nightmares: of me suffocating in a locked storage closet, of shouting voices that rang in my ears, and of evil spirits dressed in black habits waiting and searching for me. Finally, I could no longer combat the unresolved grief. It had come over me slowly, over the years. I was thirty years old and the imprinted memories still remained. The passage of time could not erase the festering memories. I reflected on my past. I could see how my experiences at St. Francis and at home clung to the outer edges of my life and it seemed to affect me more in the fall because this was when I went back to school. I was conditioned to accept the discomfort of emotional and physical abuse with stoicism.

In order to heal, I had to validate the trauma I had suffered in the boarding schools. My self-esteem had been assaulted. The purveyors of Christian teachings had drained and stomped me. Their approaches and censorship had taken my identity and my language. I had buried this immense loss in my subconscious. But I knew the answer to my healing was out there somewhere. I had no religion, no God, only emptiness, wastelands, and black holes.

When my grandfather died I felt like I lost another tie. I went to his place in Grass Mountain and I thought of the influence he had on my life. I thought about my childhood. I had been an innocent child, so vulnerable. I walked along the Little White River. I saw a fallen cottonwood lying across the river, and the smell of rain brought back the memories of Bad Nation, of my great-grandparents and my grandparents. I quietly sat in the shadows of the cottonwoods above the river, watching a deer and her two fawns drinking water and feeding as it began to drizzle. Times of family togetherness were like snapshots in my mind. These memories had sustained me and would eventually help in my journey to healing. As a small child, I remember telling my great-grandmother I had heard ceremonial songs in the middle of the summer nights and she would say, "Oh, Awa, you were just dreaming." The government had forbidden our beloved sacred rites; the churches condemned them as pagan or devil worship. The threat of a jail term kept my relatives from involving us in the religious ceremonies. No wonder my great-grandmother had sent "long journey food," wasna, to us that first year at St. Francis.

Finally, changing my reality became my conscious choice. I remember my grandfather saying, "You choose to live or you choose to exist—that's your choice. It's all a part of living, to persevere is a reflection of one's most inner beliefs—one's philosophy and we tried to teach you Lakota philosophy." I began to see myself in a new light. I had become cynical and numb to spirituality. I knew I had to direct myself to the specific goal of relearning what I thought I had lost and to create a future for myself and for my family. I concentrated on Mitakuye Oyasin, my relationship with the universe, with the forces of nature, with my human family, with the animal nations, and with the plant nations. I had always known the Lakota did not even have a word for religion, because it is an integral way of life.

At last, the profound teachings of the Lakota came back to me. Being Lakota was not a temporary illusion. I cannot tell the day I left the hurt behind. There is no magical number or date. It was a slow and gradual process, one step at a time. But slowly the pieces of the puzzle fell into place. I had diligently held in my heart the ancient Lakota teaching of my family. The healing didn't happen overnight; the pain didn't end in one day, and it didn't leave me entirely, but finally a new strength filled my body and heart. My spirit was no longer tied to the trauma of the abuse.

The crisp autumn days, calls from the birds on their migration south, the sun shining through the changing color of the maple leaves, the rust-colored scrub oak and yellow cottonwood leaves, all of these validated the memories of an innocent child and brought many memories to the surface for me to scrutinize. I began to let go of the anger and grief when I realized that it was not my fault. I was no longer that bad child, the child that could not learn the correct way to speak English.

I know the healing began with the trees. The rustling trees of

Grass Mountain whispered to me. They drew me into their embrace, pulled at my heart, and rescued me. I tied prayer ties into an old, old Rosebud pine, and the trees became my prayer partners again, and I began to make my peace. Prayers came to me from nowhere, and everywhere; my prayers were no longer empty and memorized. I cut my hair in the ritual of the Lakota grieving process. I wept when I attended our ceremonies; I wept when I prayed under the cottonwood at the Sundance. I touched the Sundance tree planted deeply over the heart of the buffalo and the sacred pipe. I looked up into its branches, saw the sacred tobacco prayer ties and flags of red, yellow, blue, white, black, and green reaching toward the sun, sending prayers into the universe. I remembered that this sacred tree was rooted in peace and goodness. The clear and sharp smell of sage and cedar reached out to me and the smoke drifted over me like a gentle touch. I trembled with a deep pain in my chest as the drummers sang, "Tunkasila, wamayankayo, le miyeca nawajinyelo, Grandfather, behold me, it is me." I remembered how my great-grandparents had prayed every morning as the morning sun rose in the east. Their beautiful, expressive Lakota words—how very strong their faith had been. How could I have forgotten such a beautiful ritual? I had felt I had been forgotten. Those words closed my throat with emotion. Now I knew that the spirits of my ancestors prayed with me and for me.

I wept under the willows in the circular womb of the sweat lodge, emerging wet and feeling the strange and wonderful power of being reborn. It permeated every cell—the very core of my being, filling me with the wonder and mystery of life, an indescribable living awareness. I wept as I tied prayer ties onto a cedar tree, trying to remember the correct way to say heyoka prayers. At times, I thought I would never quit crying. Ceremonies and prayers exhilarated and uplifted me, filling the dark holes of prejudice that had been inflicted upon me. I was finally able to return to a world I loved. I no longer felt isolated. I experienced what I had heard happened when someone died, "Unci maka sina kiye"; yes, grandmother earth had taken me into her shawl again. I looked outside myself and I felt I was a part of creation again. Revelation had come to me. I was at last reclaiming what I had been taught from the beginning: to have pride in who I am, to know my language, my history, and my culture, and to know my relatives. I finally realized that for most of my life, I had been like a person who followed a broken compass, not really knowing in which direction to go. I had lived a life without spiritual direction.

From then on, early morning picnics in the gray stillness of autumn revived me. My children and I would bundle up in the crisp fresh autumn air and sit on a high hill above Grass Mountain and watch the low mists move along the valley floor, settling into the dips and in between the hills before the morning sun peeked over the great rolling hills. I would think of how fortunate I was to have had such wonderful great-grandparents and grandparents.

Through the course of my journey, anger had been like that mist, cloudy and unclear around my soul. As I worked through this anger, I began to enjoy long walks with my own children. We had evening picnics on a high hill in Grass Mountain overlooking the valley, and I felt the leaves of all colors welcoming me home. I told my children the stories told to me by my relatives. I had kept these in my heart where they would never be lost. I showed them plants I helped my grandmother collect as food and medicines. I picked sage and rubbed it between my fingers and held it to my children to smell. We picked wild fruits and teas. I'd told them of the summer evenings in Bad Nation, how we danced when my great-grandfather sang with his hand drum. I knew my great-grandfather valued bilingualism as I told them of how he spoke to us in Lakota and Cheyenne, and I told them the winter night stories.

I sat with my children around the kitchen table preparing for a wacipi (pow-wow or dance), giving them each a project to work on, beading little buckskin bags, adding fringes and tiny tinkling bells while I told them stories about past wacipis. I also told them about how the bell was used at St. Francis Mission. Two such conflicting experiences, the bells of happy times at the wacipi and the bells of sad times at St. Francis. I told them how my father loved and composed music, writing notes on sheet paper as he played on his clarinet or saxophone late into the night, and then I told them about my piano lessons. I told them how our ceremonial songs were almost lost. I remembered how my father's music and my great-grandfather's traditional songs echoed down the valley in Bad Nation. I told them about how the children of Bad Nation made their beds in the hay rack when we wanted to sleep outside, lying there, pointing out certain star constellations, listening to stories and to the beautiful music of my father. As I spoke, these stories returned to me, rushing through space and time. Reminding me of the wonderful and beautiful Lakota spiritual foundation that my tiospaye had given me. Reminding me that my relationship with all of my relatives has not been severed.

I thought of Chief Sitting Bull's words: "If you lose something important to you, go back and search for it and you will find it." If only I had kept in my heart all of the gifts given to me by my great-grandparents and grandparents throughout my life. My spirit and my heart had always been connected to the universal energy of the wisdom of my ancestors, nature's resources, and to my knowledge of Mitakuye Oyasin. But as a child, I was victimized by an evil conspiracy when I was susceptible. I had almost lost it all. The shunning, the ostracizing, the humiliation and abandonment, the internalized oppression almost took my life. I had tried to live my life by the values demonstrated by my relatives, but I had been crushed in the attempt.

The story of my survival began with those gifts of memories, and my lessons of those memories gave me back that spiritual foundation. They confirmed my beliefs and gave me a lifelong source of strength which I had not realized I had. I rebounded with this strength, with my culture and heritage intact. It was not easy to discover my own voice, to forage for new thoughts concerning the education of my children. I realized that the answer lies in having Lakota culture and language taught in the reservation schools. So my husband and two friends, Jim and Belva Kauley, and I went door to door to every house in our community with a survey asking the parents if they wanted Lakota culture and language taught in the school. The survey was well received with only two people disagreeing with our attempts. Thus, Indian Studies was established into the school district for the first time.

The healing in my grandfather's words came to me without apology to anyone: "Have pride and dignity, you are Lakota. Get an education, search for wisdom, taku oyale ki iyeyin kte. Seek and you shall find." I knew my grandfather's views on education were the great strength of the Lakota nation.

My great-grandparents and grandparents instilled values in me that prevailed over the anger and despair and finally made me incapable of hating anyone. But the devastating experiences in the boarding schools created wounds that took many years to heal. They made me stronger and more determined to change the way our children are educated. Although those wounds healed, they scarred my views of Christianity. Christianity is merely an empty form of faith to me. I know that if I live by the true Lakota values, my spirit will survive. I have found peace within my heart through the religion of my ancestors. This is the legacy left to me by my Whirlwind Soldier tiospaye. This story will never be forgotten, it will be recorded, it will be told by my children to their children and passed on to the coming generations and it will become part of our oral tradition.

Glossary of Dakota and Lakota Words and Phrases

Dakota—friends or allies; also used to refer to the dialect of the Sioux language

hanbleceya—vision quest

hanmikceka—dress mocassins

heyoka—contrary person, clown

hocospu—scabs

Hunkpapa—campers at the opening of the circle

hutab—downstream

Ikce Wicasta—the common people

inahni—hurry

inkpata—journey

ishtimila—little one

Itazipco—Sans Arcs or Without Bows

Kabubu/cokin—skillet bread

Kimimila-skanyeca—butterflies

kiyukanpi—makes room for them

kunsi—great grandmother

Lakol wicohan—Lakota beliefs

Lakota—friends or allies; also used to refer to the dialect of the Sioux language

Lakota Oyate—Lakota people
lala—grandfather
lowanpi—ceremony
mahto—bear
mitakuye Oyasin—we are all relatives
Ooenupa—two kettles
oyate sica—bad nation
papa—dried meat
sica or sika—bad
sicanju—burnt thigh
Si Hanska—Long Foot
sihasapa—blackfeet
Sinte Gleska—Spotted Tail
siyoko—devil
taku oyate ki iyeyin kte—seek and you shall find
timpsila—wild turnips
tiyospaye—extended family group
Tunkashila—Supreme Spirit
unci—grandmother
uncicila—great grandmother
wacipi—dance
wakanyega—unique beings, children
Wasicu—white people
waskuya—corn syrup
wasna—dried meat
wastunkala—dried corn
wazuya—adventure
Wopila—Thanksgiving
wouranwala—gentleness and meekness
woyake kinikiyan—bringing back the stories

Index

Except for parents and relatives with different surnames, family members are listed under the authors in the index.—JWM

acculturation, 183, 202, 205
Alcatraz Island, 208
Alcoholics Anonymous Group (AA), 49
alcoholism, 48, 49, 97, 126–29, 147, 204, 205
Amiotte, Art, 62
Amiotte, Lowell, viii
Arikara Indians, 16
Armstrong (formerly Dewey) County, 1
assimilation, 45, 52, 60, 74, 106, 107, 165, 176, 184, 197, 202, 204
Attack Him, Cordelia, 60
Augustana College's Center for Western Studies, viii

Bad Nation (Oyate Sica Tiyospaye), 160, 162, 184, 186, 188, 192, 198, 209, 212, 213
Big Coulee Day School, 106
Bird, Jackie, 128
Bird, Laura Renville, 92
Bird Song Woman, 37
Black Elk Speaks, 71
Black Hills State University, 45, 67, 69, 70, 72, 75
boarding schools. ix, 25, 26, 28–30, 35, 36, 45, 74, 94, 95, 106, 140, 141, 157, 164, 165, 196–97. See also education; mistreatment of children
Brewer, Lenny, 65
buffalo, 3, 9
"Butterfly Girl's Path," 13, 16

camp activities. See community programs
Carlisle Indian School, 92, 202, 209
Carnegie Mellon University, 80
Catholic Church, 99, 159, 161, 162, 172, 187, 193, 204, 205, 209
ceremonies, 79, 80, 87, 100; Sweat lodge, 78, 100
Cherry Creek, 4
Cheyenne Eagle Butte School, 64
Cheyenne River Sioux Reservation, 1, 3, 4, 13, 16, 19, 30
Child, Brenda J., v
chokeberry syrup, 10
Christianity, 78, 79, 114, 115, 135, 152, 153, 183, 197, 214. See Catholic Church; Quakers
Christmas celebration, 184–86
college education, 24, 69–72, 75, 76, 150, 151
community programs, 59–61

Cook-Lynn, Elizabeth, viii
Crow Creek Indian Reservation, vi
Cull, Kenyon, 133, 144
Curry, Karla, 65, 66

Dakota language, vi, 93, 94, 95, 137, 159
Dakotapi, 95
Dawes Act, 198
Dilworth School and town, 126, 127, 131, 137, 142
dream or vision, 74, 75, 76, 77, 78
Dudley, Joseph Iron Eyes, 99
dugout living, 8
Dupree, 5

Eagle Butte, 5
education, 53, 64, 84–86, 88, 89, 107, 119–21, 147, 151, 157, 164, 199, 200, 202
Eldridge, Arlene Keoke, 92
Enemy Swim District, 101, 102; Enemy Swim Day School, 106
excommunication, 195

Fair Labor Standards Act of 1938, 112
Fargo-Moorhead area, 110, 116, 126, 128, 130, 131, 142. See Moorhead, MN
Fetal Alcohol Syndrome (FAS), 81
Flandreau Indian School, 199–201
Fools Crow, 208

games and playing, 21, 22, 102, 103, 110, 125, 177
German, Owen, 94, 125, 150
Grant, Emma Redearth, 93
Grass, Etta, 49
Gros Ventres. See Hidatsa tribe
gumbo, 5, 6

hanbleceya, 83
hanmikceka, 168

health services, 138, 139
Hidatsa tribe, 4, 16
high School studies and activities, 64–68
Hill, Roberta, viii
hocospu, sheep, 9
Hopi students, 66
Hunkpapa Band, 4, 16
Hutab, 49

Ikce, Wicasta, vii, viii, 91
Inahni, 11
Indian Child Welfare Act, 41
Inkpata, 48
integrated theme-based approach, 84
Iron Cloud, Willis, 31
Iron Moccasin, Bill, 30
Ishtimila, 11
Itazipco, 5

Janis, Janice, 63, 65, 66
Jesuits, 201–4
Jones, Jemima, 94–97, 102, 104
Jordan, Susan Defender, 4

kabubu bread (also called cokin [a skillet bread]), 10, 185
Kauley, Belva and Jim, 213
Keoke, Etta Grant, 92, 94, 95, 98, 124, 136
Keoke, Jacob, 92
kimimila-skanyeca, 15
kiyukanpi, 92
kunsi, 93, 94

Lake Traverse Reservation, 91, 97, 100, 104
Lakol Wicohan, 183
Lakota beliefs, 72, 82, 191, 192, 206, 208, 210–14. See also Lakota culture
Lakota culture, 45, 60, 62, 65, 71, 72, 78, 88, 161, 166, 170, 174–76, 182–

Index

84, 187, 204–6, 213. See also Lakota beliefs
Lakota language, vi, 50, 71, 74, 84, 88, 89, 178, 180, 183, 184, 193, 194, 197, 200, 204, 205, 213
Lakota medicine men, 77, 86
Lakota people, 3, 25, 61, 160, 182
Lakota philosophy, 82, 87, 191, 192, 208, 210–14. See also Lakota culture
The Lakota Times, 91
Lame Deer: Seeker of Visions, 71
Lee, Lanniko, vii, viii; Uncle Alvin, 4; Aunt Arlene, 21, 23, 31; Aunt Celia, 19; Uncles Cal and Dave, 8; father, 6–28; Grandma Jenny, 30, 37–39, 41; grandmas, 4, 13, 16, 21, 24, 26; grandpas, 5, 21–23, 29, 38, 40; Lee, Dewey (brother), 23; mother, 4, 10, 17, 19, 20, 25, 26; Unci Eunie, 8, 9, 12, 16, 20; Unci Susan, 8, 22, 23, 29
Little Wound School, 80
Lone Hill, Karen, vii, viii; Amos (grandfather), 59; Bessie Rock (grandmother), 46; Ethel Weston (mother), 46, 54, 56, 57; Hobart (uncle), 46; Kim (daughter), 69, 71–73, 75, 79–82; Lamoine (brother), 46; Leonard Leo (brother), 47; Lester (great uncle), 47; Lester Howard (brother), 47, 48, 63, 67); Llewellyn (father), 46, 56, 57, 68, 69; Lorna (cousin), 50, 52; Lucille (sister), 46, 51, 54; Sid (brother), 46, 55, 63; Sydney (grandfather), 46.
lowanpi, 77
Lower Brule, 35

Mahto (Bear) Butte, 20
Mandan Indians, 16
Manderson Day School, 63

The Man to Send Rain Clouds, 76
Marshall, Joseph III, viii
Mdwakantonwan Band of the Dakota, 59
Memory Songs, viii, 159
menstrual customs of the Lakota, 58, 59
Minneconjou Lakota, 4, 13, 16, 37
Minnesota uprising of 1862, 59, 100
Mississippi River, 13
Missouri River, vii, 1–3, 6, 7, 12, 16, 17, 25, 40–43. See Oahe Dam
mistreatment of children, vi, 26–28, 36, 53–55, 57, 92, 163, 166, 170–75, 177–81, 187–90, 193, 194, 201–4, 213
Mitakuye Oyasin, 42, 167, 191, 206, 210, 213
Momaday, N. Scott, viii
Moorhead, MN, 108, 116, 127, 128. See Fargo-Moorhead area
Mossman, Burton, 5

Navajo students, 66
Northern State University, 1

Oahe Dam, 24, 25, 37–39, 41, 42
Oak Lake Writers' Society, viii
Oglala Community School, 63
Oglala Lakota College, vii, 45, 83, 84
Oglala of Pine Ridge, 16
Old Agency Day School, 26, 106
One Flew Over the Cuckoo's Nest, 71
Oohenupa Tiyospaye, 4
Owen, Amanda Tiomanipi, 94

papa, 21, 185
Peever School, 146, 147, 150
Peever, South Dakota, vii, 106, 140, 146
Pennsylvania State University, 159, 167, 201
Pentecostal Church, 114

Pick-Sloane Project, 24
Pine Ridge, South Dakota, 63, 66, 69, 76, 208
Pine Ridge Reservation, 45, 68, 74, 75
Porcupine, South Dakota, 45, 46, 52, 53, 59, 62, 63, 69, 74
Porcupine Day School, 47, 50, 52, 56, 59, 61, 62, 63, 80, 82
Porcupine Singers, 75
Pourier, Denise, 62
powwow, 65, 99, 100, 105, 157
Presbyterian Church, 59, 99

Quakers, 203
Quinn, Tom, 118

racism or prejudice, 87, 88, 93, 107, 114, 118, 127, 152, 155
Red Cloud School (Holy Rosary Mission), 64
Red Pheasant, Martha, 4
Renville, Florestine Kiyukanpi, vi, vii, 91; Adrienne (sister), 106, 108, 110–14, 123, 125–30, 142–44, 148, 149; Blossom Keoke (mother), 91, 92, 114, 116, 117–19, 123–25, 128, 129, 144, 146, 147; Byron (brother), 126, 137, 144; Chyrel (sister), 113, 126, 137, 144; DelRay (son), 155, 157; Gabrielle (daughter), 154, 157; Mandis (brother), 45, 97, 106, 113–15, 118, 119, 121–23, 126, 137; Merle (brother), 126, 137, 146; Naomi (sister), 107, 108, 126, 127, 129, 130, 142, 143; Peter (grandfather), 92; Robert (father), 91, 95, 97, 114–17, 119, 122–25, 128, 129, 144, 146, 147; Roberta (sister), 97, 113, 114, 116, 119, 121, 123, 125, 126–28, 131, 137, 146, 150; Sarah Sheldon (grandmother), 92; Scott (son), 157

Renville, Gabriel, 100–2
Reorganization Act, 198
Rosebud Boarding School, 196, 198
Rosebud Reservation, 2, 70, 75, 159, 160

St. Francis Mission School, viii, 64, 161, 162, 168, 171, 173, 176, 186–88, 192, 195, 201–4. 2–6. 207, 208, 210—CHRISTINE, WHAT IS 2–6.?-AM
St. Mary's Episcopal Boarding School, vii, 132, 133, 134, 136, 137, 140, 143
St. Mary's Episcopal Church, 98, 99, 103, 136
Sica Hollow, 103
sica or sika (bad), 168
Sicanju, 12
Si Hanska (Long Foot), 92
Sihasapa Band, 4
Sinte Gleska University, 75, 159, 201
Sisseton-Wahpeton Community College, 91
Sisseton-Wahpeton Tribe, vii, 91, 92, 100
Sitting Bull, 4, 213
siyoko (devil), 49
South Dakota State University, 1, 45, 57, 91, 94, 151, 152
Spotted Tail, Chief, 176, 202
Standing Rock Reservation, 1, 4, 16, 17, 19
stories, 18, 23, 35, 58, 183, 184, 198
Strong, Mrs. Isabella, vi
sundance, 65, 77, 78, 155, 211
sweat lodge. see ceremonies

teachers: Miss Ebner, 52; Mrs. Gooch, 53; Mrs. Hendershot, 50, 51; Miss Hodges, 31–35; Mrs. Hunke, 62; Mrs. Katt, 62; Mrs. Patnoe, 55, 57; Mrs. Williams, 57

Theisz, Dr. Ronnie, 75
Thompson, Jenny Renville, 145
timpsila, 185
tiyospaye, 4, 195
tiyukan, 48, 49
Todd County School, 64
Trevine, Robert, 127, 137
tuberculosis, 107
Tunka Shila, 11, 211
Turtle Mountain Chippewa students, 66
Two Dogs, Edna Lone Hill, 49, 50
Two Eagle, Faith, 55
Two Stars, Solomon, 101
Two Tails Gilbert, Luke, 3

Unci (grandmother), 4, 8, 9, 11, 12, 13, 16, 20, 21, 22, 23, 30, 37, 38, 41; Unci Eunie, 13, 16; Unci Susan, 18, 24; Uncicila (great grandmother), 168
University of South Dakota, 81

Venegas, Hildreth Two Stars, 103
Vere, Reverend, 131, 132, 134, 141, 142, 143
Vietnam, 171

wacipi, 212
wakanyega, 182, 205
wasicu, 39, 100, 105
waskuya, 104
wasna, 140, 179, 210
wastunkala, 185
wazuya, 162

Weber State University, 91
Welch, James, viii
Weston, Charmaine, 55, 56
Weston, Jeannette, 57
Weston, Martha Red Wing, 46
Weston, Samuel, 59
Weston, Suzanne White Bull, 46
Whirlwind Horse, Anthony, 62
Whirlwind Horse, Louis, 62
Whirlwind Soldier, Lydia, viii, 159; Clement (brother), 166; Elizabeth Cook (great grandmother), 182, 186, 195, 199, 200, 209–11; George (great grandfather), 186, 195, 200, 209–11; Grace (aunt), 197–99; Homer (grandfather), 195, 197–201, 207, 209, 213; Julia (grandmother), 182, 197–99
Whirlwind Soldier Tiyaspaye, 214
White actions and attitudes, 96, 97, 100, 101, 106–8, 112–15, 117–19, 130, 132, 137–39, 144, 146–49, 151–54, 157, 158, 191, 204
White Bull, Ella Pine Bird, 58
Winnebago Indians, 13
Woodard, Charles, viii
wopila, 83
Wounded Knee II, 208
wouranwala, 87
Woyake Kinikiyan: An Anthology of Dakota/Lakota Storytellers, viii, 91

Yanktonai, 12

Zuni students, 66